MW00811630

Palgrave Studies in Animals and Literature

Series Editors
Susan McHugh
English Department
University of New England
Biddeford, ME, USA

Robert McKay
School of English
University of Sheffield
Sheffield, UK

John Miller
School of English
University of Sheffield
Sheffield, UK

Various academic disciplines can now be found in the process of executing an 'animal turn', questioning the ethical and philosophical grounds of human exceptionalism by taking seriously the nonhuman animal presences that haunt the margins of history, anthropology, philosophy, sociology and literary studies. Such work is characterised by a series of broad, cross-disciplinary questions. How might we rethink and problematise the separation of the human from other animals? What are the ethical and political stakes of our relationships with other species? How might we locate and understand the agency of animals in human cultures?

This series publishes work that looks, specifically, at the implications of the 'animal turn' for the field of English Studies. Language is often thought of as the key marker of humanity's difference from other species; animals may have codes, calls or songs, but humans have a mode of communication of a wholly other order. The primary motivation is to muddy this assumption and to animalise the canons of English Literature by rethinking representations of animals and interspecies encounter. Whereas animals are conventionally read as objects of fable, allegory or metaphor (and as signs of specifically human concerns), this series significantly extends the new insights of interdisciplinary animal studies by tracing the engagement of such figuration with the material lives of animals. It examines textual cultures as variously embodying a debt to or an intimacy with animals and advances understanding of how the aesthetic engagements of literary arts have always done more than simply illustrate natural history. We publish studies of the representation of animals in literary texts from the Middle Ages to the present and with reference to the discipline's key thematic concerns, genres and critical methods. The series focuses on literary prose and poetry, while also accommodating related discussion of the full range of materials and texts and contexts (from theatre and film to fine art, journalism, the law, popular writing and other cultural ephemera) with which English studies now engages.

Series Board:
Karl Steel (Brooklyn College)
Erica Fudge (Strathclyde)
Kevin Hutchings (UNBC)
Philip Armstrong (Canterbury)
Carrie Rohman (Lafayette)
Wendy Woodward (Western Cape)

More information about this series at
http://www.palgrave.com/gp/series/14649

Kári Driscoll · Eva Hoffmann
Editors

What Is Zoopoetics?

Texts, Bodies, Entanglement

Editors
Kári Driscoll
Utrecht University
Utrecht, The Netherlands

Eva Hoffmann
Whitman College
Walla Walla, WA, USA

Palgrave Studies in Animals and Literature
ISBN 978-3-319-64415-8   ISBN 978-3-319-64416-5   (eBook)
https://doi.org/10.1007/978-3-319-64416-5

Library of Congress Control Number: 2017948707

Cover illustration: Blue Whale Fluke - eco2drew/Getty Images

Printed on acid-free paper

This Palgrave Macmillan imprint is published by Springer Nature
The registered company is Springer International Publishing AG
The registered company address is: Gewerbestrasse 11, 6330 Cham, Switzerland

CONTENTS

NOTES ON CONTRIBUTORS

Marcel Beyer is an award-winning poet, novelist, and translator based in Dresden, Germany. Three of his novels, *Spies* (2000), *The Karnau Tapes* (1997), and *Kaltenburg* (2012) have been translated into English. He is the recipient of numerous awards, including the Kleist Prize (2014) and the Büchner Prize (2016).

Michaela Castellanos is a Ph.D. candidate in English Literature at Mid Sweden University. Her research interests lie in animal studies, the environmental humanities, and risk studies. She is the European editor of *Resilience: A Journal of the Environmental Humanities*, a member of the research network Cultural and Literary Animal Studies (CLAS), and a member the European Association for the Study of Literature, Culture, and the Environment (EASLE).

Catherine Clover is an artist based in Melbourne, Australia. Her multidisciplinary art practice explores an expanded approach to communication through voice and language and the interplay between hearing/ listening and seeing/reading. She teaches at Swinburne University (MA Writing, BA Media), Melbourne, and RMIT University (BDes Interior Design), Melbourne, and holds a practice led Ph.D. (Fine Art) through RMIT University.

Kári Driscoll is Assistant Professor of Comparative Literature at Utrecht University in the Netherlands. He holds a Ph.D. (2014) in German Language and Literature from Columbia University. He has published on zoopoetics in the works of Franz Kafka, Hugo von Hofmannsthal, and Luigi Pirandello. He is the coeditor of *Book Presence in a Digital Age* (Bloomsbury 2018) and, with Susanne C. Knittel, of *Memory after Humanism*, a special issue of *Parallax*, 22, no. 4 (2017). He is also an award-winning translator.

Eva Hoffmann is a Visiting Assistant Professor at the Department of German Studies and Gender Studies at Whitman College in Walla Walla, WA. She received her Ph.D. at the University of Oregon at the Department of German and Scandinavian, in 2017, and has a graduate certificate in Women's and Gender Studies from the University of Oregon. She has published articles on Franz Kafka, Hugo von Hofmannsthal, and Orhan Pamuk.

Joela Jacobs is Assistant Professor of German studies at the University of Arizona. She earned her Ph.D. at the University of Chicago and works on the intersection of German literature with animal studies, environmental humanities, and Jewish studies. She has published articles on monstrosity, multilingualism, literary censorship, biopolitics, animal epistemology, critical plant studies, and contemporary German Jewish identity. Her current book manuscript maps a microgenre of circa 1900 grotesque German literature that creatively animates nonhuman life-forms to answer the question what it means to be human in the modern world.

Belinda Kleinhans is Assistant Professor of German at Texas Tech University. She received her Ph.D. in German from the University of Waterloo (Ontario) in 2013. Her research interests are in the areas of biopolitics in literature, cultural and literary animal studies, literary texts, and the philosophy of language, and issues of representation. She has mainly published in the field of cultural animal studies.

Peter J. Meedom teaches English and Comparative Literature at the University of Oslo (Norway), where he earned his Ph.D. with a dissertation on the relationship between personal and impersonal life in the works of Döblin, Jahnn, Giono, Céline, Barnes, and Woolf. He is editor of the Scandinavian Journal of Nature Criticism, *Ny Jord*.

Nicolas Picard is a Ph.D. candidate in Francophone literature at the Sorbonne Nouvelle-Paris III University (Joint Research Unit THALIM: Paris III, CNRS, Ecole Normale Supérieure). His dissertation focuses on zoopoetics in French literary prose (1896–1938).

Rodolfo Piskorski recently completed a Ph.D. in Critical and Cultural Theory from Cardiff University, Wales and is currently University Teacher in Portuguese at the School of Modern Languages there. His research focuses on the interface between animality and textuality. His work has appeared in *The Journal of Literary Theory*, *Humanimalia*, and *The Journal of the Institute for Critical Animal Studies*, among others.

Matthias Preuss is a Ph.D. candidate with the DFG graduate program "Das Dokumentarische. Exzess und Entzug" at the Ruhr-Universität Bochum in Germany and is member of the researcher network for Cultural and Literary Animal Studies (CLAS). He is currently examining the documentation of environmental anomalies by exploring the poetic strategies of early ecology as a nexus of biology, politics, and economy as well as the epistemic strategies of realist and naturalist literature in the last third of the nineteenth century.

Sebastian Schönbeck is a Ph.D. candidate at the Julius-Maximilians-Universität Würzburg in Germany. He holds a scholarship of the German Academic Scholarship Foundation and is currently working on his dissertation, entitled "Animals in the Poetics of Enlightenment." His research interests include German and French literature of the eighteenth and nineteenth century, (literary) animal studies, environmental humanities, genre theory, and deconstruction.

Paul Sheehan is Associate Professor of English at Macquarie University, Sydney, Australia. He is the author of *Modernism, Narrative and Humanism* (Cambridge UP, 2002) and *Modernism and the Aesthetics of Violence* (Cambridge UP, 2013), and coeditor of "The Uses of Anachronism," a special issue of *Textual Practice* (2012). Most recently he has published essays on James Joyce, Cormac McCarthy, and posthuman bodies, and is currently working on a collaborative project entitled Transnational Coetzee.

Ann Marie Thornburg holds an MFA in Poetry from the University of Michigan Helen Zell Writers' Program where she was also a Zell Postgraduate Fellow in Poetry. She was also a Human-Animal Studies Fellow at Wesleyan University. She is currently pursuing a Ph.D. in Anthropology at the University of Notre Dame, Indiana, investigating human and free-ranging dog relations, focusing on questions of transience and mobility.

Introduction: What Is Zoopoetics?

Kári Driscoll and Eva Hoffmann

In *The Animal That Therefore I Am*, Jacques Derrida famously recounts his experience of being caught, naked, in the gaze of his cat. In the prolonged reflection on the human–animal relationship that follows, Derrida posits that within the Western tradition there are two fundamentally distinct types of discourse regarding the animal: "In the first place there are texts signed by people who have no doubt seen, observed, analyzed, reflected on the animal, but who have never seen themselves being seen by the animal" (Derrida 2008, 13, trans. mod.). In these philosophical and scientific texts, animals are only ever the objects of observation, and, to quote John Berger, "the fact that they can observe us has lost all significance" (Berger 1991, 16). This first category contains almost all of Western philosophy and science. In the second category we find primarily texts by "poets and prophets" (Derrida 2008, 14), and, indeed, as Derrida affirms, "thinking concerning the animal [*la pensée de l'animal*], if there is such a thing, derives from poetry. There you have a thesis: it is

K. Driscoll (✉)
Utrecht University, Utrecht, The Netherlands

E. Hoffmann
Whitman College, Walla Walla, WA, USA

© The Author(s) 2018   1
K. Driscoll and E. Hoffmann (eds.), *What Is Zoopoetics?*,
Palgrave Studies in Animals and Literature,
https://doi.org/10.1007/978-3-319-64416-5_1

what philosophy has, essentially, had to deprive itself of. It is the difference between philosophical knowledge and poetic thinking [*une pensée
poétique*]" (7). Poetic thinking, by implication, is in some sense synony-
mous with "*la pensée de l'animal,*" which, in turn, would be a form of
thinking that has taken account of the fact that what we call "the animal"
can look at *us* and, "in a word, without a word, *address*" us (13).

Even more strongly, Derrida suggests that the experience of being
looked at by an animal, of seeing oneself being seen through the eyes
of a nonhuman, represents the starting point for thinking: "The animal looks at us [*nous regarde*, also: concerns us], and we are naked
before it. Thinking perhaps begins there" (29). Indeed, this hypothesis
is already announced in the title of his lecture—"L'animal que donc je
suis"—which places "the animal" in the position usually occupied by
the Cartesian *cogito*. All thinking, Derrida appears to be saying, is ultimately "animal thinking," in that it comes *after* or, indeed, *follows* from
this encounter with "the animal," and this is what Western philosophy
has—in and for the sake of its very essence—sought to forget. Poetry, by
contrast, would be defined as that form of thinking that has not forgotten, but has continued to "think" or to "think through" the question
of the animal, repeatedly, "endlessly, and from a novel perspective" (6).
Not all poetry, perhaps, and certainly not in a unified or systematic way
that would justify speaking of a single, coherent tradition or movement.
Nevertheless, there is and has undeniably been a certain affinity between
"poetic thinking" and "animal thinking," whose precise articulation will,
of course, vary greatly depending on the historical, cultural, linguistic,
and geographic context and a host of other factors, but which is ubiquitous enough to merit its own name: *zoopoetics*.

The general consensus seems to be that the term "zoopoetics" was
first used by Derrida in a rather offhand allusion to "Kafka's vast zoopoetics" (6). While Derrida does not elaborate on this further, the reference to Kafka is instructive because of the specific way animals and
animality figure in his writings. One of the first commentators to pick
up on Kafka's zoopoetics was Walter Benjamin, in his 1934 essay written
on the tenth anniversary of Kafka's death. A key component of Kafka's
work, Benjamin writes, is the excavation of that which has been forgotten, and this operation is inextricably linked to the figure of the animal.
Animals, for Kafka, are "repositories of the forgotten [*Behältnisse des
Vergessenen*]," and "Kafka never tired of listening to the animals to hear
that which has been forgotten [*den Tieren das Vergessene abzulauschen*]"

(Benjamin 1999, 810, trans. mod.). Returning to Derrida's text, we might say that zoopoetics involves not only seeing but also precisely this attentive listening—a practice of "listening otherwise" (cf. Driscoll 2017)—to the animal in order to recover something that has been forgotten or repressed. For Kafka, an unavoidable effect of this auscultation of the forgotten is the reanimalization of language. The Western, carno-phallogocentric tradition has consistently sought to disembody language, to transcend the physical, animal part of the human. Thus, as Benjamin observes, one's own animal body is the "most forgotten Other [*die vergessenste Fremde*]" (Benjamin 1999, 810) of language. It is for this same reason, he writes, that "Kafka called the cough that erupted from within him 'the animal.' It was the vanguard of the great herd" (ibid.). Kafka's "vast zoopoetics," then, is also a poetics of the body, of the sudden reminder of one's own corporeality, and hence of one's own animality.

This brings us to Benjamin's most important observation, which is simultaneously the most often overlooked, but which should have far-reaching consequences for how we approach not only "Kafka's vast zoopoetics" but zoopoetics in general. Immediately after observing that Kafka never tired of listening to his animals for traces of the forgotten, Benjamin writes: "They might not be the goal, but without them it can't be done [*Sie sind wohl nicht das Ziel, aber ohne sie geht es nicht*]" (ibid.). That is to say: Kafka's poetics is a zoopoetics not because his texts are *about* animals, but because the animals that inhabit his texts serve as a necessary and unsubstitutable means to particular, as yet inscrutable, poetic ends. Without them it can't be done. But what is "it"? We may never know, and indeed, the answer will be different each time, but whatever "it" may be, it contains the whole of zoopoetics.

Each of the fourteen essays collected in this volume can be seen as an attempt to answer this question by means of one or more specific texts, from a variety of traditions and periods, all of which engage, explicitly or implicitly, with the complex relationship between animality and poetic language—the entanglements of bodies and texts. Taken together, these essays present a rich and multifaceted collection of responses to the question of zoopoetics, not only in terms of the individual literary texts themselves, but also with regard to the methods and approaches of literary animal studies. That is to say, the intersection between "poetic thinking" and "animal thinking" is a characteristic not merely of poetry, but also of a certain mode of reading and criticism; the essays that follow are, thus, conceived as both studies and examples of zoopoetics.

To reiterate: zoopoetic texts are not—at least not necessarily and certainly not simply—texts *about* animals. Rather, they are texts that are, in
one way or another, predicated upon an engagement with animals and
animality (human and nonhuman). In short, their "poetic thinking,"
(i.e., the way they reflect on their own textuality and materiality), on
questions of writing and representation, proceeds via the animal. This,
moreover, has implications for how we, as readers and scholars in animal
studies and literary studies—and literary animal studies—approach these
texts. One of the most important implications of Benjamin's claim that
the animals themselves might not be "the goal" of zoopoetics but rather
its unsubstitutable "medium" is that we need not fear or mistrust the
metaphorical, symbolic, and allegorical meanings embodied by literary
animals, so long as we do not make the mistake of reading these nonhuman presences *only* or *simply* as metaphors—as arbitrary and interchange-
able ciphers for the "real" or "intended" meaning. This approach has, of
course, been endemic to traditional approaches to animals in literature.
As Margot Norris writes in *Beasts of the Modern Imagination*, a foundational work of literary animal studies, "It seem[s] that nowhere in literature [are] animals to be allowed to be themselves, to refer to Nature
and to their own animality without being pressed into symbolic service
as metaphors, or as figures in fable or allegory (invariably of some aspect
of the human)" (Norris 1985, 17). The single-minded determination
to interpret the animals "out" of literary texts constitutes another form
of forgetting and disappearance (cf. McHugh 2009a, 24), which a zoopoetic reading would seek to counteract. At the same time, we should
also be wary of claiming to recover the animals "themselves," lest we
ignore their specifically *literary* and *poetic* character. In short, the white
whale in Melville's *Moby-Dick* is not *just* a metaphor; but he's also not
just a whale. He is, if anything, an *animot* (Derrida 2008, 47–48), or
a "figure" in Donna Haraway's sense, namely a "material-semiotic
knot" (Haraway 2008, 4). The task of a zoopoetic reading is precisely
to explore what lies between these two extremes, the mutual imbrica-
tion and entanglement of the material and the semiotic, the body and
the text, the animal and the word.
    In this sense, zoopoetics may also be seen as an exercise in what
Derrida calls "limitrophy" (Derrida 2008, 29) or "feed[ing] the limit,
[…] complicating, thickening, delinearizing, folding, and dividing" (ibid.)
it, multiplying differences and discontinuities, in order to show how the
limit is not "single and indivisible" but rather multiple, fractured, and

folded in on itself in myriad complex and often contradictory ways. The task, therefore, is not to "blur" or "efface" the boundary between humans and animals—or rather, between "what calls *itself* man and what *he* calls the animal" (30)—in favor of a "homogeneous continuity" (ibid.), but rather to insist on the irreducible multiplicity and heterogeneity contained in those categories. This is important to keep in mind in order to counteract the inadvertent tendency, even within animal studies, to reify the category of 'the animal' by taking it for granted that everything from spiders to dogs to whales falls under the purview of the field. This is a tendency to which zoopoetics is, of course, not immune either. It makes a difference that Moby-Dick is a whale (even if he is not *just* a whale) and not a dog or a spider, and hence strictly speaking, we would need to distinguish between cetopoetics, cynopoetics, and arachnopoetics, and so on—and, indeed, many of the contributions to this volume do just that (e.g., the chapters by Michaela Castellanos, Joela Jacobs, and Matthias Preuss).

If it is, nevertheless, meaningful and important to speak of zoopoetics as a poetics of animality more generally, it is not because of the legitimacy of "the animal" as an ontological category, but rather because of its function as a discursive one, namely as the "other" of the human. Animals, more so than other forms of life such as plants, are obviously agential beings that operate at roughly the same speed and scale as humans and have their own perspective on the world around them: animals *look at us* in a way that trees and rivers—or, for that matter, other humans—do not, and this is what has always made them "good to think," as Claude Lévi-Strauss famously put it (Lévi-Strauss 1963, 89). Animals, in short, have always served as both a mirror and a screen for the human, a site of negativity against which "the human" has been defined. Yet this also means, as Kari Weil writes, that "[t]he idea of 'the animal'—the instinctive being with presumably no access to language, texts, or abstract thinking—has functioned as an unexamined foundation on which the idea of the human and hence the humanities have been built" (Weil 2012, 23). As our understanding of animal language, culture, and morality develops, she continues, so must our view of the nature of the human and the humanities. This is a further reason why a zoopoetic intervention into literary studies may be necessary, as the traditional insistence on reading literary animals as metaphors and allegories for the human has not only served to occlude the complexity and material-semiotic recalcitrance of these nonhuman presences, subsuming the diversity of literary animals under the singularity of "the animal," it has *also* tended to assume a singular and universal human experience or condition that would be self-evidently represented by the former. Thus, such reductionist reading practices have served to perpetuate an epistemological framework that takes "human" to mean white, male, heterosexual, able-bodied, rational, and so forth.

A central concern for zoopoetics—conceived both as an object of study and as a methodological problem for animal studies, and for literary studies more generally is, thus, the question of representation: Who or what is being represented by whom or what and in what way? What, in this context, would it mean for literary theory and criticism to let animals "be themselves"? And how can and do representations of animality help us to come to a more inclusive and complex understanding of what it means to be human? Questions of representation are especially important for animal studies because nonhuman animals simply "cannot speak for themselves, or at least they cannot speak any of the languages that the academy recognizes as necessary for such self-representation" (2012, 4). This problem is compounded within *literary* animal studies because there are, strictly speaking, no "actual" animals in literary texts that "we" might allow to "be themselves": there are only words, or rather, *animots*. A zoopoetic approach to literature must take the implications of this fact seriously, and the contributors to this volume, many of whom are both scholars and poets or artists in their own right, resist the tendency to press animals "into symbolic service" as metaphors and allegories for the human, and instead are attentive to the specific ways in which animals operate in literary texts as "functions of their literariness" (McHugh 2009b, 490).

Much of the nervousness within animal studies surrounding the metaphorical and/or semiotic conception of animals stems from the suspicion that "such a conception serves ultimately to assimilate the animal to a fundamentally logocentric discourse" (Driscoll 2015, 227) that reduces the question of the animal to the question of legibility. In this context, it is important to stress that our encounters with animals in the "real" world are also *both* material *and* semiotic, and hence that the relationship between "real" animals and "literary" animals is not that of an original to a copy, but rather reciprocal and irreducibly entangled. Roland Borgards, one of the founders of literary animal studies, has argued persuasively for the inclusion of animals and plants in the collective production of meaning, suggesting that we read animals and their textual traces as "material metaphors" (Borgards 2015, 180; cf. 2012). More importantly, the encounter between humans and other animals leaves a trace in the text that cannot be translated into meaning. Along similar lines, albeit in a Derridean rather than a Latourian vein, Rodolfo Piskorski has proposed "zoogrammatology" (cf. Piskorski 2015) as a method for reading these animal traces. In his contribution to this volume, Piskorski develops the concept of *arche*-animality (in reference to Derrida's concept of *arche*-writing) as a framework for a zoopoetic reading of Clarice Lispector's novel *The Apple in the Dark* that complicates traditional understandings of metaphoricity. These considerations serve as a further indication of the way in which the figure of the animal and of animality presents "a specific problem *to* and *for* language and representation" (Driscoll 2015, 228).

Following the principle of "limitrophy" to trouble and complicate the binary distinction between man and animal, the contributions to this volume explore new ways of reading animal figures both in canonical texts and in lesser-known works, tracing the question of zoopoetics across a variety of genres and historical periods and taking material-semiotic exchanges between human and nonhuman animals into account. Thus, in their zoopoetic readings the authors of this volume pay attention to animals not only as the objects of literary representation, but also as actively involved in the *production* of the very materiality of the text. In so doing, this volume expands on existing approaches to zoopoetics and engages with the question on how zoopoetics should proceed. By granting animals an active role in the making of poetry, a zoopoetic approach defies the long-held belief within the history of Western philosophy and the humanities in general that the human as the ζῷον λόγος ἔχων is the only animal that possesses language. In other words, animals not only have their own languages in which they communicate, but they also influence us in our production of language, and specifically in the making of poetry. Literary animals are therefore imbricated in the lives of actual animals—and vice versa.

Zoopoetics, thus, takes both human and nonhuman animals to be not only the objects but also *agents* of representation. This brings us close to Aaron M. Moe's conception of zoopoetics, whose central tenet is that "nonhuman animals [...] are makers" and that "they have agency in that making" (Moe 2014, 2):

The etymology [of zoopoetics] also suggests that when a poet undergoes the making process of *poiesis* in harmony with the gestures and vocalizations of nonhuman animals, a multispecies event occurs. It is a co-making. A joint venture. The two-fold foci of zoopoetics—that nonhuman animals are makers and that this making has shaped the form of human poems— illustrates how animals *animate* […] and therefore bring the sensuous world to the surface of the written page. (2014, 2)

Emphasizing agency as "the first focus of zoopoetics" (Moe 2013, 4), Moe argues for the empowerment of nonhuman animals and their "bodily *poiesis*" in the poetic process. As Michaela Castellanos notes in her chapter in this volume, however, Moe's model often tends to assume a rather straightforward "translation" from the "real" animals' bodily *poiesis* to the poetic text. It also implies a hierarchy of representation, whereby poetic texts that result from encounters with "real" animals are somehow more "zoopoetic" than ones that engage with purely cultural animals and animality. Leaving aside the difficulty of determining whether a particular poem is the record of an *actual* encounter and engagement with an animal "in the flesh," it seems arbitrary and above all reductive to discount the agency of textual or cultural animals in coshaping zoopoetic texts. Rilke's iconic animal poem "The Panther," for example, was inspired not only by his visits to the *Jardin des Plantes*, but also by a statuette of a panther he had encountered in Rodin's studio. The former is just as much a "figure" in Haraway's sense as the latter, and it is precisely the combination of these two impressions, these two encounters, along with innumerable others that are both natural and cultural, human and animal, real and imagined, that constitutes the "material-semiotic knot" of the poem.

Furthermore, while it is of course crucial for a zoopoetic approach that we acknowledge the agency of both human and nonhuman animals by regarding poetic and other forms of artistic expression as a "multispecies event," we must also keep in mind that the agency of nonhumans in these processes has been and continues to be quite limited. That is to say, an overly affirmative focus on agency runs the risk of obscuring how animals function both as a symbolic and as a material resource, which turns animals into a form of capital or biopolitical animal matter, as Nicole Shukin (2009) suggests. The authors of this volume, for example Matthias Preuss, Belinda Kleinhans, and Michaela Castellanos, extend the logic of biopolitics to the animal body in their zoopoetic readings, and point to the precariousness that is involved. Matthias Preuss expands on Moe's zoopoetics by proposing to understand literature as expression, as text, and as secretion. His reading of Ovid's *Metamorphoses* accounts for the materiality of animal matter, while challenging the notion of empowerment and agency by pointing to the historical exploitation of animal skin and secretion in the material production of literature. This, too, is a "multispecies event" of sorts, albeit one quite different from the reciprocal pleasure of making that Moe appears to envisage.

Furthermore, the mimetic aspect of a zoopoetic reading that focuses on a joint "bodily energy" between species runs the risk of reiterating categorization and tends to ignore the fluidity of "becoming" with which many zoopoetic texts imagine alternative forms of life. In this volume, Peter Meedom's contribution on Djuna Barnes's *Nightwood* challenges our understanding of species and presents a zoopoetic reading that makes other forms of life and kinship formations legible. Meedom's chapter illustrates how zoopoetic approaches to literature share some of the concerns and interest of queer theory, as Eva Hoffmann also points out in her contribution. These chapters highlight the need for zoopoetics to engage with intersectional analysis: zoopoetics can and must not only challenge our conceptions of both "the animal" and "the human"— while being attentive to the specific historical moments from which these categories emerge—but also investigate how these categories intersect with constructions such as race, gender, and sexuality. In that regard, zoopoetic approaches to language and literature can inform other discourses, and be informed by them, for example critical race studies, gender studies, disability studies, etc., by investigating the central role of animality in the way we construct and perceive identity and differences.

What Is Zoopoetics? is divided into three sections, "Texts," "Bodies," and "Entanglement," each comprising four chapters. All three of these terms are central to our conception of zoopoetics, and hence all of the chapters engage with the entanglements of textuality and corporeality, the encounter between human and nonhuman meanings and forms. Nevertheless, we have grouped these twelve essays according to the relative emphasis they give to these elements. The first section focuses on questions of language, metaphoricity, and narrative, in short on the semiotic side of the "knot," whereas the second section is primarily concerned with the materiality of literary animals. The final section brings these two sides together, focusing on interspecies encounters and the complex interplay between word and world that emerges when species meet. In addition to these twelve essays, we have the great privilege of being able to include two texts by Marcel Beyer, one of the great contemporary "zoopoets." These ruminations on writing, communication, language, and representation frame and complement the discussions at the heart of this book.

The first chapter, by Nicolas Picard, is entitled "Hunting Narratives: Capturing the Lives of Animals." In it, Picard explores the structural analogy between hunting and hermeneutics, and what this means for practices of zoopoetic reading. "Hunting narratives," thus, refers both to stories about hunting as well as the hunt for narratives. To a certain extent, he writes, "We hunt to be able to tell stories. The pleasure of narration is as important as the pleasure of the hunt, since it is, in the end, the pleasure of predation." Belinda Kleinhans's chapter sheds light on the more sinister side of linking predation and narration. Focusing on literary animals in the work of Günter Eich, particularly his "moles," Kleinhans explores how Eich's zoopoetics seeks to "undermine" the complicity of language in oppressive regimes of power (specifically National Socialism). Continuing the theme of animality and language, Joela Jacobs's contribution traces the motif of attributing speech to dogs from postmodern internet memes such as "Doge," which plays with ungrammatical language, to modernist canine narratives by Oskar Panizza and Franz Kafka, which tie in with the tradition of the eloquent "philosopher dog." Jacobs argues that language undoes the difference between human and animal in these texts by introducing epistemological and ontological doubt which destabilizes the perception of self and other for both the narrating dogs and the human readers. Concluding the "Texts" section, Sebastian Schönbeck's chapter proposes a zoopoetic reevaluation of the genre of the fable, which, he argues, has been unjustly maligned by literary animal studies as being quintessentially anthropocentric. Through a careful analysis of Heinrich von Kleist's repurposing of one of La Fontaine's fables in his essay "On the Gradual Production of Thoughts Whilst Speaking," Schönbeck explores the interrelation between aesthetics, poetics, political philosophy, and natural history in Enlightenment thought.

Section two begins with a chapter by Rodolfo Piskorski on Clarice Lispector's novel *The Apple in the Dark*. Departing from an inherent ambiguity in the Portuguese term for giving birth ("dar a/à luz," which, depending on whether it is written with an *a* or an *à*, means either to "give [someone] to the light" or to "give the light [to someone]"),

Piskorski develops a rich and complex reading of the poetics of light and dark in the novel, which he relates to the figure of animality, or, more specifically, *arche*-animality, an "articulating supplement" that both precedes and makes possible the distinction and transition between nature and culture. Following on from this, Michaela Castellanos's chapter approaches Herman Melville's *Moby-Dick* as a zoopoetic text that probes the contingencies of the categories human and animal through the narrator's language. Castellanos situates whales in the cultural and historical context of early nineteenth-century America and argues that the anxiety over categorization of animal bodies mirrors the uncertainty of how to comprehend racialized bodies. Eva Hoffmann's chapter, "Queering the Interspecies Encounter: Yoko Tawada's *Memoirs of a Polar Bear*," presents a zoopoetic reading of the queer kinship in Tawada's novel that runs counter to the heteropatriarchal logic of procreation and family structures, and illustrates how the lives of three generations of polar bears are intricately intertwined and entangled with those of their human companions, from which new narratives and forms of writings emerge. While the first three chapters of this section explore the role of gender, race, and sexuality in the production and rendering of animal bodies, Paul Sheehan's chapter, which brings this section to a close, takes up the problem of the real and metaphorical disappearance of animal bodies. Through a reading of texts by W. S. Merwin and Richard Skelton, Sheehan imagines a zoopoetics of extinction predicated on absence and mourning for lost species.

The third section begins with the paradigmatic figure of entanglement: the spider. In his chapter, Matthias Preuss presents three different zoopoetological (or rather arachnopoetological) figures inhabiting Ovid's *Metamorphoses*. Whether the spider's relation to the text is read as "spinning," "weaving," or "secreting," each of these three figures implies both a semiotic and a material component, which furthermore has important implications for the conception of the animal as the *medium* of zoopoetics. Peter Meedom's "Impersonal Love: *Nightwood*'s Poetics of Mournful Entanglement" shifts the discussion toward the relationship of personal and impersonal life in Djuna Barnes's *Nightwood*. Focusing primarily on the seemingly incoherent ramblings of the "gender-bending quack" Matthew O'Connor, Meedom explores how the novel addresses the entanglement of personal lives in the impersonal life of the earth, calling for an impersonal love attuned to loss. Figures of loss and mourning also animate Ann Marie Thornburg's chapter, in which she reads two poems—one by Diane Seuss and one by Carl Phillips—that revolve around an encounter between a human speaker and an animal, which end in gestures of letting go of the other. Rather than signaling the speaker's giving up on relating or giving into vague celebrations of difference, however, these gestures, Thornburg argues, are supported by processes of self-scrutiny that acknowledge the precarity of relating. In the closing chapter, multimedia artist Catherine Clover presents and comments on her textual field recording, *Heading South into Town*, which follows the motion of a journey from Melbourne's suburban north to the center of the city and details a contingent interaction between people and birds through hearing, listening, voicing, speaking, and reading. In the chapter, she considers her creative work through a reflexive process, including how artistic thinking can work with and through the current ecological crisis and what art offers. The motif of human-bird interaction is then taken up in the volume's coda, written by Marcel Beyer, in which he meditates on the various forms of communication that take place between him and the birds on the balcony of his apartment, and how it relates to his work as a writer.

Acknowledgements The editors would like to thank all the contributors for their hard work and everyone at Palgrave who helped us bring this to fruition. Special thanks to Marcel Beyer for agreeing to be part of this volume. Thanks also to Niels Springveld for carefully proofreading all the chapters and for compiling the index, and to Susanne Knittel for her help and support.

Utrecht and Eugene, May 2017

WORKS CITED

Benjamin, Walter. 1999 [1934]. Franz Kafka: On the Tenth Anniversary of His Death, trans. Harry Zohn. In *Selected Writings, Volume 2, Part 2 (1931–1934)*, ed. Michael W. Jennings, Howard Eiland, and Gary Smith, 794–818. Cambridge, MA: Belknap Press of Harvard University Press.

Berger, John. 1991 [1977]. Why Look at Animals? In *About Looking*, 3–28. New York: Vintage.

Borgards, Roland. 2012. Tiere in der Literatur – eine methodologische Standortbestimmung. In *Das Tier an sich. Disziplinübergreifende Perspektiven für neue Wege im wissenschaftsbasierten Tierschutz*, ed. Herwig Grimm and Carola Otterstedt, 87–118. Göttingen: Vandenhoeck & Ruprecht.

———. 2015. Kapitel 61: *Stubb Kills a Whale*. Asche. *Neue Rundschau* 126 (1): 173–185.

Derrida, Jacques. 2008. *The Animal That Therefore I Am*, trans. David Wills and ed. Marie-Louise Mallet. New York: Fordham University Press.

Driscoll, Kári. 2015. The Sticky Temptation of Poetry. *Journal of Literary Theory* 9 (2): 212–229.

———. 2017. An Unheard, Inhuman Music: Narrative Voice and the Question of the Animal in Kafka's 'Josephine, the Singer or the Mouse Folk.' *Humanities* 6 (2): art. no. 26. https://doi.org/10.3390/h6020026.

Haraway, Donna J. 2008. *When Species Meet*. Minneapolis: University of Minnesota Press.

Lévi-Strauss, Claude. 1963. *Totemism*, trans. Rodney Needham. Boston: Beacon Press.

McHugh, Susan. 2009a. *Animal Farm*'s Lessons for Literary (and) Animal Studies. *Humanimalia* 1 (1): 24–39.

———. 2009b. Literary Animal Agents. *PMLA* 124 (2): 487–495.

Moe, Aaron M. 2013. Toward Zoopoetics: Rethinking Whitman's 'Original Energy'. *Walt Whitman Quarterly Review* 31 (1): 1–17.

———. 2014. *Zoopoetics: Animals and the Making of Poetry*. Lanham, MD: Lexington Books.

Norris, Margot. 1985. *Beasts of the Modern Imagination: Darwin, Nietzsche, Kafka, Ernst, and Lawrence*. Baltimore: Johns Hopkins University Press.

Piskorski, Rodolfo. 2015. Of Zoogrammatology as a Positive Literary Theory. *Journal of Literary Theory* 9 (2): 230–249.

Shukin, Nicole. 2009. *Animal Capital: Rendering Life in Biopolitical Times*. Minneapolis: University of Minnesota Press.

Weil, Kari. 2012. *Thinking Animals: Why Animal Studies Now?* New York: Columbia University Press.

Prelude: I Observe with My Pen

Marcel Beyer

I

In his book *Im Tierpark belauscht* [*Overheard at the Zoo*], a collection of anecdotes published in 1965, Heinrich Dathe writes that "years ago" (as if animals in captivity, like things, existed beyond our reckoning of time), particularly on days when there had been lots of visitors, in the corner pavilion of the erstwhile monkey house, the staff of the Leipzig Zoo would frequently discover a suspiciously large assortment of jewelry and other personal items. Only through "careful and covert observation," Dathe writes, were they able to discover how these "mirrors, silk scarves, straw hats, caps, gloves, spectacles, lorgnettes, ladies' umbrellas, pencils and fabric flowers," to say nothing of the "keys, wallets, handbags and purses," had found their way into the cage of these two sooty mangabeys (also known as white-naped mangabeys, *Cercocebus atys*).

At this point in Dathe's monkey anecdote, as I am faithfully retelling it here, we can already begin to see that "observation" and "observation" are two fundamentally distinct activities, depending on whether we are dealing with a text or not. For there is no way the zoo staff can actually have discovered such a hoard of stolen treasures in the mangabey

M. Beyer
Dresden, Germany

© The Author(s) 2018
K. Driscoll and E. Hoffmann (Eds.), *What Is Zoopoetics?*,
Palgrave Studies in Animals and Literature,
https://doi.org/10.1007/978-3-319-64416-5_2

15

cage at closing time. After all, Dathe himself reports that the zookeeper regularly had to deal with distressed visitors during opening hours complaining of having lost something.

Naturally, in telling his story, Heinrich Dathe is employing a simple dramaturgical trick in order to get the reader's attention: allowing us to share in a curious observation—implicitly announcing that the mystery will be solved at the end. And although one observation follows the other ("faster than I can tell it," as he writes at one point), unlike in a classic detective story, it makes no difference for Dathe's narrative that his description of the floor of the monkey cage strewn with straw hats, spectacles and handbags cannot possibly correspond to any empirical observation, nor that it stands in direct contradiction to observations made elsewhere in the text. The reader, meanwhile, presumably an avid zoogoer himself, might well balk at the reference to car keys and wallets left behind in the monkey house: Would anyone actually leave the zoo without having regained possession of such indispensable items? Instead of solving this initial mystery step by step, Dathe's anecdote piles mystery upon mystery, in a gesture parallel to that of the two sooty mangabeys whose cage, if not in reality then certainly in the text, gradually fills up with purloined objects.

Nevertheless, the reader can be certain that the narrator will present him with a solution in the end, and it would be a simple matter to recount the rest of the story if it weren't for the fact that Dathe more or less surreptitiously constructs a triangular constellation of observers—zoo animals, zoogoers, zookeepers—that is at once highly revealing and highly vexing. If we strip away the genteel, jaunty tone and the rather tiresome humor, which hinges entirely on a "classic" role reversal between man and ape, as well as the general aversion to primates evinced by Dathe's frequent use of words such as "capricious," "underhanded," "cunning," "thieving," and "wicked"—in short, if we try to disregard the rhetorical ornamentation (but then again, style *is* character)—what we are left with is this: the zookeepers observe the two monkeys adopting different roles in order to observe the zoogoers as they satisfy their curiosity.

The one monkey, crouching on the floor of the cage, stretches his arm out through the bars. A visitor, "touched" (Dathe writes) by the gesture of the open paw, which he (the visitor, according to Dathe) interprets as a "hand held out imploringly," leans out over the railing in order to give the monkey something to eat, or else to tap him on the palm of his "hand" with a spectacle case or a fountain pen. Meanwhile, the other mangabey, perched on a pole higher up in the cage, is looking "down with feigned nonchalance at the people assembled outside his abode." As soon as a zoogoer comes sufficiently close, this unobserved observer— and not, as one might expect, his accomplice down below, sitting by the bars of the cage, "innocently rolling his eyes"—snatches the spectacle case from the zoogoer's hand or the hat from their head, whereupon the two mangabeys withdraw in order to "rip their loot to pieces" (i.e., to examine the object).

Here the unstable observer constellation collapses. There is no question of a timely intervention by the zookeeper, or even by the author himself in his capacity as a practicing animal psychologist. On the contrary, Dathe stresses that this "modus operandi" was employed by the two mangabeys "repeatedly and with a consistent degree of success." The monkeys now shift their attention from the curious zoogoer to the object they have seized, while we instead become aware of another observer position, namely that of the other visitors who have observed the events as they unfolded.

The observer constellation collapses—and the result is shame. The "victim" feels ashamed, certainly in front of the other visitors, and certainly also for having allowed his keys or his spectacles to be taken from him, so that he is now in a certain sense naked. Ashamed also because he has no alternative but to call the zookeeper and confess his misfortune. But above all, no doubt, he feels ashamed because compared to the two monkeys, he has proved the less observant observer.

Now, it would be completely beside the point to criticize Dathe's anecdote for being illogical, or to accuse the author of representing the process of observation in a way that is not "true to life." Having read this occasional piece, which bears the title "Two Partners in Crime," one is more likely to feel that one has learned something about the difficulties of communicating observations as such. These difficulties are not merely the result of the text's formal constraints, the generic narrative conventions of the anecdote, but rather, and I am quite certain of this, come to the fore whenever a text seems to speak to our desire as readers to ignore the distinction between observation and written observation. Writing is not a procedure for "recording" observations, but rather a process that can spur observation. "Writing things down," as these two sooty mangabeys from the pen of Heinrich Dathe teach us, is at best an illusion.

Thus, it comes as no surprise when, at the end of his tale, Dathe again draws the reader's attention to a writing implement: "It was a singularly impressive sight to see a fountain pen dispatched with one bite," he reports, as if to allow this animal, symbolically at least, to cross the inviolable line between writing and nonwriting mammals. "At this, the ink ran out of corners of the ape's mouth like blueberry soup. The observers erupted into enthusiastic applause."

II

In September 2012, I attended a conference in Würzburg, where, in the breaks between sessions—the discreet charm of cultural and literary animal studies—a photograph of Derrida's cat was passed around. So this was she: the assuredly real, singular, living, mortal, emphatically nonsymbolic, nonallegorical, nonconceptualizable, nonwritten and nonwriting cat, whose daily routine included seeing Derrida every morning, in the bedroom or in the bathroom, naked. And we looked at her, and we felt no shame.

III

Over the past 15 years I have tried repeatedly to read Vladimir Nabokov's *Lolita*, but have so far not managed to get beyond the astonishing critical apparatus in Dieter E. Zimmer's German edition and Nabokov's own afterword, entitled "On a Book Entitled *Lolita*," which, as result, I have now in fact read multiple times.

Of all the various ostensibly autobiographical statements Nabokov made about his novel, none has remained as consistently vexing to his readership as the comment in this afterword that the "first throb" of what would eventually become *Lolita* had been prompted by a newspaper article he happened upon in late 1939 or early 1940 while in Paris. The story was about an ape—a chimpanzee? an orangutan?—held captive at the Jardin des Plantes, who, after months of coaxing by a scientist—a zoologist? an art historian?—became the first of his species to produce a charcoal drawing. "This sketch showed the bars of the poor creature's cage."

Apart from the rather trivial parallelism in the fact that Humbert Humbert writes his account from behind bars, there is hardly anything in the novel that would recall that "initial shiver of inspiration," even if the

PRELUDE: I OBSERVE WITH MY PEN 19

narrator does describe his eyes as "ape eyes" and his ear as an "ape-ear," Lolita's feet as "monkeyish," and once refers to Lolita's hand as a "paw" and to his own as an "ape paw." Humbert even describes a trip that the two of them take to a zoo in Indiana, where—Robert Musil sends his regards from the Villa Borghese—"a large troop of monkeys lived on a concrete replica of Christopher Columbus' flagship."

The real-life counterpart to the zoo in the novel was quickly identified as the Mesker Park Zoo in Evansville, Indiana—its current website features a rubric entitled "Kinderfun." But despite decades of searching, Nabokov scholarship has so far failed to locate the zoopoetic source material he identifies for his novel: there was no such newspaper story, nor an artistic ape at the Jardin des Plantes at the beginning of the Second World War.

In the course of this frantic search, scholars have, however, "discovered" a whole range of apes who drew and painted, as well as a chimpanzee at the Berlin Zoo who in 1938 took pictures from inside his cage with a Leica: one of his photographs shows the bars of his cage, behind which we see a group of smiling zoogoers, and, on the far left-hand side, a camera pointed at the chimp. Scholars have also tracked down a chimp named Cookie who, in 1942, under the direction of his owner H. Huber Clark, took pictures of his observers from inside his wire-mesh-reinforced cage in New York; and another chimp, also named Cookie, who, 1949, under the auspices of the *Life* photographer Bernhard Hoffman, took a group photo of visitors to the St. Louis Zoo, after having spent the previous nine years patiently sitting for zoogoers' photos himself.

The attendant role reversal between observers and observed which these photographs "document" recalls Heinrich Dathe's mangabey story, particularly given that both cases—here a camera, there a fountain pen—involve a tool which man employs to reassure himself of his view of the world and hence his identity.

Behind the bars of the ape cage, a man. This becomes more than a superficial gag if we consider the possibility that Nabokov's image of the ape who draws the bars of his cage might refer to another image altogether, a nightmare vision from the imaginary photo album of the writer's profession, now presumably unfamiliar to most literary scholars, but which continues to haunt the minds of writers to this day. And it will have been just as vivid for Nabokov in 1951, when he began writing *Lolita*, as in 1957 when he wrote the afterword that contained the simian origin story, because this image had, with an unheard-of intensity, raised the question of what, in the best, or, indeed, the worst case, a writer could be.

This photograph, if it were to exist, would show a row of outdoor cells just north of Pisa. Steel cages, some reinforced with wire mesh, with a piece of tar paper provide shelter from the elements. In the photograph, taken in late May or early June of 1945, one would see, inside one of these cages, the poet Ezra Pound. Whether he kept his eyes downcast or stared directly at the photographer from inside his "gorilla cage," silently condemning him for taking the picture—it would be impossible, even after intensive scrutiny, to say for certain whether Pound's face, deeply furrowed by anti-Semitic frenzy, or his lifeless eyes, revealed something akin to shame.

IV

"Ape art" has been around for a hundred years. The first known scientist to give paper and pencil to a chimp—a male named Yoni—was Nadezhda Nikolaevna Ladygina-Kohts, who did so in 1913, in the zoopsychological laboratory at the State Darwin Museum in Moscow. Like Nabokov's imaginary ape, Yoni also drew lines across the page, even though, as far as we know, in this case the artist was not a "poor creature" kept in a tiny cage and subjected to the inquiring gaze of daily visitors.

In the public imagination, or so it seems to me (if I may venture a hypothesis), it is only after 1945 that the image of the ape who paints, draws, or takes photographs becomes separated from that of the vaude-ville monkey who does tricks or the organ-grinder's sidekick in the colorful costume: in other words, a monkey trained by men to imitate man. Whether this shift has to do with the fall of National Socialism, under which all spheres of life and human expression had been regarded from a perspective of racism, or whether the wholesale biologization of art in the Nazi period had simply moved to a different area—either way, from this point forward, each new piece of tangible evidence provided by these zoological experiments in occupational therapy gives rise to the familiar debate as to whether these simian artworks represent proof that the self-evidently close relationship between humans and great apes is in fact "even closer" than anyone had imagined. Because, look—the verdict, so curiously at odds with this "ontological intuition"—aren't they "just beautiful"? How absurd and repugnant, how ominous this "just beautiful," which unites the idea of an "evolutionary mammalian aesthetics" with "natural beauty" à la Riefenstahl. A drawing by a chimp; a painting by an orangutan: "At first I thought it was degenerate art, but then, when I discovered who the artist was, I recognized its true value."

If we now move on from the countless works by apes on paper and canvas (perhaps "signed" "Cheeta" and given the title "Untitled" by an art dealer) and instead turn our attention to postwar ape photography, another vertiginous dimension opens up. The simple addition of the optical apparatus suffices to make a whole series of thorny problems disappear almost automatically. Suddenly, the viewer is relieved of the burden of having to prove his artistic sensibilities by pondering whether this or that primate's work is more reminiscent of an unfinished Käthe Kollwitz sketch or a late Jackson Pollock, or perhaps rather the early stages of a Bob Ross, particularly if you used to watch his show on an old television set with an indoor aerial and bad reception. Similarly, the question of whether apes draw a connection between observation and pictorial representation fades into the background. If a chimpanzee or a gorilla snaps a photo, it makes no difference whether they are able or indeed feel the need to "capture" their sense impressions. We have long since grown used to the idea that a photograph can be a nonintentional form of representation. But if we are willing to concede that humans produce images "by accident," as the art historian Peter Geimer terms it, then we must be willing to concede the same for an animal. Apes do not take photographs of what they observe; they observe *and* take photographs.

This is where it gets interesting. An animal makes use of a camera, the archetypal documentary apparatus, in order to document ... what, exactly? In the case of Koko the gorilla, whose self-portrait was on the cover of the October 1978 issue of *National Geographic*, the question is still relatively easy to answer: looking in the mirror, this primate, trained in the use of the camera, is documenting the classic mirror test—as if she herself were the ethologist hoping to provide proof of the capacity for self-awareness in a nonhuman animal. But while this answer feels implicitly compelling, it does not resolve the problem of what the relationship here is between observation and photography. After all, what Koko is seeing through the viewfinder is in fact not her own face, but rather the camera which covers it almost completely. Perhaps she is actually looking at the mirror-inverted "Olympus" logo above the lens; perhaps she is staring at her hands holding the camera.

In a widely publicized PR stunt by the Schönbrunn Zoo in early December 2009, the female orangutan Nonja was given a digital camera which automatically uploaded the pictures she took to a Facebook account that had been set up in Nonja's name. Within the first few days, she and her fellow orangutans had taken more than a hundred pictures, receiving a raisin each time they pressed the shutter-release button. Even more spectacular than the marketing success are the pictures themselves, of whose existence the orangutans at Schönbrunn Zoo remain entirely unaware. Viewing these images, it quickly becomes apparent that you are witnessing the inspection of an object which the orangutans consider to be a raisin dispenser—and yet you constantly find yourself wishing that they were inspecting a camera.

We see: clouds of wood shavings. An armpit. The edge of a window. A pair of eyes. A blurry section of light-colored ground. Dark skin. In the background, an orangutan looking at another orangutan who is looking at a camera. More wood shavings on the ground. A foot. A crumpled white cloth. An eye. A nose. A tuft of hair. Ropes swinging in the air. Upper lip, row of teeth, tongue—pressed against the camera lens. A smooth tree trunk, stripped bare of its bark. Light.

Schönbrunn Zoo never tire of pointing out that for the orangutans, this digital camera, which they would occasionally use as a projectile, was a toy like any other. And like so many other toys that came before and after it, this one clearly lost its appeal after just a few weeks—there appear to be no exact dates, as if animals in captivity, like things, existed beyond our reckoning of time. Photographs taken in late April 2011, not by the apes themselves, show Nonja and Sol, another female orangutan, building towers out of big, brightly-colored Legoesque bricks.

This was not a rigorous ethological experiment, just something to keep the orangutans occupied. But when we look at Nonja's photographs, we cannot help but wonder what it is that we observe when we observe. From which, remarkably enough, nothing develops.

V

In the Nabokov Museum in St. Petersburg, on October 13, 2012, under the watchful eye of the museum guard in the darkened room immediately to the right of the entrance, I tried—in contravention of the regulations and in vain—to capture a sharp image, not of an ape-chewed fountain pen, but rather of three pencil stubs supplied with bite marks by Vladimir Nabokov himself.

The caption by the display case informs me that these were a gift to the museum by the author's son in 1999. A special gift indeed, for in these blunt pencil stubs, each equipped with a brown, turquoise, or gold eraser cap, respectively, the visitor may perceive not only an example of "Nabokov's favorite writing tool," but, insofar as his eyesight will allow it in the semidarkness, he is also invited to imagine that the little, irregular markings in the lacquer represent "traces of the writer's teeth."

VI

Observation—herein lies the "magical" turning point—is both a natural behavior and a cultural technique. And we, as scholars, artists, and writers, focus our attention with growing curiosity on an imaginary point where we hope to be able to discern the transition from the one to the other.

Ink in the corners of a chimpanzee's mouth. A photograph of a cat that is decidedly not a symbol. The bars of a cage in the Jardin des Plantes. Abstract art above the living room sofa, unsigned, "Untitled." A steel-reinforced cell at the US Army Disciplinary Training Center between Pisa and Viareggio. A series of photographs taken in the sun-filled Orangutan House at the Schönbrunn Zoo. Three tooth-marked pencil stubs.

I observe with my pen.

Translated by Kári Driscoll

PART I

Texts

Hunting Narratives: Capturing the Lives of Animals

Nicolas Picard

Zoopoetics such as it has developed in France over the past ten years under the auspices of Anne Simon, seeks "specifically to highlight the stylistic, linguistic, narrative and rhythmic means by which writers restore the diversity of animal behaviors and worlds, as well as the complexity, historical and otherwise, of human-animal interactions" (Simon 2015, 217).[1] As Simon reminds us, the term, which Jacques Derrida was one of the first to use in reference to Kafka (cf. Derrida 2008, 6), refers to the Greek notion of ζῷον [zōon], which designates the living being, the animate (Simon 2015, 219), deriving ultimately from the verb ζάω [záō] evoking the idea of living, of breathing, of being among the living, or in its transitive use, "to make life," or "to give life." Zoopoetics further-more refers to the notion of ποίησις [poíēsis], which defines creation, the action of doing according to a certain knowledge, and the notion of "poetics," understood in its broadest sense as a method that questions the properties of literary discourse. "Zoopoetics" is, thus, the study of those living beings that move and breathe, examining the way in which

N. Picard
University of Paris III: Sorbonne Nouvelle, Paris, France

© The Author(s) 2018
K. Driscoll and E. Hoffmann (eds.), *What Is Zoopoetics?*,
Palgrave Studies in Animals and Literature,
https://doi.org/10.1007/978-3-319-64416-5_3

27

creative language constructs textual animals. How does human literary language embody beasts of flesh and blood? How has this strong connection between φύσις [*phúsis*] and λόγος [*lógos*] been established?[2] How have the lives of animals been disseminated or transcribed in human language? That is to say, how have the ways in which animals shape their *Umwelten*, their expressive behavior, their rhythms, their voices, emotions, forms, ornaments, and styles, been captured in poetic language? "Zoopoetics," Simon writes, "links the inventive, or even foundational power of creative language and the primordial expressivity of the living—the *poiein* of the *zōon*" (2017, 83). While speech (λόγος) has served to sanction the anthropological difference (i.e., the ontological superiority of man and the existential poverty of animals), it is through poetic language that writers have sought to (re)establish the connection between man and the rest of the creation.

In order to understand this complex form of poetic knowledge, which reveals multiple ways of figuring animal lives, and to change the way we look at animals in literary texts and in the world at large, zoopoetics draws on other disciplines that have deepened their reflection on animals and the living world (e.g., ethology, zoology, zoosemiotics, phenomenology, history, ethics, anthropology, and ecology). In short, zoopoetics integrates interdisciplinary perspectives that, because they change the way we look at animals, also allow us to reevaluate literary norms and uncover new corpora in the history of literature, bringing to light a wealth of unknown and marginal works that have been overlooked. I am thinking in particular of the corpus of rural literature, anchored in the French soil and closely linked to specific regions, which has until very recently been excluded from the field of criticism and ignored by official literary history. In France, the rural world, which "is of major interest for its proximity to both domestic and farm animals" (Romestaing and Schaffner 2014, 6), has been largely disregarded since the nineteenth century because of its lack of interest in the city and the idea of progress, or because it is not *avant-garde*. Another reason is the effect of the anthropological difference, that is to say, the anthropocentrism of Western philosophy which, at least since Descartes, has denied animals' emotions, rationality, subjective world, culture, and individual history. Many French writers of animals and rurality, by contrast, had, well before their time, proclaimed "the end of the human exception" (Schaeffer 2007). I am thinking in particular of those authors of the early twentieth century who did not view humanity as an exception with dominion over all of creation, but rather asserted an ontological equilibrium between humanand nonhuman animals.

Indeed, at the end of the nineteenth century and in the first decades of the twentieth century, the status of the animal in Francophone literature underwent a considerable shift. Whereas literary animals previously had been the protagonists in fables, fairy tales, and legends, serving predominantly as metaphors, symbols, or allegories of the human,[3] around the turn of the century they increasingly acquired "subject" status with a personal experience and a rich emotional life. Literary animals became living beings with complex semiotic and cognitive abilities, even being recognized as friends and family members. The various roles these animals embody bear witness to the economic, scientific, cultural, political, and legal changes that had taken place in France during the nineteenth century, especially from 1850 onward. These literary animals came to be seen and represented in a more concrete and specific way—as living beings rather than mere metaphors—and, moreover, in this respect they also come closer to humans (cf. Romestaing and Schaffner 2014, 10–11). Game animals occupy a privileged position in many of these works, testifying to the writers' passion for hunting, both as a personal pursuit and as a more bookish practice. In what follows, I will consider works by four different authors, all of which revolve around the hunt. While the hunting practices presented in these texts are very diverse, all are exercised in the plains, woods, and forests of France in the first half of the twentieth century. The earliest of these, *Le Roman de Miraut*, is a biography of a hunting dog, written in 1913 by the Franc-Comtois Louis Pergaud (1882–1915), in which the author recounts episodes of hunting "*à la billebaude*," whereby the hunter moves through the territory with or without precise objectives and hunts whatever small game the dog raises (mostly birds, hares, and rabbits). "La chasse au sanglier" ("The Boar Hunt," 1923) by the Gascon writer Joseph de Pesquidoux (1869–1946), by contrast, evokes what is known as drive-hunting, where trackers and dogs noisily drive the game in the direction of the hunters lying in wait. In "Chasse de nuit" ("Night Hunting," 1934), Gaston Chérau (1872–1937) tells of a rare wild cat hunt with dogs in Haut-Berry. This text, as well as "Automne" and "Les Seigneurs noirs" which will also be discussed, forms part of *Chasses et plein air en France*, a 1934 collection of nature and hunting stories in which Chérau gives expression to his passion for and conception of hunting. Finally, in his novel *Raboliot* (1925), Maurice Genevoix (1890–1980) focuses on hunting with dogs, with night lights and rabbit snaring. The novel tells the life story of a poacher who, caught in the act of illegal hunting and unable to stop, is forced to flee and live in the woods. In *La dernière Harde* (*The Last Hunt*, 1938) and *Forêt voisine* (*Neighboring Forest*, 1931), Genevoix focuses on deer hunting with hounds in the medieval tradition—as an allusion to Gaston Fébus's *Book of the Hunt* (1388).[4] Contrary to traditional hunting texts, *La dernière Harde* does not merely set out the hunter's point of view: it imagines the way in which the deer experience the hunts and how they foil the hunters' traps. What is more, this novel presents the biography of one of the members of the herd, the Red Stag.

As a literary motif, the interest in hunting is connected to capturing animal lives and our relationship to them. In fact, hunting embodies a paradigm of animality (Simon forthcoming)—pursuit and flight, capture, struggle, assimilation, even fusion between humans and animals. It implements, and this also explains why narrative constitutes its preferred mode of expression, an anthropological path toward animals and a "logic of the limit" or "limitrophy," which—according to Derrida—is not only "what abuts onto limits but also what feeds, is fed, is cared for, raised, and trained, what is cultivated on the edges of a limit" (Derrida 2008, 29). It raises an important issue of what it means "[*t*]*o follow* and *to be after*" (10) the animal. It also questions the anthropological difference: Does hunting define humans in sharp opposition to nonhuman animals? Are the hunted animals in turn deprived of language, rationality, and subjectivity? All the writers discussed in this chapter were passionate about animals, and, moreover, three of them—Joseph de Pesquidoux, Louis Pergaud, and Gaston Chérau—were hunters (Genevoix was a fisherman, although he also knew hunting), and as such they had observed and traversed the worlds of animals that inhabited the regions they knew so well. In what follows, I will show how their hunting narratives give an intimate and accurate picture of the sorts of empathic relationship that humans establish with animals and use their *mētis* to track them down. In other words, I will study how, and why, in experiencing the deciphering of animal traces, animal lives are both questioned and configured. Finally, I will show how the gesture of predation governs the practices of writing and reading, determining the structure of the narratives.

SIGNS, CLUES

Hunting effectively questions animal otherness because it is a medium, because the capture of the animal is delayed and occurs at the end of the process of predation. Hunting always presents itself as an irrepressible passion: obedient to their impulses, the hunters go hunting untiringly, looking for prey; hunters such as Raboliot cannot resist this "need for nocturnal hunting" (Genevoix 2001, 201), this "hunting instinct" (202), which urges him "to obey the eternal counsels which come from the earth and the clouds, the clear orders that rise in [him] with the same peaceful slowness as the white moon rising over the fields" (202). The hunt, thus, begins with a call to which the hunters respond: "From the familiar sky, the native lands, mysterious calls come to you, voices secret and well known, a thousand persuasive presences that pull you, like a thousand grasping hands, out of bed [*mille présences persuasives qui vous tirent, comme avec des mains, hors du lit*]" (201). The night is saturated with animal signs, some of which constitute a mystery to be unveiled, the others calling for recognition and reappropriation. To catch prey, we must first identify and interpret the signs that refer to them: acoustic signs, but also visual, olfactory, or even tactile signs. They inform us about the identity and the behavior of the animal. If the sign is unidentified, we see it as a track [*trace*], that is, as an indication of an animal's passing. The track is a sign that the hunter is looking for, and implies, an epistemic goal. It contains a potential meaning insofar as it must be interpreted, but the interpretation may be limited, depending on the nature of the tracks or on the knowledge of the interpreter. For example, Fanfare, questioned by the Duke to whom he makes his report, has not been able to identify precisely the nature of the animal:

A boar? What kind of boar? A grand old boar, a boar of the fourth year, a sow? ... Fanfare [...] hesitates; he cannot say for sure: "I'm afraid the tracks were not clear. There was gravel around the hold. Impossible to tell by the dew claws, by the rear prints, by anything at all. All that I can say is that there is a boar on the grounds of the Bondrée." (Genevoix 2000, 607)[5]

For the most part, the animal track takes the form of a *footprint*: it is the mark left by the pressure of a body on the ground, the physical production of a living organism, a mark of identity or a metonymy of the animal being which testifies to its sex or its species thanks to the morphological characteristics it reveals. Like all animal tracks, it constitutes a *clue*, "a sign that seems to protrude towards the one who discovers it" (Hamou 2007, 191), like those "frail fragments of ivory scattered on the sand and the moss [...] bones, the disjointed skeletons of beasts [*bestioles*] put to death by the little predators with short legs, and which the necrophores have finished stripping" (Genevoix 2000, 615): "From the moment you begin to notice them, they seem to leap out at you [*il semble qu'elles vous sautent aux yeux*]" (ibid.).

The term "clue" appears very frequently in the hunting narratives to describe the methods used to capture animals. Looking for a dangerous boar, the hunters:

> head towards the nearby marl-pit [...] because they want to gather clues, to see if by any chance it has gone in that direction, and if so where it went from there. They walk the length of a field, traverse a heath. [...] And the first clues come into view. They see a copse of pines that look like they've been bled to death, all splintered and torn where the beast has sharpened its tusks. There is rooting in the loamy soil, and, on the bank of a stream, a deep wallow that bears the imprint of a massive body. (Pesquidoux 1923a, 7)

The clue triggers inductive reasoning because the hunter needs to know the causes (what animal, what behavior) by apprehending the meanings in which it is inscribed. This interpretative approach is often explained within a logical framework (perception, interpretation/cognition, conclusion/evaluation, decision/action), as in the previous passages. This corresponds to what the American pragmatist philosopher Charles Sanders Peirce calls "abduction," a form of inductive reasoning which "consists in studying facts and devising a theory to explain them" (Peirce 1934, 5.145). It is "the process of forming an explanatory hypothesis. It is the only logical operation which introduces any new idea" (5.172). It is "logical inference, asserting its conclusion only problematically or conjecturally, it is true, but nevertheless having a perfectly definite logical form" (5.188). Although Peirce uses the syllogistic model to expound his theory,[6] he stresses the fact that abduction has a natural and intuitionist origin: "Man's mind has a natural adaptation to imagining correct theories of some kinds" (5.591). Abduction has, in fact, both a rational and a creative dimension: the examination of the facts—the clues of the animals' passing—spontaneously gives rise to a hypothesis, a new idea

which one must verify experimentally *a posteriori*. The abductive process is a semiotic and cognitive process which allows us to structure and
increase our epistemic experience and knowledge—which, in the case of
the hunters, will be zoological knowledge.

Carlo Ginzburg, who unites abduction with the conjectures of doc-
tors, historians, and philologists, also explains that, by deciphering the
clues, the hunter configures a "cognitive" and "epistemological" model
(Ginzburg 1989, 96), a "paradigm" behind which lies "what may be the
oldest act in the intellectual history of the human race: the hunter squat-
ting on the ground, studying the tracks of his quarry" (105). Ginzburg
points out that the evidential data "[are] always arranged by the observer
in such a way as to produce a narrative sequence, which could be
expressed most simply as 'Someone passed this way,'" and specifies that
perhaps the actual idea of narration "may have originated in a hunting
society, relating the experience of deciphering tracks" (103).[7]

THE ANIMAL GRIMOIRE

The interpretation of animal tracks on the ground is a decryption of what
Simon calls an "animal book" (Simon 2011, 173), composed of all the
signs they produce (visual, olfactory, sonorous, tactile). La Futaie, the
"whipper-in" [*piqueux*][8] of Genevoix's *La dernière Harde*, is a master in
this art:

> At the very moment when the two deer were about to re-enter the enclo-
> sure of the Orfosses, he in turn had taken the hounds in the direction of
> the ponds. He had not seen anything move. The fact that others, rather
> than being wary of the fresh print, still legible, written on the soft ground
> as though on the white page of a book, had let the hounds go astray on
> the hot scent of the stag—this, once more, was no fault of his. Nor, for
> that matter, was it the fault of the hounds, who had as always simply fol-
> lowed their instinct and naturally followed the trail of the easier prey.
> (Genevoix 1988, 110–111)[9]

The world is a book, the earth a blank page, the footprint of the old deer
of the Orfosses a sign written on its surface, readable for La Futaie who
knows how to perceive it, but the trace is invisible to the other hunters
who follow the dogs on the track of the young stag. These animal traces,
thus, "transform the 'blank page' of the earth into a deceptive book,

designed to lead the interpreter [*l'herméneute*] down the wrong track (in every sense of the word)" (Simon 2011, 174). The hunter must learn to read, to understand "the tricks of physical writing (writing on *phúsis*)" (ibid.). By deciphering the singular writings of the animals, the hunters have access to their stories; they internalize them and reproduce them. Sometimes they can get a complex overview of these stories, so the animal book takes the form of a personalized biography. Sometimes they only glimpse a part of it and the story loses itself in a horizon of meaning to be elucidated, if the hunter so wishes: "A certain path through the forest, still dry a fortnight ago, retained all the tracks: here a deer has followed it for five hundred yards; there, a herd of hinds and its leader crossed it at an angle, without hurrying" (Chérau 1934b, 115).

Genevoix provides a very interesting conception of the "animal book," which, as Simon underlines, is a "revitalization" (Simon 2011, 173) of the ancient metaphor of the book of nature, invoking what Hans Blumenberg (2007 [1986]) calls "the legibility of the world." Genevoix describes it as a "grimoire,"[10] a word that appears in French in the sixteenth century. According to Littré, "grimoire" derives from "gramaire," "gramare," a variety of "grammaire," the study of Latin which was unintelligible to the common people and was viewed as an occult science.[11] We can infer from this the idea of an *animal grammar* written on *physis*, which contains an occult meaning insofar as it is not accessible to ordinary mortals. One has to be an experienced *grammarian*—an experienced hunter—to be able to decipher the obscure animal texts that constitute this metaphorical "grimoire." This book contains an esoteric and mysterious meaning which no longer reveals the eternal truths of the divine book of nature, but the behavioral and existential truths of animals:

> He looked on the ground cluttered with brushwood, deciphering, in haste, a grimoire full of meaning. Tracks zigzagged, capriciously, where the rabbits leapt about at night; others, proceeding in a straight line, testified to the passage of the hares; the print of a predator marked the slope of a ditch; a feather fluttered, imprisoned in a bramble; and everywhere, mixed in with the vegetal humus of the soil, animal detritus, the carcasses of small rodents, bones as brittle as fish bones, scattered droppings, caught the eyes and the mind of Raboliot. (Genevoix 2001, 221)[12]

For a seasoned exegete such as Raboliot, this "grimoire full of meaning" can be read like a palimpsest of myriad intersecting and superimposed texts produced by animals. These texts of varying lengths are recent and always perishable because they are organic. The animal grimoire is fundamentally polyphonic as each text, that is, each signifying combination of signs,[13] each "sequence of events"[14] that the hunter reconstructs, corresponds to a behavioral trajectory that reveals a singular history and exposes a style of writing which is a "style of existence" (Macé 2011). From the point of view of the hunters who interprets them, theses texts are nonlinguistic, corporeal, and evanescent. For the author and the reader, they are both linguistic and nonlinguistic. This process of deciphering is both a semiotic investigation, insofar as the hunter perceives and interprets signs and apprehends a "moving and constantly changing semiosis" (Hallyn 2005, 244), and a hermeneutic analysis, because he seeks to elucidate a hidden and symbolic meaning, an animal mystery proceeding from the supernatural which overlaps with the natural.[15]

Although Genevoix's grimoire needs a skilled exegete, Raboliot manages to decipher it intuitively. Chérau's hunters of a wild cat, by contrast, although experienced, are lost in the meandering of its olfactory traces (which the dogs follow): They are caught in an "inexplicable tangle [*indébrouillable écheveau*]" (Chérau 1934a, 31). The hunters make "almost a complete circle around the castle" (33) before proceeding "east through the wooded outcropping in the direction of the Allier" (33). When they reach the great moat, the gamekeeper thinks the cat will "go left to reach Meyland" (34), but in fact it goes right along "the ridge that dominates the chaos of the Grosses Roches" (34). "[I]nstead of going down in the hell of the Grosses Roches" (36), however, the cat's tracks reappear "in the great wood, right towards the center" (36): the hunt then splits in two and the hunters have to "shout to keep track of each other" (36). The cat, meanwhile, frustrates the gamekeeper's expectations, proceeding "directly towards the castle and the farm" (37): "What manner of beast was this that was capable of accomplishing such a journey only to come leaping back almost like a stag? [*qu'était-ce que cette bête capable d'accomplir un tel trajet pour revenir au lancer presque comme un chevreuil*]" (37). The reader is lost in the threads of a tangled narrative, the animal text constituting a labyrinth:[16] The cunning cat leads its pursuers into the impasses of a meaning that constantly escapes them: "[It is] a kind of sorcery" (37). The animal is, thus, held to practice a form of black magic, wielding supernatural powers that situate it beyond and below the human order. We can see how the relationship between human and animal can be abyssal. This example shows that the animal is everywhere at once: "The animal is there before me, there close to me, there in front of me—I who am (following) after it.

And also, therefore, since it is before me, it is behind me. It surrounds me" (Derrida 2008, 11) on a physical and symbolic level. The human is defined in relation to the animal which it pursues: "I am inasmuch as I am *after* [après] the animal" (10).[17] As long as the animal is not captured and because it is the object of an unsatisfied desire, it haunts the hunter/reader in the form of powerful mental images. As a mystery, it lives within us; it inhabits our deepest psychological structures. In a sense, then, whenever we chase the animal through forests and texts,[18] we are trying to make these dormant images of animals and the narratives in which they are caught correspond to the images of the concrete and textual animals that we capture.[19]

THE SCHEMATISM OF HUNTING

Philippe Jousset argues that predation lies at the foundation of language and collective imaginary and, therefore, at the foundation of literature and the dynamism of culture. Hunting, he writes, constitutes "the schematism of literature" (Jousset 2007, 59). The origin of narrative should undoubtedly be placed in the animal organism itself. Indeed, it is arguably instinctual in nature, for, as René Thom writes: "When the predator wakes up, he is hungry and he only thinks of eating by capturing an external prey. But this prey must be found, and therefore sought" (Thom 1991, 83). If hunting is the schematism of literature, then "the prey and the predation of the prey are at the origin of meaning" (Quignard 1990, iv–v, qtd. in Jousset 2007, 60). Jousset asks,

> "What do our stories tell us?" or, more broadly, "what are we fictionalizing?" The answer would probably be: we recite the thousand and one possibilities of the predation scenario and, more importantly, as soon as the practical needs of "communication" are not in the first rank (which are often satisfied without the help of language or very incidentally through its medium), we recite the scenarios of the virtualization of this predation. (2007, 45)

Writers and readers are hunters of meaning who constantly reproduce the archaic gesture of predation. They simulate the processes of capture, (re)create narratives, and hunt linguistic and imaginary prey. Writers such as Gaston Chérau and Joseph de Pesquidoux embody this link between hunting practices and narrative practices, because in their texts they fictionalize the scenes of hunting that they experienced firsthand, or they draw on their experiences as hunters in order to invent other scenes. They create hunting narratives that reproduce schematically the biological processes of predation. These narratives develop as the hunting parties unfold; they live and die according to the rhythm of the hunts they evoke.

Furthermore, literary hunting narratives have a strong oral tradition. Chérau highlights this in the preface to his book when he specifies that his narratives are the reformulation of the "stories of hunting, stories of beasts, insects, trees, stories of beautiful nature" (Chérau 1934a, 7) that he told his comrades during World War I. Similarly, when he recalls the hunters' meetings in *Le Roman de Miraut*, Louis Pergaud underlines the fact that "when four hunters gather, it is usually to speak of hunting" (Pergaud 1948, 210): "And on the feast of Saint Hubert the two fellows gave a detailed account of the events of their morning hunt, while breaking bread and having a drink" (140); "while reminiscing about the first outings of all of their now-deceased hounds, taking turns telling hunting stories each more wonderful than the next, the two companions got dutifully drunk at Fricot's in fitting celebration of that memorable day" (123); "they told many hunting stories that were edifying and admirable, and, others that, while touching on more profane subjects, were nonetheless colorful and very tasty" (202).

As these passages demonstrate, to a certain extent, we hunt to be able to tell stories. The pleasure of narration is as important as the pleasure of the hunt, as it is, in the end, the pleasure of predation. Pascal Quignard goes so far as to write that the aim of hunting is to "come back and tell" (Quignard 2002, 142–143, qtd. in Jousset 2007, 216). In the terms elaborated by anthropologist Marcel Jousse, the hunter "mimes" the last hunt: he "replays" it orally by narrating the hunt he has experienced and internalized (Jousse 2008). In other words, he relives in his narration the phases of the experienced action of the hunt in the order he saw them occur. And he "irradiates them in body, manual, laryngo-buccal style" (675), then in graphic and literary style if he is also a writer like Louis Pergaud, Gaston Chérau, and Joseph de Pesquidoux. However, linguistic predation nourishes biological predation, as Chérau reminds us by reporting a technique of "crow hunting" with glue that he has himself experienced: "It is a story I read in a book of hunting, in the days of my youth, and my spirit of an enraged little trapper had given himself without restraint! I experimented with the process" (Chérau 1934c, 161). The monumental *Bibliographie générale des ouvrages sur la chasse* developed at the end of the nineteenth century by Roger Souhart, which collects works published in Europe since the fifteenth century, gives some measure of the extent of the phenomenon. Hunters are passionate about hunting and books, oral narratives, and written narratives. If, according to Marcel Jousse, "the mouth is at once instrument of speech and instrument of manducation" (Jousse 2008, 401), the hand of the writer, an instrument of writing, replays or prolongs its action. The gastronomic motif we find in the narratives of Joseph de Pesquidoux corroborates this idea: The animal is not only killed, it is also consumed.[20] Thus, by linking gastronomy and hunting textually, de Pesquidoux reminds us that writers and readers also feed on words and symbolic prey. What René Thom calls the "predation loop" (Thom 1991, 176) ends with the manducation and the ingestion of the animal, in the fusion between the predator (the writer, the reader) and the prey (the literary animal).

This ritual consumption of the animal is the end point of the anthropological path to it. The animal ends up literally within the human being, whether it is a physical animal that is converted into chemical energy, or whether it is converted into symbolic energy as a textual beast.[21] The state of "privation" dear to Aristotle, which according to Thom expresses a "lacuna of form" (1974, 176), is, thus, momentarily filled up until the desire for capture reappears, until the writer is again hungry for animals and produces new hunting narratives. This insatiable desire for otherness bears witness to Derrida's concept of "carno-phallogocentrism" (Derrida 1995, 280). It is a "dominant schema" that implies "carnivorous virility" and "installs the virile figure at the determinative center of the subject" (ibid.). Sacrificing and eating animals is done under the primacy of the human's speech and reason (*lógos*), a primacy established by phallocratic societies (dominated by male power).[22] The schematism of hunting implements the schematism of carno-phallogocentrism, which is the "dominant schema of subjectivity itself" (281). Thus, if the ingestion of the hunted animal presupposes, on a biological and symbolic level, the fusion between the human subject and the animal, on an ethical level it reinstates anthropological difference. The hunter—the human—constructs himself by opposing the animal, which appears in the end to be the one that can be killed and eaten, or, in a "sublime refinement," "eaten well" (283), if we follow Joseph de Pesquidoux's texts. What of the animals themselves, then? Do they, in these hunting texts, only serve to define human subjectivity and domination? Is there a way to avoid the logic of carno-phallogocentrism? Insofar as they are concerned with this "conception-appropriation-assimilation of the other [animal]" (281), these literary hunting narratives necessarily inscribe themselves in this logic. However, they also and maybe most importantly figure poetics of the *zōon*, which questions and constructs animals lives through semiotic and hermeneutic processes: their capacity to write texts—their languages, their intelligent behaviors, and their experiences and individual stories. In our corpus, thus, hunting proves to be ambivalent: it is an expression of the human's carno-phallogocentric domination and the construction of the existential thickness and subjectivity of animals. It is both a passion for animals and a passion for capture. For Genevoix, de Pesquidoux, Chérau and Pergaud, animals remain an object of desire and mystery: The quest for animal lives ends only in order to perpetuate itself.

NOTES

1. "[La zoopoétique] a plus particulièrement pour objectif de mettre en évidence les moyens stylistiques—linguistiques, narratifs, rythmiques—que les écrivains mettent en jeu pour restituer la diversité des comportements et des mondes animaux tout comme la complexité—y compris historique—des interactions hommes/bêtes." Unless otherwise indicated, all translations from the French are by Kári Driscoll. I would like to thank both him and Eva Hoffman for their thoughtful comments and detailed suggestions for revision.
2. From a perspective of the phenomenology of language, for example. See on this subject Jean-Claude Coquet (2007).
3. This, however, does not prevent these literary animals from conveying precise zoological knowledge. On this subject, see Zucker (2002, 37) and Sebastian Schönbeck's chapter in this volume. In addition, it should be noted that even before this shift, literary animals did not serve merely or exclusively as symbols of the human. Cynegetic literature, for example, has, from the Middle Ages onward, interrogated the figure of the living animal by highlighting the aptitudes and subjectivity of hunting dogs, as well as the ways of life and ruses of prey animals. In his introduction to Phébus's *Livre de la chasse*, Marcel Thomas goes so far as to describe the work as "the first outline of a veritable natural history" (1986, 19). For the Anglophone context, see Susan Crane's *Animal Encounters* (2012), which explores the complex intersubjectives involved in human-animal interactions in medieval Britain.
4. On the medieval hunting tradition, see Strubel and de Saulnier (1994). Among the texts discussed are "Chace dou cerf," a brief, anonymous

poem written around the middle of the thirteenth century, as well as
Henri de Ferrières's long poem *Les livres du roy Modus et de la royne
Ratio* and Gace de La Buigne's *Roman des deduis,* both written in the
second half of the fourteenth century.

5. "Un sanglier? Quel sanglier? Un porc entier, un tiers an, une laie? ...
   Fanfare [...] hésite; il ne peut pas se prononcer: 'les traces n'étaient mal-
   heureusement pas claires, il y avait du cailloutis autour du fort. Impossible
   de juger aux gardes, aux traces de derrière, à rien. Tout ce qu'il est permis
   de dire, c'est qu'il y a un sanglier dans l'enceinte de la Bondrée.'"

6. "The surprising fact, C, is observed; / But if A were true, C would be
   a matter of course, / Hence, there is reason to suspect that A is true"
   (Peirce 1934, 5.188).

7. At the same time, a conceptual mode of knowledge that aims for a more
   mediate and more general concrete reality (the animal) also emerges from
   this intuitive process of deciphering traces. Hans Blumenberg thus invites
   us to consider how primitive man invented the "prototypical concept: the
   trap. It is the realization of thought in the compact sense: a device whose
   application, arrangement, suspension and retrieval allow someone absent
   to make something absent his prey. The trap is cognitively matched to the
   prey for which it is set: its shape, its strength, its behavior and its movements.
   Whoever is better at thinking catches more prey" (Blumenberg forthcoming).

8. The "piqueux" runs the hunt and is responsible for the hounds.

9. "[A]u moment juste où les deux cerfs allaient rentrer dans l'enceinte des
   Orfosses, il avait pris, par ordre, les grands devants vers les étangs. Il n'avait
   donc rien vu sauter. Que d'autres, au lieu d'être mis en défiance par un
   volcelest pourtant bien lisible, inscrit sur la terre molle comme sur la page
   blanche d'un livre, eussent laissé s'emballer les chiens sur la voie chaude du
   daguet, encore une fois ce n'était pas sa faute. Celle des chiens non plus,
   d'ailleurs, qui ce jour-là comme d'habitude avaient suivi leur instinct de
   forceurs, et naturellement bondi sur les traces d'une proie plus facile [...]."

10. My discussion here is inspired in part by Anne Simon's commentary on
    this passage in Genevoix's *La dernière Harde,* in which she refers to
    "hunting as a grimoire." Hunting, as she observes, can be seen as a "mise
    en abyme of hermeneutics"—though she does not develop this point fur-
    ther—and as an implementation of what Ginzburg calls "the evidential
    paradigm" (1989): a cognitive and epistemological model based on the
    interpretation of clues (Simon 2011, 170–176).

11. "Gramare" comes from the Latin "grammarium," from "gramma" in
    lower Latin ("letter, something written, drawn"), which, in turn, derives
    from the Greek γράμμα ("letter," "written mark") and from the verb
    γράφειν ("to write," "to draw").

12. "[Raboliot] regardait le sol encombré de broussailles, il déchiffrait sur le terrain, en hâte, un grimoire chargé de sens. Des passées zigzaguaient, capricieuses, où les lapins boultinaient la nuit; d'autres, s'étirant droit, révélaient les meusses des lièvres; un pied de fauve marquait le talus d'un fossé; une plume vibrait, prisonnière d'une ronce; et partout, mêlés à l'humus végétal, des débris animaux, de menues charognes de rongeurs, des os frêles comme des arêtes, des crottes, des fientes éparpillées, sollicitaient les yeux et la cervelle de Raboliot."

13. According to Thomas A. Sebeok, "messages can be constructed on the basis of single signs or, more often than not, as combinations of them. The latter are known as texts. A text constitutes, in effect, a specific 'weaving together' of signs in order to communicate something" (2001, 7).

14. Umberto Eco thus defines the notion of text: "The sequence of events investigated by a detective can be defined as a text" (Eco 1983, 204; cf. Thouard 2007, 80).

15. "And immediately, with the unseen animal, with the land where it lurks, the supernatural relation of signs is established [*Et tout de suite s'instaure avec la bête non vue, avec le pays de sa guette, la relation surnaturelle des signes*]" (Doumet 1992, 15).

16. Michel de Certeau writes to this effect that sometimes the reader is "like a hunter in the forest, he spots the written quarry, follows a trail, laughs, plays tricks, or else like a gambler, lets himself be taken in by it" (1984, 173).

17. On this subject see Ravindranathan and Traisnel (2016, 147–148).

18. For Walter Benjamin, "the text is a forest in which the reader is hunter" (Benjamin 1999, 802); according to Terence Cave, "tracking is like the reading of a narrative, and vice versa" (Cave 2002, 251). Many authors emphasize this homology between hunting and the processes of writing and reading. René Thom goes so far as to postulate that "the great syntactic structures stem from the formal structure of the great interactions of biological regulation, for example the transitivity which generates sentences of the type SVO (subject-verb-object)" (Thom 1991, 197). Biological predation would thus be "a prototypical instance of transitive action ('the cat eats the mouse')" (ibid.).

19. Vilém Flusser imagines the prehistoric genesis of such images: "Let us take as an example the oldest of the images known to us (that of a pony in Pêche-Merle). It concerns representation being held in rock faces. The maker of the image stepped away from a pony, looked at it and transmitted what he briefly saw to the memory of the wall. And he did this in such a way that others would recognise what they saw. And he did all these immense complex things so as to be able to use what he saw as an orientation for future actions—like the hunt for ponies" (Flusser 1988, 10, qtd. in Ieven 2003).

20. See, for example, "La chasse au sanglier" (Pesquidoux 1923a, 1–12) and "Menu gascon" (Pesquidoux 1923b, 97–109).
21. Thom calls this transformation into symbolic energy "neurulation": "the absorption by the animal of a symbolic prey, which will become its nervous system, thus justifying the assertion that the predator is its prey" (Thom 1974, 115).
22. Carol Adams emphasizes the same idea, which she calls "The Sexual Politics of Meat": "the assumption that men need meat, have the right to meat, and that meat eating is a male activity associated with virility" (Adams 2010, 4). In the early twentieth century in France, and still nowadays, ritual hunting, killing, and eating animals seem to act as "mirror and representation of patriarchal values" (241).

WORKS CITED

Adams, Carol J. 2010. *The Sexual Politics of Meat: A Feminist-Vegetarian Critical Theory*. New York: Continuum.

Benjamin, Walter. 1999. *The Arcades Project*, trans. Howard Eiland and Kevin McLaughin. Prepared on the basis of the German volume, ed. Rolf Tiedemann. Cambridge, MA: Belknap Press of Harvard University Press.

Blumenberg, Hans. 2007. *La Lisibilité du monde*, trans. Pierre Rusch. Paris: Editions du Cerf.

———. Forthcoming. *Lions*, trans. Kári Driscoll. London: Seagull Books.

Cave, Terence. 2002. *Recognitions: A Study in Poetics*. Oxford: Clarendon Press.

Certeau, Michel de. 1984. *The Practice of Everyday Life*, trans. Steven Rendall. Berkeley: University of California Press.

Chérau, Gaston. 1934a. Chasse de nuit. In *Chasses et plein air en France*, 17–67. Paris: Stock.

———. 1934b. Automne. In *Chasses et plein air en France*, 115–118. Paris: Stock.

———. 1934c. Les Seigneurs noirs. In *Chasses et plein air en France*, 156–161. Paris: Stock.

Coquet, Jean-Claude. 2007. *Phusis et logos: Une phénoménologie du langage*. Vincennes: Presses Universitaires de Vincennes.

Crane, Susan. 2012. *Animal Encounters: Contacts and Concepts in Medieval Britain*. Philadelphia: University of Pennsylvania Press.

Derrida, Jacques. 1995. 'Eating Well,' or the Calculation of the Subject, trans. Peter Connor and Avital Ronell. In *Points... Interviews, 1974–1994*, ed. Elisabeth Weber, 255–287. Stanford: Stanford University Press.

———. 2008. *The Animal That Therefore I Am*, trans. David Wills and ed. Marie-Louise Mallet. New York: Fordham University Press.

Doumet, Christian. 1992. *Traité de la mélancolie de Cerf*. Paris: Champ Vallon.

Eco, Umberto. 1983. Horns, Hooves, Insteps: Some Hypotheses on Three Types of Abduction. In *The Sign of Three: Dupin, Holmes, Peirce*, ed. Umberto Eco and Thomas A. Sebeok, 198–220. Bloomington: Indiana University Press.

Flusser, Vilém. 1988. *Krise der Linearität*. Bern: Benteli.

Genevoix, Maurice. 1988 [1938]. *La dernière Harde*. Paris: Flammarion.

———. 2000 [1931]. Forêt voisine. In *Trente mille jours*, 563–677. Paris: Omnibus.

———. 2001 [1925]. Raboliot. In *Romans et récits de la Loire*, 181–327. Paris: Omnibus.

Ginzburg, Carlo. 1989. Clues. Roots of an Evidential Paradigm, trans. John and Anne C. Tedeschi. In *Clues, Myths and the Historical Method*, 96–125. Baltimore: Johns Hopkins University Press.

Grandjean, Antoine. 2012. Lisibilité du monde et mondanéité de la lecture (À partir de Blumenberg). *Cahiers philosophiques* 128: 85–97.

Hallyn, Fernand. 2005. Pour une poétique des idées: le livre du monde, ou les ramifications d'une métaphore. *Bibliothèque d'humanisme et de renaissance* 67 (2): 225–247. Paris: Droz.

Hamou, Philippe. 2007. 'The Footsteps of Nature'. Raisonnement indiciaire et 'interprétation de la nature' au XVII e siècle. Quelques considérations historiques et épistémologiques. In *L'Interprétation des indices. Enquête sur la paradigme indiciaire avec Carlo Ginzburg*, ed. Denis Thouard, 189–210. Lille: Presses Universitaires du Septentrion.

Ieven, Bram. 2003. How to Orientate Oneself in the World: A General Outline of Flusser's Theory of Media. *Image & Narrative* 3 (2). http://www.imageandnarrative.be/inarchive/mediumtheory/bramieven.htm.

Jousse, Marcel. 2008. *L'Anthropologie du geste*. Paris: Gallimard.

Jousset, Philippe. 2007. *Anthropologie du style. Propositions*. Pessac: Bordeaux Academic Press.

———. 2012. *En Proie aux mots. Action et affection en littérature*. Paris: Hermann.

Macé, Marielle. 2011. Styles animaux. *L'Esprit Créateur* 51 (4): 97–105.

Peirce, Charles Sanders. 1934. *Pragmatism and Pragmaticism*. Vol. 5 of *the Collected Papers of Charles Sanders Peirce*, ed. Charles Hartshorne and Paul Weiss. Cambridge, MA: Belknap Press of Harvard University Press.

Pergaud, Louis. 1948 [1913]. Le Roman de Miraut, chien de chasse. In *Œuvres de Louis Pergaud II*, 11–316. Paris: Mercure de France.

Pesquidoux, Joseph de. 1923a. La chasse au sanglier. In *Chez nous. Travaux et jeux rustiques II*, 1–12. Paris: Plon.

———. 1923b. Menu Gascon. In *Chez nous. Travaux et jeux rustiques II*, 97–109. Paris: Plon.

Quignard, Pascal. 1990. *Petits traités*. Paris: Adrien Maeght.

———. 2002. *Abîmes (III)*. Paris: Grasset.

Ravindranathan, Thangam, and Antoine Traisnel. 2016. What Gives (*Donner le change*). *SubStance* 45 (2): 143–161.

Romestaing, Alain, and Alain Schaffner. 2014. Romanesques animaux. In *Animaux d'écriture. Le lien et l'abîme*, ed. Alain Romestaing and Alain Schaffner, 9–23. Paris: Classiques Garnier.

Schaeffer, Jean-Marie. 2007. *La Fin de l'exception humaine*. Paris: Gallimard.

Sebeok, Thomas. A. 2001. *Signs: An Introduction to Semiotics*. Toronto: University of Toronto Press.

Simon, Anne. 2011. Chercher l'indice, écrire l'esquive: l'animal comme être de fuite, de Maurice Genevoix à Jean Rolin. In *La Question animale. Entre science, littérature et philosophie*, ed. Jean-Paul Engélibert, Lucie Campos, Catherine Coquio, and Georges Chapouthier, 167–181. Rennes: Presses Universitaires de Rennes.

———. 2015. La zoopoétique: un engagement proprement poétique en études animales. Interview by Alain Schaffner. In Approches de l'animal, ed. Alain Romestaing and Alain Schaffner. Special issue of *ElFe XX–XXI* 5: 217–228.

———. 2017. Du peuplement animal au naufrage de l'Arche: la littérature entre zoopoétique et zoopoéthique. In French Ecocriticism, ed. Daniel A. Finch Race and Julien Weber. Special issue of *L'Esprit Créateur*, 57 (1): 83–98.

Souhart, Roger. 1886. *Bibliographie générale des ouvrages sur la chasse. La vénerie et la fauconnerie*. Paris: Chez P. Rouquette Editeur.

Strubel, Armand, and Chantal de Saulnier. 1994. *La Poétique de la chasse au Moyen Age. Les Livres de chasse du XIVè siècle*. Paris: Presses Universitaires de France.

Thom, René. 1974. *Modèles mathématiques de la morphogenèse*. Paris: Bourgois.

———. 1991. *Esquisse d'une sémiophysique. Physique aristotélicienne et Théorie des Catastrophes*. Interéditions: Paris.

Thomas, Marcel. 1986. Fébus Aban! Introduction to *Le livre de la chasse*, by Gaston Phébus, 9–34. Paris: Philippe Lebaud.

Thouard, Denis. 2007. Indice et herméneutique: cynégétique, caractéristique, allégories. In *L'Interprétation des indices. Enquête sur la paradigme indiciaire avec Carlo Ginzburg*, ed. Denis Thouard, 75–89. Lille: Presses Universitaires du Septentrion.

Zucker, Arnaud. 2002. Sur les fables ésopiques, morale de la fable et morale du récit. *Anthropozoologica* 36: 37–50.

"You Cannot Escape Your Moles": The Becoming-Animal of Günter Eich's Late Literary Texts

Belinda Kleinhans

I

Günter Eich's writings teem with animals. While animals could be seen as just the objects of his writing, with the emergence of his prose poems *Moles* in 1967, Eich states "Moles are what I write [*Was ich schreibe, sind Maulwürfe*]" (Eich 1973, 7), thus complicating the relationship between the animal in the text and the animal *as* text. The unique symbiotic relationship the animal enters into with the literary text moves Eich's zoopoetics close to what Akira Mizuta Lippit calls "animetaphor": "The animal becomes intertwined with the trope, serving as its vehicle and substance. [...] the animal is already a metaphor, the metaphor an animal" (Lippit 2000, 165). One could also say that in Eich's case, the text is already an animal, and the animal a text. The blurred line between language and animal(ity) in Eich's writing unravels standard preconceptions of language and meaning in a playful way and can be read in the context

B. Kleinhans
Texas Tech University, Lubbock, TX, USA

© The Author(s) 2018
K. Driscoll and E. Hoffmann (eds.), *What Is Zoopoetics?*,
Palgrave Studies in Animals and Literature,
https://doi.org/10.1007/978-3-319-64416-5_4

45

of the crisis of language in post-World War II German literature. In his 1959 Büchner Prize speech, Eich explicitly addresses the problems of power and language following the existence of a Reich Ministry of Public Enlightenment and Propaganda, stating that "power configures language for its own needs" in order to "force humans into behavior conducive to power, to adjust them and make them definite" (Eich 1991a, 4: 621).[1] "*Gelenkte Sprache*," controlled language, is for Eich a language that is clear-cut, unambiguous, and that offers answers instead of questions.

Gelenkte Sprache is a language that is in the service of power and steers ("*lenken*") people in a certain direction. As a language that used to be in service of fascism, *gelenkte Sprache* carries with it the possibility of turning life (*bíos*) into mere material existence (*zoē*). Eich comments on this in his 1958 radio drama "Festianus, Märtyrer": "Our sins are moles [*Unsere Sünden sind Maulwürfe*]" (1991a, 3: 491). These "sins," often taken to refer to Eich's work during the Third Reich (cf. Vieregg 1996), can, with the animetaphor of the *Moles*, be understood in the context of Eich's critique of "the unconscious of language, of *logos*" (Lippit 2000, 165), which, responding to Third Reich biopolitics, corresponds to the possibility of language to "render" life in the sense of Shukin (2009, 20). Language, enriched historically and culturally with a variety of rendering practices, is always to a certain degree *gelenkte Sprache*, outside of the conscious awareness of the language user who nonetheless is steered in a certain direction through the implications and unconscious aspects of language. Accordingly, Eich writes in 1968 "You cannot escape your moles [*Deinen Maulwürfen entgehst du nicht*]" (Eich 1991a, 1: 322), opening up an interesting tension between text, animal, and language user: One cannot escape one's "moles" (one's language, or the power of discourse), yet Eich develops a playful language in which the "moles" can escape us, rendering a language of power inert. To demonstrate this hide-and-seek of textual animals and to understand Eich's zoopoetics, I will analyze some of his later literary texts through the lens of Lippit's animetaphor and Shukin's concept of rendering. This will enable me to highlight (a) how poetic language, as a distinct response to Third Reich language use, is employed to remind us of the rendering tendencies always already inherent in language (especially in postfascist times), and (b) how linguistic playfulness and writing that sustains rather than resolves paradoxes can counter the rendering tendencies of language.

II

The question of an animal (or language) deliberately escaping us appears as early as 1955 in Eich's poetry cycle *Botschaften des Regens* (*Messages from the Rain*). The animals in the poem "Tauben" ("Pigeons" or "Doves") shed light on the later *Moles* in their simultaneous tangibility and elusiveness (from language, from logos). The pigeons become the animetaphor for the un/ambiguity of decipherable signs that are simultaneously readable and unreadable and that mock our attempts to grasp them. The choice of bird, pigeons/doves (both are "Tauben" in German), is especially significant in this context. Traditionally, doves symbolize (decipherable, understandable) messages, be it a messenger bird or a biblical reference to Noah's Ark. The zoopolitical aspect enters the poem also through the choice of animal, as humans and pigeons/doves have a longstanding tradition of dominance and control that highlights the "inescapable contiguity or bleed between *bios* and *zoē*, between a politics of human social life and a politics of animality that extends to other species" (Shukin 2009, 9). Accordingly, pigeons/doves were used as carriers of messages for thousands of years, including both world wars, their domestication for sport (racing), for breeding for specific physical characteristics, and for use as food. Especially by means of pigeon keeping, breeding, and hunting, man has had a lasting effect on this species. These activities subject the animal to a form of rendering that embed it into social semiotic and material currencies (21), which also become visible as explicit violence in the changes in this species and the extinction of the passenger pigeon in 1914 as a direct result of massive overhunting. Eich's poem echoes some of these uses with a warning in the third stanza of the poem:

Du bist nicht ihr Herr [...]
wenn du Nachrichten an ihre Federn heftest,
wenn du Zierformen züchtest, neue Farben,
neue Schöpfe, Gefieder am Fuß. (Eich 1991a, 1: 105–106)

you are not their master [...]
when you fasten messages to their feathers,
when you breed curious variants, new colors,
new crests, or tufts of feathers about the foot. (Eich 1991b, 27)

In postfascist Germany, the reference to being someone's master, as well as breeding techniques, is reminiscent of breeding plans for the German people during the Third Reich (cf. Gerhard 2005), while also reminding us that even that does not grant one complete mastery over another living thing.

While the concern for rendering life and referencing biopower builds the backdrop for the poem, Eich's text is more interested in the disappearance of the animal from the human grasp and its shift away from logocentric models, which is not only a mark of his animetaphor, but also a central interest of the zoopoetics of his texts. Accordingly, the introduction of the pigeons in the text in the first stanza already removes them somewhat from human access, placing them high above the human, stating:

> Taubenflug über die Äcker hin, –
> ein Flügelschlag, der schneller ist als die Schönheit.
> Sie holt ihn nicht ein, sondern bleibt mir
> als Unbehagen zurück im Herzen. (Eich 1991a, 1: 105)

> Flight of pigeons over the ploughed fields—
> a wingbeat more swift than beauty
> that cannot catch up with such speed
> but remains in my heart as disquiet. (Eich 1991b, 27)

Human concepts, such as beauty, are unable to catch up with the speed with which the pigeons' wings are moving, which fill the human onlooker with disquiet [*Unbehagen*]. The human is unable to establish contact with the animals, and his tools for conceptualization, such as "beauty," "cannot catch up with" the animal high above, drawing attention to humans' limitations. The pigeons escape the grasp of human concepts, yet the human onlooker doesn't escape the unsettling presence of the animetaphor, pointing to something animalistic outside of language.

Just as "you cannot escape your moles," the lyrical I cannot escape the impression of the pigeon animetaphor which haunts the second stanza in the form or an eerie, nonexistent laughter: "As if the laughter of pigeons too could be heard / in front of the dovecotes, dwarf dwellings painted green" [*Als wäre auch Taubengelächter vernehmbar / vor den Schlägen, den grün gestrichenen Zwerghäusern*] (1991a, 1: 105; 1991b, 27). The use of the subjunctive "as if" removes the birds once again from the human grasp, commenting on the man-made structures of "dovecotes, dwarf dwellings" with a mocking sound that is only imagined by the lyrical I. This laughter echoes the critique of controlling structures Eich cites in his Büchner Prize speech and hints at what he calls "anarchic instinct": "When I hear that [power] is already preformed in the animal world and is a consistent phenomenon of societal order [...], then I set against this my anarchic instinct: Isn't all use of power trivialized and relieved of suspicion in this way?" (1991a, 4: 620). The pigeons' ghostly laughter in the second stanza highlights two things: Firstly, the pigeons are nowhere to be seen or heard around the dwellings created to control them, rejecting the "power" the dwellings stand for; and secondly, the act of laughing (even though imagined) expresses the anarchic instinct that clearly mocks the hubris of human understanding and control of life. Consequently, the lyrical I begins to "wonder" (1991b, 27), opening up the ambiguities of meaning of the textual animal. Here, Eich's language renders meaning and facts ambiguous and favors complex relationships and questions over answers, which he always suspects of being in the service of power. He labels his work on language, which can be seen in the line of poststructuralism and deconstruction, an "anarchic instinct" and writes: "I have a certain intent, namely the intention to the anarchic, because with everything I write I am, at base, turning against agreement with the world [*Einverständnis mit der Welt*], not only the social world, but also the objects of creation, which I thus reject" (1991a, 4: 510).

The rejection of creation or a certain agreement with how the world is plays out then in the remaining two stanzas of the poem: "I advise myself to be afraid of pigeons. / You are not their master, I say [...] / Put no trust in your power" [*Ich rate mir selbst, mich vor den Tauben zu fürchten. / Du bist nicht ihr Herr, sage ich [...] / Vertrau deiner Macht nicht*] (1991a, 1: 105–106; 1991b, 27). This challenge to man's mastery over the birds points toward an order beyond the limited anthropocentric worldview of mastery and control. The pigeons—still partly visible in the first two stanzas through their flight, their earthward glances, their plumage and feet—slowly elude the humans' limited perspective; humans are overcome by a feeling of disquiet and even fear, acknowledging

daß neben deinesgleichen heimliche Königreiche bestehen,
Sprachen ohne Laut, die nicht erforscht werden,
Herrschaften ohne Macht und unangreifbar,
daß die Entscheidungen geschehen im Taubenflug (1991a, 1: 105–106)

that beyond your kind there are hidden kingdoms,
languages without sounds that cannot be fathomed,
dominions without power and unassailable;
that decisions are made by the pigeons' flight. (1991b, 27)

The German original here was translated literally by Hamburger as "without power" to distinguish it from "powerless." This distinction may point to the fact that while their kingdoms are running indeed without power (i.e., not rendering others), they are not, in the grand scheme of things "powerless" or weak. In the wake of postfascist Germany, which is still grappling with its inheritance of dreams of power and control through the biopolitical rendering of others, this line reads as a reminder that power is not always achieved through obvious means, and that "dominions" and even "kingdoms" can exist that do not subscribe to a power through hierarchies and control of others.

This last stanza highlights that the anthropocentric regime of power/knowledge cannot capture everything. Rather, the existence of other regimes beyond our ken is revealed. The secret and unassailable nature of these dominions points to the limitations of an anthropocentric perspective. Language, as a system for creating meaning, is included in this critique of an anthropocentric worldview, as there are "languages without sound" that defy categorization. Eich's use of pigeons deepens his critique of anthropocentric models of understanding, as carrier pigeons were used to carry decipherable human messages. In the context of this poem, however, they are the carriers of hidden meanings and signs that are indecipherable for humans. The text enacts at the same time the attempts of domestication (of text, of language, of animal) and the simultaneous resistance to it. Only the animal in the text can do this, though, as those orders are anthropocentric and logocentric. This is where the zoopoetics of Eich's poem offers us a line of flight into silence and "languages without sound."

III

The simultaneity of tangibility and elusiveness of literary animal and meaning that the poem "Pigeons" enacts determines the existence of the new genre *Moles*, which Eich first published in 1967. These prose poems, a symbiosis of text and animal, add to the ambiguity of the literary animal and meaning the level of text genre itself. Often described as "Unsinnspoesie" (nonsense poetry) and understood as the epitome of his "anarchism" (cf. Neumann 1981), the *Moles* divided the critics—maybe also because they seem to take the idea of languages that are unassailable quite literally. While the pigeons in the poem hint at a line of flight outside or beyond language, yet do not directly interfere with language, Eich's prose poems literally burrow through language like their namesake, the mole, burrows through the soil. Through this process of undermining language, they approach Lippit's notion of animetaphor with "language as a perforated and solvent body"—the mole's ground—which "lacks density, finitude and definite borders" (Lippit 2000, 160). The ensuing production and concurrent dissolution of meaning is closely tied to the specificity of the textual animal. The mole activates standard associations such as blindness and a life in darkness. Light has been a well-established metaphor for truth since Plato, whereas a life in darkness, or blindness, symbolizes ignorance. While on a semiotic level, the meaning of the mole seems clear, the fact that the animal lives below ground and digs tunnels through the ground (which can also be understood as the metaphorical ground on which we stand—language or truth), dissolves the clarity of meaning and lends the moles the quality of an animetaphor. Aura Maria Heydenreich comments that it is a central trait of the mole "to move in the impenetrable, in the resisting ground— and thus to endanger human regimes whose allegedly safe foundation is the ground. In this way, the mole engages in sub-version in a literal sense" (Heydenreich 2007, 180).

What makes the moles of particular interest for a zoopoetics is the fact that they not only feature in the text as diegetic animals (cf. Borgards 2012, 90), but that the mole is, in fact, the textual genre itself: "Moles are what I write, their white claws turned out, the balls of their toes are pink [*Was ich schreibe, sind Maulwürfe, weiße Krallen nach außen gekehrt, rosa Zehenballen*]" (Eich 1973, 7–8; 1991a, 1: 318). The use of the mole here, both as a product of the writing process, as well as a diegetic animal with a physical presence, opens a productive tension between text and animal. Labeling these short prose pieces *Moles*—blind animals living in darkness—marks them as subversions of discourses on progress and enlightenment (knowledge), but also of language. They, thus, perform a becoming-animal of language where language is alive (cf. Lippit 2000, 136) and the text shifts away from purely logocentric modes. The *Moles* can be read as a metalanguage, as instead of using language as a reference system that references ideas or objects, the *Moles* reference language and normative speech itself (Kohlenbach 1982, 84). Hence, they are very close to the animetaphor Kári Driscoll establishes for the rats in Kafka's "Erinnerungen an die Kaldabahn," because they burrow through the language the narrator is using and have "the power to make language 'other' and to dispossess its user of exclusive ownership" (Driscoll 2013, 26). Because the "moles" are at the same time diegetic text animals and the text (genre) itself, any time a mole appears, meaning oscillates between the diegetic animal and the function of animal writing. This leads to an interesting relationship between author and text: The author's text is not solely his text, as the mole offers resistance to the writing process and unsettles meaning. It is also ambiguous whether the moles are burrowing through the text or whether the moles are the text. They, thus, pose a question similar to the one Driscoll raises regarding Kafka's zoopoetic animals: In these instances of zoopoetry, is language still a house built and inhabited by humans (2013, 32), or are the textual animals actually shaping the metaphors and figures of speech, ultimately making language *their* house?

The tension between author(ship), text, and a traditional logic of language is exposed in "Preamble" via wordplay on speed and thought: "My moles are faster than you think [*schneller als man denkt*]. If you think they're over where the rotten wood and stone's [*Mulm*] flying, they're already off in their tunnels chasing down a thought" (Eich 1973, 7–8; 1991a, 1: 318). The double reference to thought here first addresses the expectations of a reader ("faster than you think"), and second, that thoughts underlie language. The moles burrow through language, which makes mole writing faster than thought and suggests that the narrator does not simply record preformed thoughts, but rather follows the logic of the textual animal's movement. The moles also pile up detritus [*Mulm*]—soil, rotten wood and stone, a reference to the unconsciousness of language that leaves traces behind, in postfascist Germany the remnant of fascist language use that is still discernable and that many of Eich's literary colleagues are fighting against as well. Yet the mole is not where language abuse, the detritus, is piled high, meaning that it does resist totalitarian language use; rather, it draws attention to its existence in everyday language and makes this unconscious aspect of language visible through its activity.

The fact that the moles (not the author) are chasing down thoughts becomes the guiding principle for the logic of the highly associative *Moles* texts. The text defies traditional modes of writing and understanding; its language avoids subscribing to any preexisting system of classification or citation and, thus, also avoids the traps of linguistic totalitarianism which shaped the Third Reich. Accordingly, the text continues: "You could film their speed electronically by sticking some blades of grass down through [*an eingesteckten Grashalmen*]" (Eich 1973, 7–8). The apparent contradiction between electronic measuring devices and blades of grass defies expectations and is instead inspired by the image of a mole moving close under the surface of the grass. The pseudoscientific aspect of this procedure can remind the reader of the pseudoscientific research connected to racial science which was conducted in the early twentieth century and which, like the blades of grass, always only moved on the surface of its object without producing any reliable scientific deep knowledge. The references to the speed of the animal highlights the diegetic existence of the animal, which can be filmed and observed, its speed measured by scientific methods. However, because they are always "faster than you think," Eich's tongue-in-cheek comments about moles illustrate that, even though we think we can grasp animal (or any other's) existence (and also their referential meaning) via recordings and measurements, it always escapes us. Eich intentionally breaks with common logic, because, as he states, "It isn't the content, it is language that works against power [*Es sind nicht die Inhalte, es ist die Sprache, die gegen die Macht wirkt*]" (1991a, 4: 624).

On the metaphorical level, the statement about the mole's speed can be read in connection with the cognitive process, because they chase down thoughts, yet are also "always a few meters ahead of all the other noses [*Andern Nasen einige Meter voraus*]" (1973, 7–8; 1991a, 1: 318). The idiom "jemandem eine Nasenlänge voraus sein" (to be ahead of someone by a nose) gains an additional meaning in this context: "Being ahead of the others" is significant for the everyday understanding of the text as well as for a deeper reading, because the *moles* (both text/genre and textual animal) run ahead of readers' cognitive processes. The associations that are started through language use and common sayings in each *Mole* are often immediately abandoned, like the detritus, and, thus, point to the unconscious workings of language. The animetaphor then misleads its reader: "The topography of the texts shifts at any moment, the mole is always ahead of the reader. Hypotheses are formed and discarded, perspectives opened which prove immediately misleading—the burrowing movement of the mole shapes their poetic texture"

(Heydenreich 2007, 200). Heydenreich draws a connection between the poetic texture of the *Moles*, and Deleuze and Guattari's line of flight:

> The line of flight becomes the poetological principle. Because the direction of meaning of the texts cannot be determined; because there are no leading thoughts which could culminate in a punch line; because the direction of reading has to hold on to trains of thought and thought intersections which disorient the reader. [...] language enters a new territory, completely unclaimed from conventions. (ibid.)

While Heydenreich devotes considerable attention to genre, she overlooks the diegetic nature of the animals in Eich's prose poetry. After all, the texts can only achieve this line of flight and a space of semantic openness as a specific function of their textual animals. As Eich declared in his "Preamble," it is the textual animals who are ahead of others, and harmful: "My moles are destructive [*schädlich*], make no mistake. The grass above their tunnels dies off; which of course just makes it more apparent" (Eich 1973, 7–8, trans. mod.). The image of the dying grass over the moles' tunnels must be taken seriously, as it highlights the undermining of a world (and also language) structured by humans that is being destroyed by the textual animals. While the dying grass can be "read" by human observers and points to the existence of the mole underground, the animal is "too fast" and cannot be captured. Following the logic of the text, it is the moles who are in control of the text—not the author or reader. Their pervasive invasion of meaning, alteration of associative courses, and resistance to metaphorical meanings force the reader to use language with care, because the moles undermine it and hollow it out, and it might give way at every reading step.

The textual animals stand for anarchy and the liberty of spaces in-between, clearings outside of human systems and regulations, a type of "hidden kingdom," as in the poem "Pigeons." The moles' kingdom, the text, becomes as unassailable as the dominions of the pigeons, because the moles constantly work the competing meanings that arise from their references, yet they never resolve the ensuing tension. In postfascist Germany, a language that is "anarchic," a language of critique and questions—a poetic language, "experimental, radical [...] [that] contradicts official language rules" (1991a, 4: 624) is the only kind of language that avoids totalitarian structures and, thus, rendering of life. The dying of the grass could in this context be seen as something positive, as the dying of official language rules and standard expressions which serve totalitarian language. The *Moles* assail the stability of language and the clearings they create (or the molehills that make us stumble), but do not get us any closer to capturing the mole itself—arising from the continuous effort to break the referentiality and metaphoricity of language. "Preamble" explicitly references the Grimm fairy tale of the hare and the hedgehog: "Hey we're over here [*Wir sind schon da*] they could yell, but then they'd only feel sorry for the hare" (1973, 7–8).[2] The call "wir sind schon da" ("Hey we're over here") is repeated several times in the fairy tale and references the moral code that informs it. However, Eich's text plays with the expectation of the reader regarding this cultural reference: "The game with words in the idiomatic expression is highlighted and thus the proverbial phrase is pushed back into its literal meaning" (Martin 1995, 315). The "schon" (already), taken literally, points to a kind of always-already thereness of the mole, and the unconsciousness of living language which becomes visible in the animetaphor and undermines the firm ground of being, truth, and logos. At the same time, it also points to the "Da-sein," the presence and existence of the mole, and their eerie presence reminds us of Eich's warning: "You cannot escape your moles" (Eich 1991a, 1: 322). One cannot escape the manipulative side of language which is always already there, preformed, outside of one's control, and can, when used uncritically, lead to a linguistic totalitarianism in the service of biopolitics. Language is always faster than we are, leading us astray.

In accordance with the break in referentiality, the cultural reference to the moral code in the *Moles* is immediately retracted and the referential level broken by adding, "They'd only feel sorry for the hare." The text, through this unexpected turn in thought, actively seeks to counteract the reader's incursions into its territory. The *Mole* expresses pity toward the proverbial hare, and yet it remains unclear for the reader whether this pity is reserved for the semiotic function the hare fulfills in the tale, because it silences the reference to "real" animals or whether the moles express sympathy for the futile effort of the diegetic hare, who can neither keep up with the speed of the moles, nor with the cleverness of the hedgehogs. The play of meaning makes this an animetaphor which "stands for the simultaneous production and dissolution of meaning" (Driscoll 2013, 26); however, in this instance, the animetaphor does not point toward a realm outside of language, but rather plays linguistic traditions and language games off against one another. The effect achieved for the reader is a forced reflection on the animals in sayings, fables, fairy tales, and other language games, and on their simultaneous status as diegetic and semiotic animals. It also reveals the traps that are inherent in preformed chains of associations that common language use invites—or compels—humans to follow. The breakdown of logical coherence in the text created through its many ambiguities, contradictions, and turns in thought subvert the manipulative power in language that shapes thought.

The connection between text and animal is especially pronounced in the *Mole* "Dem Libanon" ("To the Lebanon"). The title, which reads like a dedication, serves as an alienation effect because the whole text has, besides the title, nothing to do with the Lebanon, misleading the reader. Rather, it is a signpost to the Other for German readers in the 1960s, an exoticism which stands in for all the others they know nothing about. In the *Mole*, verses by the expressionist author and poet Georg Kulka turn into animals:

> He has known for a long time now that his verses were hooded crows, sometimes also rooks. Quadrupeds [*Vierfüßer*] would stay longer in the room, iambic hares, trochaic marmots [...]. Really he was waiting for both common ravens and fallow deer, but this combination was rare [...]. You always have to check your verses in Brehm. (Eich 1991a, 1: 307)

The resistance to (linguistic) control of the textual animal is especially striking here: Even though Kulka created these textual animals in the first place and should, as their creator, be in control, they withdraw from his influence by not staying "longer in the room" or refusing to show up in combinations he finds useful. The line between animals as pure text (allegories or metaphors) and animals as diegetic—or even real—becomes permeable, too: Poetic devices such as metrical feet turn into animal feet, and it becomes impossible for the reader to determine whether "Vierfüßer" refers to four metrical feet, a poetic form, or diegetic quadrupeds. The fluidity between physicality and figure of speech, exemplified by the "Vierfüßer," points to a world that is not grounded in a referentially stable language (cf. Lippit 2000, 137–138). The reference to Brehm further breaks with the purely semiotic use of animals by introducing a highly popular zoological reference book (first published in 1860). It draws attention to the fact that animals—in the text as well as in the wild—are always both material and semiotic, because the "scientific knowledge" that is reproduced in Brehm culturalizes nature and is historically as well as culturally situated.[3] Through these cross-references, omissions of classifications, orienting references, and subversions of stable meanings, authority is undermined (Kohlenbach 1982, 79). The move from poetic language to zoological references also blurs the line between scientific, quasi-objective language and general language use and exposes both as anthropocentric discourses that can only be countered in the quasi nonsense of these experimental *Moles*. It is the authority of existing things and their representation in language, the existence of firm knowledge that is subverted and hence rendered useless. The mismatch between the title dedication "To the Libanon" and the content gains new meaning with the demand to verify truths in a dictionary. As the title (or entry dedication) does not illuminate or produce accurate knowledge about the Lebanon, encyclopedias, especially under fascism, have not produced reliable knowledge, but rather propagated political worldviews in order to manipulate people.[4] To counter this, Eich's *Moles* bring chaos and "anarchy" into seemingly stable, unambiguous language games. The absolute deterritorialization of meaning is then proposed as an escape from the discourse that constitutes and binds the subject.

IV

By referencing normative speech itself, the animetaphors moles are uniquely suited to uncover the dark or unconscious side of language which, in postfascist Germany, is connected to the idea of rendering life, and to the inherent violence this type of rendering in normative language possesses. The playful texts hence gain sinister overtones that point toward a commodity fetish as discussed by Shukin (2009). "Preamble" highlights the "rendering life" of the moles by naming their potential use as delicacies or as coats: "Their many enemies enjoy them as delicacies; their thick coats are prized" (Eich 1973, 7, trans. mod.). Drawing attention to the "prized coats" situates the animal firmly in a discourse of life as specter, as a purely material means of capital (Shukin 2009, 39). The *Mole* reminds us that animals in modern society built on animal capital have value mainly as a rare collectors' items. The prose poem reflects this back from the animal in a sarcastic way: "Traps are set, and they run right into them blindly. [...] Wear us as lining for your coats, we're coat fodder! That's what all of them think [*Tragt uns als*

Mantelfutter, denken sie alle]" (Eich 1973, 7, trans. mod.). By ascribing
these thoughts to the textual animals and assigning the personal pronoun
"we," the prose poem draws the reader over to the animals' side, elicit-
ing not only sympathy for the moles, but also outrage at the fact that
the value of their lives are reduced to mere "coat fodder." It also demonstrates that, once on the track of this type of thinking, these "traps"
of assigning value based on the material value of life become inescapable, and the moles have to run "blindly" into them. The fact that the
moles are textual animals and, thus, cannot really be worn as coat fodder extends the problematic aspect of rendering onto the literary level, in
which the author always renders the animal. We, thus, arrive at the double entendre of rendering as proposed by Shukin, where it is at once the
mimetic act of making a copy (or here, a text), and the industrial boiling
down and recycling of animal (or with the Holocaust in mind, human)
remains (2009, 20). Modes of speech and modes of action intersect in
the aspect of rendering.

The materialist critique of life in biopolitical times that is raised in the
mention of delicacies and coat lining shows up again in the *Mole* entitled
"Winterstudentin mit Tochtersohn" ("Winter Student with Daughter-
Son"), which comments on the care the moles require: "My moles are
washed and brushed daily. This is arranged by a specialist [*Fachkraft*], a
winter student" (1991a, 1: 318–319). This focus on the physical presence of the textual animal breaks with purely semiotic meanings. Their
grooming by a "specialist" seems to refer, once again, to the exploitation
of the animal for coat linings and, thus, its appropriation as a commodity fetish. This rendering of animal life in material ways in the text, in
post-Holocaust Germany, takes on a particularly sinister undertone as it
is well known that the bodies of victims of concentration camps were,
like animals, completely rendered; while not turned into "coat fodder,"
their skin and hair were used to produce other, bizarre commodities. We
are—with this sinister truth not only about animal capital, but also biopower under fascist regimes—reminded of Eich's iconic dictum that "our
sins are moles [*Unsere Sünden sind Maulwürfe*]" (1991a, 3: 491). And
while the industrial practice of rendering human bodies seems to have
come to a halt for the moment, it finds its continuation in the rendering
of animal bodies, both based on the same principle. Thus, our sins are
moles in several ways. They are underground, negated and ignored until
they disturb the surface, but they are also in language, as the moles move
through language, and will pop up at unexpected moments, reminding

us of our historical heritage, carried in language. In light of the commodity fetish in the *Moles*, this seems to underscore a materialist critique
of life in biopolitical times as expressed by Shukin.[5]

However, in the typical mode of Eich's zoopoetics, the text immediately changes direction, proving once again that it is "faster than
thought" and undermines readers' expectations. This change in direction
(and, thus, also referentiality) allows Eich's text to challenge the notion
of animal capital and its appropriation as a cultural sign or reference. The
text proceeds to describe the "specialist" in seemingly absurd terms: "In
the evenings, she learns yoga techniques, wants to take her exam this
summer in India. This is extravagant [*ausgefallen*] enough for my moles. [...]
My winter student has blue hair, but her German is deficient" (1991a, 1:
318–319). With this unexpected move and the seemingly random pieces
of information about the caretaker, the text "undermines all systems and
instead engages in philosophical deconstruction" (Rollin 1996, 44). The
clear preference of the moles for this "specialist" that is expressed in the
statement "extravagant enough" assigns the moles agency that, as commodity fetish, seemed to have been lost before. The preference of the
moles requires the unexpected: "I have tried in vain to hire a sodomite.
They exist only in psychoanalytical reports and in the Old Testament"
(Eich 1991a, 1: 318–319). The *Mole* draws attention to the dissocia-
tion of language and truth by pointing out that sodomites do not exist,
except as a construct, thus, negating truth and language representability.
The chasm between word and reality is opened and allows the "inflow of
the fantastically or absurdly 'Other' into closed meaning- and language
realms [...] Reality is to be perceived as deception, as unreal, as farce"
(Joachimsthaler 2009, 102). As Jürgen Joachimsthaler states, the succes-
sive, quickly changing linguistic images, which seem to be determined
more by alogical sequencing and associations, determine themselves
the meanings of the text (ibid.) and enable a separation of signifier and
signified, even a disentanglement of identity and language. The "reality"
or truth of categories is dissolved.

The "anarchic" aspect of the *Moles* shows itself here as the liberty with
which labels are used, and the subsequent meaninglessness of language.
Consequently, the winter student's German is "deficient," and what is
more "she doesn't know any other languages, it is congenital [*Andere
Sprachen kennt sie nicht, es ist angeboren*]" (Eich 1991a, 1: 318–319).
Because she is unable to understand or communicate in any language,
her position shifts closer to the animal (traditionally conceptualized as

mute), and yet this muteness gives her power over the desperate narrator who is unable to connect to her on a conversational level:

> A quarter-hour daily I have to tickle the soles of her feet. [...] Yes, I say to my winter student; she still understands this best [*das begreift sie noch am besten*]. You are beautiful, I say, but even here it is getting more difficult, she gives me her soles [...] most of my sentences do not interest her. (ibid.)

The narrator has to resign himself to offer "Liebesbeweise," demonstrations of love, in the form of feet tickling, as she doesn't care about his sentences. These "Liebesbeweise" also allow for another reading of the grooming, one of care. Both readings stand side by side in the *Moles* and are a marker of their zoopoetics where language is freed from its common referentiality and, thus, deconstructed in order to counter power discourses. "Contexts are evoked that mutually undermine each other and, thus, subvert any semantic consistency of the text" (Heydenreich 2007, 488). Her congenital inability to speak languages could be connected to the Other in language, and that we are always to a certain degree outside of language, as highlighted by the animetaphor. It also highlights the arbitrariness of speaking or belonging to a language and culture, which challenges the primacy and superiority of one language over another (cf. Derrida 1998). The rejection of value statements such as "you are beautiful" do not make any sense to her, because they subscribe to anthropocentric and arbitrary categories of value and beauty in which she is not interested. This moment also connects back to the poem "Pigeons," where beauty is unable to capture the birds' flight. The *Mole*, thus, folds language in on itself, embraces the "unrestricted variability of combinations and the limitless exchangeability of words and phrases" (Heydenreich 2011, 508).

Eich's zoopoetics relies on the movement of the animal through the text to produce a criticism of language that forms a critique of anthropocentric and logocentric systems which, in the context of postfascist Germany, gains additional urgency. The material aspect of the text is closely related to a politics of rendering and suggests that one "cannot escape" the logic of rendering, which is deeply embedded in language use and cultural associations. Because of their specificity, the animals have an intertextual or literary agency that transcends unambiguous language use and shakes the foundations of logocentrism—and, thus, opens up a space of playful anarchism which, while remaining conscious of discourses of rendering, nonetheless undermines it, creating a language that is "unassailable." The references to animal abuse and violence that are clearest when his texts resist meaning least (i.e., in the breeding of the pigeons, and in the fur coat lining of the moles) suggest that any anthropocentric and logocentric language already implies a type of violence or fascism (of meaning) that you "cannot escape." His solution, achieved through zoopoetics, is a playful language game where meaning is always suspended and reference is provisional and pending. Eich's animals and their close connection to a critique of language and power (especially after fascism) point to a change of the meaning and function of textual animals after the experience of fascist language abuse. In Eich's texts, animals become subversive animetaphors—at the same time inside of language and its border—simultaneously pointing to and hollowing out structures of rendering.

NOTES

1. Unless otherwise indicated, all translations from the German are my own.
2. English-speaking readers might be more familiar with a similar version found in Aesop's fable "The Tortoise and the Hare."
3. Brehm, though claiming to be a zoological reference book, adds a lot of culturally preformed knowledge that cannot be verified by animal observation and thus embeds the animals he lists in a strong anthropocentric frame.
4. For example, "Meyers Lexikon" from 1936–1942 or the Duden edition from 1933 show significant and politically motivated deviations that not only comply with but actually propagate the anti-Semitic and totalitarian worldview.
5. On the relationship between "rendering" and zoopoetics, see also the chapters by Castellanos, Hoffmann, and Preuss in this volume.

WORKS CITED

Borgards, Roland. 2012. Tiere in der Literatur – eine methodologische Standortbestimmung. In *Das Tier an sich. Disziplinübergreifende Perspektiven für neue Wege im wissenschaftsbasierten Tierschutz*, ed. Herwig Grimm and Carola Otterstedt, 87–118. Göttingen: Vandenhoeck & Ruprecht.

Derrida, Jacques. 1998. *Monolingualism of the Other; or, The Prosthesis of Origin*, trans. Patrick Mensah. Stanford: Stanford University Press.

Driscoll, Kári. 2013. The Enemy Within: Zoopoetics in 'Erinnerungen an die Kaldabahn'. *Journal of the Kafka Society of America* 35/36: 23–35.

Eich, Günter. 1973. Preamble, trans. Stuart Friebert. *Field: Contemporary Poetry and Poetics* 8: 7–8.

———. 1991a. *Gesammelte Werke in vier Bänden*, ed. Axel Vieregg. Frankfurt am Main: Suhrkamp.

———. 1991b. *Pigeons and Moles: Selected Writings by Günter Eich*, trans. Michael Hamburger. Columbia: Camden House.

Gerhard, Gesine. 2005. Breeding Pigs and People for the Third Reich. In *How Green Were the Nazis?: Nature, Environment, and Nation in the Third Reich*, ed. Franz-Josef Brüggemeier, Mark Cioc, and Thomas Zeller, 129–146. Athens: Ohio University Press.

Heydenreich, Aura Maria. 2007. *Wachstafel und Weltformel. Erinnerungspoetik und Wissenschaftskritik in Günter Eichs "Maulwürfen."* Göttingen: Vandenhoeck & Ruprecht.

———. 2011. Die Grenzen der Axiomatik und die Kritik der enzyklopädischen Wissensordnung. David Hilbert in Günter Eichs Maulwurf Hilpert. In *Zahlen, Zeichen und Figuren. Mathematische Inspirationen in Kunst und Literatur*, ed. Andrea Albrecht, Gesa von Essen, and Werner Frick, 486–510. Berlin: de Gruyter.

Joachimsthaler, Jürgen. 2009. Die Pest der Bezeichnung. Günter Eichs Poetik der Verstrickung und der Austauschbarkeit. In *Günter Eichs Metamorphosen. Marbacher Symposium aus Anlass des 100. Geburtstages am 1. Februar 2007*, ed. Carsten Dutt and Dirk von Petersdoff, 87–119. Heidelberg: Winter.

Kohlenbach, Michael. 1982. *Günter Eichs späte Prosa. Einige Merkmale der Maulwürfe.* Bonn: Bouvier.

Lippit, Akira Mizuta. 2000. *Electric Animal: Towards a Rhetoric of Wildlife.* Minneapolis: University of Minnesota Press.

Martin, Sigurd. 1995. *Die Auren des Wort-Bildes. Günter Eichs Maulwurf-Poetik und die Theorie des versehenden Lesens.* St. Ingbert: Röhrig.

Neumann, Peter Horst. 1981. *Die Rettung der Poesie im Unsinn. Der Anarchist Günter Eich.* Stuttgart: Klett-Cotta.

Rollin, Marie Simone. 1996. Günter Eich – Ein gestürzter Mythos. In *"Unsere Sünden sind Maulwürfe." Die Günter-Eich-Debatte*, ed. Axel Vieregg, 29–48. Amsterdam: Rodopi.

Shukin, Nicole. 2009. *Animal Capital: Rendering Life in Biopolitical Times.* Minneapolis: University of Minnesota Press.

Vieregg, Axel. 1996. *"Unsere Sünden sind Maulwürfe." Die Günter-Eich-Debatte.* Amsterdam: Rodopi.

The Grammar of Zoopoetics: Human and Canine Language Play

Joela Jacobs

I

Dogs are known for their ability to learn to associate meaning with words in the human language, which has been an ongoing site of investigation and source of imagination for the human species. Short commands and word combinations elicit specific behavioral responses in dogs (Pilley 2013), and recent studies have put the potential number of words in the canine vocabulary at over 1000 (Kaminski et al. 2004; Pilley and Reid 2011). The idea of a canine gift of language is not new: a century ago, "wonder dogs" performed complicated feats such as spelling words and solving mathematical equations for paying audiences.[1] Yet, in their focus on typically human abilities, trainers and observers fell prey to the so-called Clever Hans fallacy, meaning that these undoubtedly smart dogs did not actually do the math, but rather responded to barely noticeable nonverbal cues, such as intonation, posture, and gestures, that indicated the expected response (Hearne 2007, 4–5; Cooper

J. Jacobs
University of Arizona, Tucson, AZ, USA

© The Author(s) 2018
K. Driscoll and E. Hoffmann (eds.), *What Is Zoopoetics?*,
Palgrave Studies in Animals and Literature,
https://doi.org/10.1007/978-3-319-64416-5_5

et al. 2003; Ratcliffe and Reby 2014; Andics et al. 2016).[2] While perhaps not spelling champions, dogs are nevertheless talented interpreters of human signals, which has led to a long history of imagining dogs' verbal response to our words. Contemporary dog memes are one such example that seems to be typical of the internet age and draws on the multilingual and multimedial resources of new technologies. These captioned images pick up on the notion of dogs' understanding of human vocabulary by attributing words to the animals they show. Memes such as "Yes, this is dog" and "I have no idea what I am doing," for instance, depict dogs performing anthropomorphic tasks such as answering the telephone or typing an email (Know Your Meme A, B). The comic effect of these images and their captions derives at least in part from the mismatch between canine abilities and a technologically mediated human context that is language- and communication-focused. While these memes do not show us what a dog thinks, they do provide a glimpse into how humans imagine "the dog" in postmodern times and how this view differs from modernist and premodernist understandings of canines and their linguistic skills.

Many memes in contemporary internet culture have a particularly playful approach to language and attribute ungrammatical utterances to animals.[3] The meme of the "doge," for instance, whose name is already a misspelling of the canine species designation, contains only ungrammatical sentence fragments, such as "why this happened," "so scare," and "trim 2moro" (Know Your Meme F) when the character is faced with the prospect of nail trimming. This way of speaking has become its own recognizable linguistic pattern on the internet (McCulloch 2014a), and rather than reflecting some kind of "animal language," it shares characteristics with the way humans talk to babies (infant-directed speech) and companion animals (pet-directed speech) (Burnham et al. 2002; Ben-Aderet et al. 2017). The combination of anthropomorphization and infantilization that occurs in ungrammatical language attribution might at first glance seem to reinforce ideas of human superiority in these scenarios, yet the use of memes as a commentary about the posting person's own feelings and experiences by allegorical proxy, for instance in the case of "I don't know what I'm doing," ironizes and inverts this superiority. By creating a space for the breaking of rules, both of grammar and of typical human/animal divisions and hierarchies, memes turn the depicted failure of, for instance, a dog trying to type an email with his paws into a comical success. The meme of the doge makes this creative potential particularly clear in respect to language: the usually highly enthusiastic utterances, e.g. "wow," "such tempt," "very taste" about a treat (Bowker 2014), or the meta-commentary on its own linguistic innovation, "very syntax," "so linguistics," "many spelling" (McCulloch 2014b), create an endearing speech pattern that underscores the perceived cuteness of the image and group the depicted dog in a category of beloved beings such as babies.[4] Whether by way of creative ungrammatical language or contextual contrast, dog memes base their appeal on a purposefully anthropomorphized depiction of an animal that breaks anthropomorphic rules. Regardless of whether this registers with the viewer as an ironic critique of anthropomorphism, internet culture plays in creative ways with the human/animal distinction and linguistic norms by putting human words into the animal's mouth or, rather, by captioning the animal's anthropomorphic misperformance in the human language.[5]

This postmodern play with speech norms is only the most recent rendition of a tradition of attributing language to animals and allowing dogs to satirize human behavior. Dogs have been in the dual role of the best friend and best critic of humans at least since the Cynic Diogenes, who was called "the Dog."[6] Western literature tends to portray dogs as particularly insightful and linguistically gifted: from Cerberus in Lucian's *Dialogues of the Dead* in the second century BCE to the canines of Cervantes' famous *Dialogue of the Dogs* in 1613, literary dogs tend to be experts in human matters, particularly regarding questions of philosophy. Theodore Ziolkowski (1983) has called this the tradition of the "philosopher dog," who tells his life story eloquently and is as interested in music and literature as in a juicy ham.[7] The texts of this genre play with the notion of the dog as a speaking, narrating, and communicating figure who is fluent in most major topics of human concern. The topos of the narrating dog became of particular interest around 1900 with the rise of the phenomenon of language skepticism. Modernist writers were acutely aware of the inability of language to represent anyone's perceived reality accurately, and they struggled with the arbitrariness of signs and their referents.[8] These language-philosophical concerns prompted many experiments in the arts, but they also ushered in a renewed interest in animals as narrators, particularly dogs, in many modernist texts across the Western canon.[9] Yet unlike their predecessors, these modernist philosopher dogs are skeptical of the human language, thus reflecting contemporary concerns. In what follows, I will introduce two German renditions of this type of philosopher dog, one written by Oskar Panizza and the other by Franz Kafka. The canine narrators of these texts eloquently master the human language, and also communicate with other dogs in canine ways. Yet, in keeping with the language crisis of the time, both narratives include a central encounter with other dogs during which human language fails the respective philosopher dog, which prompts an epistemological and ontological crisis. As dogs who tell stories, they constantly grate against the conditions of narration as a typically human pursuit. Yet, as memes show, imaginative and creative language can destabilize this traditional distinction between humans and animals. Through canine narration, Panizza's and Kafka's texts similarly question conventional ways of figuring animal capabilities, while acknowledging the human dependence on language-based conceptualization through their narrative form. The two texts trouble the traditional human/animal binary both through the anthropomorphic application of linguistic skills to dogs and the introduction of epistemological and ontological uncertainty, which destabilizes the perception of self and other for both the philosopher dogs and human readers. In each of the following two sections, I begin with an introduction to the respective narrative, then describe the text's view on humans and their language briefly, and finally analyze the encounters with nonspeaking dogs that raise epistemological and ontological questions.

II

In Oskar Panizza's *From the Diary of a Dog* (1892), a dog narrates a series of adventures and encounters of his life as a pet. He largely roams free in a city, which enables him to compare human and canine modes of communication directly, and his assessment is clear:

> When you watch two dogs who meet by chance and explore each other, everything is done in a few minutes. We know that he is complaining about the frost, he is going hungry, he has been beaten, he is defiant, he is suspicious; one whiff tells us everything; his soul lies open before our nose. But now watch two humans! Indeed, I can barely give an idea to those who have not seen this for themselves. What an embarrassment! Such effort in sounds and movements! [...] The frog, the sparrow, the squirrel, the crow, the stork and the wolf combined could not produce the sum of the sounds that humans need to ask each other: How are you? Are you

hungry?—Indeed, I often ask myself whether all these nonsensical and whimpering sounds mean something; whether despite this colossal effort, this race finally knows what the other thinks to himself, and what he thinks of him! [...] Whether they know something about each other?—Of the composition of their soul?—Poor species! (Panizza 1977, 159–161)[10]

The canine communication system involves all five senses: vocal signaling, body language, touch, taste, and most importantly, a scent-based system of pheromone signaling (Coren 2000, 247–253; Horowitz 2009, 67–88). The narrator's depiction of canine communication emphasizes the efficacy and depth of sensory communication by way of scent, and it relegates human vocalizations as well as gestures to a category of secondary, less successful means of expression. The aromatic is presented as a way of instantly knowing the particularities of an individual (i.e. the soul), in contrast to an abstract system of signs and gestures, which is unable to answer such a deceptively simple question as "How are you?"[11] In this paragraph, the emphasis on the olfactory, which is based on the physiologically demonstrated abilities of dogs, challenges the foundation of human epistemology, as language and gestures lead humankind into a perceived moment of crisis in which one is unable to know the other. The humans observed by Panizza's narrator are unable to pose the question "How are you?," which additionally betrays an ontological inability to know oneself. Panizza's narrator suggests that dogs escape these problems through their scent-based communication. As he also points out, canine communication focuses on the particularity of another's corporeal presence in a way that does not seem to separate body and mind. The "soul" that is laid bare by one whiff therefore appears to be a soul in the Aristotelian sense: the form or idea of the living dog, i.e. its dog-ness (cf. *De Anima* II.1–2). According to Panizza's philosopher dog, animals generally avoid the epistemological and ontological problems faced by humans, while human language is shown as a central obstacle to the perception of the world and the self, which reflects the skepticism so central to the modernist language crisis.

Yet the dog's praise of the canine language (ironically, delivered in human language) is contrasted with a moment of communicative failure between the canine narrator and another dog that suggests that the narrator's anthropomorphic skills have made him vulnerable to the same sense of loss of self as humans. Panizza's narrator attempts to interpret the experience in both the canine and the human communicative mode, but it leaves him confused and shaken in his linguistic confidence. As he says himself, he is at a loss for words and indeed becomes momentarily confused about grammar, albeit in different ways than the doge:

> I don't know how to say it — — the small bushy dog's entire body was trembling; his gestures, his gaze expressed half jubilation, half pain; his face became dumb, dodgy, embarrassed; it was odd that all salutations I had experienced so far were simply characterized by mutual information about one's own wellbeing; this one however seemed to consider that information superfluous and moved within completely different sensations, and it awakened a new, stupid idea in me. To use a crazy but short expression: It seemed to me as if the dog wanted to be I — or be me; how do you say this? — It seemed as if the bushy dog wanted less to orient himself about me, or the disposition of my soul, whether we would get along and such, but he, the bushy dog, wanted to be me, the straight-haired dog. It sounds absolutely crazy. I admit it. Yet I cannot express it any other way. — He smelled me from behind. I used to consider this a game. Yet I have to say it touched me in a peculiar way. With horror I realized how a new Dog-I opened up inside of me, which threatened to wipe out the past. I did the craziest jumps and body twists. I felt [literally: appeared to myself] like a human. (Panizza 1977, 220)

The other dog's behavior corrupts the process of "laying bare one's soul," of establishing his dog-ness via scent that makes up regular canine communication in the text. The intentions of the eagerly but silently sniffing dog seem to have changed from an epistemological quest of finding out about the other to an ontological endeavor of wanting to be the other ("It seemed as if the bushy dog wanted less to orient himself about me, or the disposition of my soul, whether we would get along and such, but he, the bushy dog, wanted to be me, the straight-haired dog."). The notion of "being become" triggers an existential crisis of language, in which the otherwise quite eloquent narrator is seemingly no longer able to express himself in either of his languages because it is unclear to him whether he is the subject or object of the encounter; that is, whether the other dog wants to be *I* or *me*. This grammatical insecurity draws attention to the fact that narrating in the human language makes the dog both the subject and the object, i.e. the "I *and* me" of the narrative. The endeavor of the strange dog to "be(come) another dog," specifically the narrating dog, turns into a "becoming-human" in the last line, in which the narrator announces that "I appeared to myself like a human" (*ich kam mir wie ein Mensch vor*). This raises epistemological doubt ("I appeared to myself" or "I seemed to myself like a human") and an ontological question that harks back to the narrator's anthropomorphic skills: am I perhaps not a dog, or not the same dog anymore? The encounter with another dog who disturbs both canine and human modes of communication (which is both the silent bushy dog and the narrator's own canine nature, since "a new Dog-I opened up inside of me") destabilizes the anthropomorphic framework from within.

The epistemological doubt raised by this philosopher dog does not stay confined to canine encounters in the text. In a telling passage that sums up the relationship of the narrator to his human side and ultimately renders modernist language skepticism even more acute, we encounter the familiar mode of pet-directed speech from the perspective of an animal:

> In the last month I counted: 12 blows with a stick; 25 kicks with the foot; 6 times beatings and blows with the fist or hand; 3 times having to endure terrible thirst; 1 time bones that were gnawed bare and hard as stone; 35 times "Cootchie-cootchie-coo, who is the nice doggie?"; circa 40 times "Goochie-goochie-goo, who is the black bow-wow?". The services on my side are: 120 licks; 370 sniffs; 500 tail-wags, and close to 699 times brown-nosing. — Each one finds their way to get by! (Panizza 1977, 178)

The narrator's list of figures equates human violence and abuse with infantilization and demeaning affection, and because of the nature of this human-animal relationship, his own canine devotion is also mere calculation. This dog has done the math and outsmarted his owner with his attunement to human expectations and social cues, thereby destabilizing the established conventions of superiority/inferiority in the human/ canine relationship and introducing epistemological doubt to the human side. The text's contrast of ungrammatical pet-directed speech uttered by humans with the canine narrator's general eloquence calls attention to and subtly subverts the infantilization just as memes do when they make dogs talk to us like we talk to them. Perhaps part of the reason for the impulse to infantilize dogs is their traditional role as observers, interpreters, and critics of humankind. After all, a companion animal tends to know more about their family than most neighbors and witnesses private moments that individuals might not even share with their partners. Akin to Derrida's encounter with his cat, dogs know us in our nakedness. They have smelled us and "our soul is laid bare" to them.

III

Thirty years after Panizza's critical canine commentator, in 1922, Franz
Kafka penned one of his most enigmatic animal texts, *Investigations* or
Researches of a Dog (*Forschungen eines Hundes*).[12] Its canine narrator
exhibits a catalog of modernist attributes: the stream of consciousness
that makes up his narrative jumps between reflections and memories that
appear decontextualized and defamiliarized. Anecdotal moments come
into focus, only to disappear without any explanation. No overt plot
coherence or conclusion emerges. Yet, instead of depicting canine experience according to the idea that animals exist in an unreflective present,
most of the canine narrator's thoughts represent an effort to make sense
of a range of past and present experiences in eloquent musings. These
investigations or researches (*Forschungen*) of the way the world works
draw attention to canine abilities of tracking clues and interpreting sensory data, and they simultaneously tie this text into the tradition of the
philosopher dog. Humans are not explicitly mentioned in the narrative,
so that their potential presence can only be identified through interpretative maneuvers. While several scholars have done so in fascinating and
skillful ways (Berg 2010; Alt 2005, 653–656), their approach betrays a
certain expectation regarding the importance and perception of humans
in the world of dogs on the part of the reader. It seems to assume that
humans are not explicitly identified by the narrating dog because he
doesn't quite know how this anthropocentric world works, i.e. his perception is impaired by his dog-ness, similar to the memes in which dogs
"don't know what they are doing" in human contexts. However, the
canine narrator of Kafka's text is fully aware of non-dogs in his world,
though they are not described in a way with which humans might like to
identify:

> Besides us dogs there are many different kinds of creatures all around–
> poor, meager, mute beings, whose speech is limited only to certain cries;
> many of us dogs study them, have given them names, seek to help them,
> educate them, improve them, etc. (Kafka 2007, 132–133)

From a dog's eye view, these linguistically limited and nearly mute creatures could very well be or include humans (Harel 2013, 52). The narrator uses typically human terms to describe the way in which dogs have
established dominion over other species by naming and categorizing

them in their studies (*Forschungen*). Dogs consider these others to be in need of assistance, education, and improvement according to canine standards, and the texts thus turns an anthropocentric framework into a cynocentric yet anthropomorphized one, in which inarticulate species are trained by eloquent dogs. Although Kafka's canine narrator does not contrast intra-canine communication with human language here explicitly, he shares with Panizza's dog a view of non-canine communication as deficient and impoverished.

The most frequently discussed scene of Kafka's text is the narrator's memory of a childhood encounter with seven dogs who stand upright on two legs, as if dancing to music. Bipedal like humans, they ironically cause the narrator (a dog who speaks like humans) to doubt their dog-ness, mainly because they appear to have forgotten the principles of canine communication, which, in turn, leads to the narrator's momentary loss of his human language skills. As in Panizza's text, this moment of epistemological and ontological doubt involves meeting and greeting rituals:

> [B]ut in the end they were dogs nevertheless, dogs like you and me; you observed them in the usual way, like dogs that you meet on the street; you wanted to go up to them, exchange greetings [...] But they–incredible! incredible!–they did not answer, acted as if I did not exist; dogs who do not respond in any way when they are called offend against good manners, a transgression for which the smallest as well as the largest dog is under no circumstances forgiven. Might they possibly not even be dogs? But then, how could they not be dogs[?] (Kafka 2007, 135–136)

The scene can be contextualized within canine meeting behavior: approaching to exchange greetings entails a trade in scent-based information via canine noses and anal glands as well as the interpretation of visual clues (Coren 2000, 247–253; Horowitz 2009, 67–88). The upright dogs encountered by the canine narrator make such an exchange impossible because their posture makes it difficult to access their anal glands and impossible for them to bring their noses near another dog's behind. Instead, this position brings the dogs face-to-face, prompting prolonged eye contact, a situation that is threatening according to canine standards and could turn aggressive.[13] At the same time, the upright dogs are baring their undersides, which is typically either a signal of appeasement and deference, or trust and relaxation in dogs (Coren 2000, 192; Horowitz 2009, 110). Imagining the scene thus—rather than a human greeting involving handshakes and questions about the other's well-being—reinforces the narrator's incredulity: these dogs are not just "rude"; they are sending mixed signals, behaving both aggressively and deferentially in canine terms, and are thus disrupting regular behavioral patterns on multiple communicative levels.

Yet ignoring someone else would be "an offense against good manners" in the human world as well, and in philosophical terms, it would render the other insignificant to such a degree as to deny their existence. A response serves to reaffirm the perception of oneself and the world, and in this scene, the breakdown of communication shatters the narrator's epistemological and ontological certainties. If the dogs *ignore* him, are they really dogs? And if the dogs ignore *him*, does he exist? Like Panizza's narrator, the encounter makes Kafka's canine suddenly wonder whether he is perhaps not, or no longer, a dog. The absence of canine communication results in a fundamental crisis of other and self for the narrating philosopher dog, which leads to the disruption of his own communicative skills:

> These dogs before me were violating the law. Great magicians they might be, but the law applied to them as well: that was something that I, a child, already knew very well. And from this point I saw even more. They really had good reason to remain silent, assuming that it was from feelings of guilt that they did so. For what a way to behave; because of the loud music I had not noticed until now that they had truly cast off all shame; these miserable creatures were doing something that was at once most ridiculous and most obscene; they were walking upright on their hind legs. Ugh! [...] I could not proceed, I no longer wanted to instruct them; they could go on spreading their legs, committing sins, and luring others to the sin of silent observation, but I was such a small dog, who could require such a difficult act of me? I made myself look even smaller than I was, I whimpered[.] (Kafka 2007, 136–137)[14]

The narrator's discomfort about the dogs' disregard for canine standards of behavior and communication culminates in a breakdown or perhaps refusal of the human language. Instead of "instruct[ing] them," Kafka's canine is whimpering (notably one of the terms used in Panizza's narrator's description of the human language), which marks an explicit deviation from the human language he uses in the rest of the narrative. He describes this sound as a human would, correctly embedded in the syntax and grammar of the narrative, but the meaning of the whimpering expression itself is inaccessible. High-pitched tonal vocalizations of dogs, such as whimpering, usually communicate discomfort (Coren 2000, 86–93; Horowitz 2009, 89–120). In this sense, we understand the communicative purpose of whimpering, but remain nonetheless excluded from the depths of its meaning for dogs. The anthropomorphic fiction of the narration is destabilized from within, highlighting the limits of human language and epistemology. Yet while the whimpering dog only momentarily resists the anthropomorphism implied by canine narration, the group of seven dogs does so in two permanent ways: they remain silent in the human language and they foreclose the reciprocity of scent-based canine communication, making themselves inaccessible to the anthropomorphic canine narrator and thus the human reader, which reinforces the ontological doubt of whether they "might possibly not even be dogs." Instead of translating from the canine world, then, the narrator is cast out of its meaning-making processes in this scene, and his whimpering, which should align him with the dogs, is in stark contrast to their silence and cuts him off from the human reader. As a result, the narrator is momentarily barred from expression and connection in both human and nonhuman language, leaving the reader to grapple with the human dependence on language for epistemological and ontological certainties. The breakdown of both human and animal communication moreover collapses the categories of the human/animal distinction by exposing the anthropomorphic constructedness of *both* sides of this binary.

IV

Postmodern memes and philosopher dog narratives reflect the idea of the dog in the human imagination by endowing the canine species with human language. The critical potential of this anthropomorphism emerges when anthropomorphic dogs run up against the limits of human language. In these moments, the traditional human/animal distinction is destabilized from both directions by undoing any certainties about the category of the animal and of the human alike. In the context of the modernist disavowal of the reliability of language and reason, Panizza's and Kafka's philosopher dogs parse out the failure of the human conception of self and other, and thereby ironically and purposefully perform an unsettling of the traditional human/animal binary from a nonhuman point of view. For these modernists, this is a fundamental epistemological and ontological crisis that begins and ends with language skepticism, during which even the nonlinguistic alternative of canine communication ultimately fails to establish secure knowledge about the self and the world. Contemporary memes, on the other hand, approach preconceived ideas of the human and the animal much more lightheartedly as simply one of the numerous binaries that are broken down in the postmodern age. They play subversively with the norms of being and knowledge, just as they do with language. What appears as ungrammatical in memes and modernism—whether it is a language-skeptical breakdown of communication or a caption on the doge—turns out to partake in the grammar of zoopoetics: the particular linguistic creativity enabled by anthropomorphized animal language that questions its own presuppositions.

NOTES

1. In Germany around 1900, the philosophizing terrier Rolf, for instance, was one of the most prominent subjects of the so-called *New Animal Psychology*, which was significantly impacted by Pavlov's behaviorist studies of dogs that won him a Nobel Prize in 1904 (Moekel 1920; von den Berg 2008; Bondeson 2011).
2. Clever Hans was a horse, but the fallacy applies equally to dogs and other species.
3. This is familiar from LOLcats, but also extends to a generation of dogs, such as Moon Moon or the doge (Know Your Meme C, D, E). Since the writing of this article, additional language patterns have appeared in the "doggo" meme, which tends to address "frens" who "bork" with a response such as "you are doing me a frighten," while the "borking pupper" might confess that he was just "doing you a bamboozle." Cf. Know Your Meme G.
4. However, the meme can invoke a notion of inept animality that would be called "derp" in internet speech, which connotes stupidity. Dictionary. com defines derp in its adjectival use as "foolish or awkward: pictures of animals making derp faces." Some iterations of the meme abuse this notion in racist or ableist ways, e.g. by mocking people with speech impediments or intellectual disabilities or non-native speakers of English, which highlights the pattern's relation to foreigner-directed speech (Uther et al. 2007).
5. For an elaboration on the (meta)communicative intricacies of play and its creativity, see Massumi (2014), and for an engagement with the interrelation of textuality and animality ("zoogrammatology"), see Pisorski (2015). See also Myers (2015) on the critical potential of anthropomorphism in cat videos.

6. The ancient Greeks called those who pestered them with uncomfortable questions Cynics. The nuances of meaning surrounding dogs in literature are explicated by William Empson (1989), who explains that "the grin of dogs seems then to have been part of their reputation for satire" (164) in Elizabethan times, whereas "the idea of the dog as a cynic […] seems to be in part a learned innovation" (ibid.). The trope of the *grinning dog* in connection with *biting satire* combines two aspects of the canine act of showing teeth, which can signal both friendly and aggressive behaviors (e.g. relaxed "smiling" vs. snarling). As *honest dogs*, satirists of the human condition are said to be "lifting their legs and pissing against the world" (*Return from Parnassus* (1601), quoted in Empson 1989, 165) with the help of the spoken or the written word. "The notion that the dog blows the gaff on human nature somehow attached itself to the ambition of the thinker to do the same" (169). In the eighteenth century, the metaphor shifts from that of an outsider to a form of praise for a respectable character, yet it maintained "the independence of the outcast […]; he does not hide the truth about himself and thereby shows the truth about us all" (168). This contrasts starkly with the idea of 'the kept dog' whose flattery is a lie (cf. 165 and 176f).

7. See also Kohlhauer (2002), Neumann (1996), Prawer (1977). One particularly prominent example of this genre is the dog Berganza, who was first introduced by Cervantes and later taken up by various authors, among them perhaps most prominently in the German tradition E. T. A. Hoffmann in *News of the Most Recent Fate of the Dog Berganza* (1814). The figure of Berganza typically tells the story of his life in a series of anecdotes that reflect on living as a dog as much as on pertinent topics of the respective intellectual zeitgeist.

8. The skepticism that language can adequately portray the world is symptomatic both of an epistemological crisis and an artistic search for a new poetic language among German modernists around 1900. Hugo von Hofmannsthal's *Chandos Letter* (1902) is usually cited as a key expression of this recognition of the limits of language in the so-called language crisis (*Sprachkrise*).

9. In 1918, Oskar Walzel confirmed the contemporary literary interest in animals 'for their own sake' in the German context, characterizing it as their "ardent aspiration to establish an empathic connection with the animal and to divine its mental processes [*Seelenvorgänge*]" (qtd. in Driscoll 2015, 214). The same time saw the publication of texts such as Thomas Mann's *A Man and His Dog* (1918), which reflects human-canine relationships. This literary trend was not limited to Germany, as Jack London's wildly successful dog novels (e.g. *The Call of the Wild* from 1903 and *Wild Fang* from 1906) show among many others, such

as Marie More Marsh's *Vic: The Autobiography of a Fox Terrier* (1892), Marshall Saunders' *Beautiful Joe: An Autobiography* (1893), Anatole France's *Riquet* and *Pensées de Riquet* (both 1900), Mark Twain's *A Dog's Tale* (1903), O. Henry's *Memoirs of a Yellow Dog* (1903), Reginald Pelham Bolton's *The Autobiography of an Irish Terrier* (1904), Olive Evelyth Hurd Bragdon's *Pup: The Autobiography of a Greyhound* (1905), Esther M. Baxendale's *Yours with All My Heart: Her Own Story, as Told by the Beautiful Italian Gazelle-Hound Fairy* (1904) and *Fairy: The Autobiography of a Real Dog* (1907), Jacinto Benavente y Martínez's *New Dialog of the Dogs* (1908), Miguel de Unamuno's *Berganza and Zapirón* (1909), Carrie Gates Niles Whitcomb's *The Autobiography of Jeremy L.: The Actor Dog* (1910), Barbara Blair's *The Journal of a Neglected Bulldog* (1911), etc. This list could arguably be extended by a range of later twentieth-century texts, for instance, Albert Payson Terhune's *Lad: A Dog* (1919), Mikhail Bulgakov's *The Heart of a Dog* (1925, censored until 1987), Sewell Collins's *The Rubáiyát of a Scotch Terrier* (1926), Virginia Woolf's *Flush* (1933), Italo Svevo's *Argo and His Master* (1934), etc., but the majority of these texts move away from the first person narrative position so central to the cluster around 1900. For more on this topic see Kuzniar (2006) and Brown (2010).

10. All quotations of Panizza's text were translated by Joela Jacobs.

11. The canine ability of knowing who one is in an instant is a popular trope, for instance in Homer's *Odyssey*, in which the dog Argos is the only one to recognize his disguised master Odysseus after his 20-year absence (17.290–327). Knowing who one is, on a fundamental ontological level, is also invoked in Levinas's (1990) account of Bobby, the dog who recognized concentration camp prisoners as men and reminded them of their humanity, after they had been dehumanized to such an extent that they seemed to have forgotten themselves.

12. The German title was formulated by Max Brod for the posthumous publication of the text. Stanley Corngold's English translation puts the word "researches" in the title (Kafka 2007), while Willa and Edwin Muir render it as "investigations" (Kafka 1988).

13. "Direct head-on approaches can be threatening to dogs, especially shy ones meeting a person or dog whom they don't know. Watch two well-socialized but unfamiliar dogs greet at the park. The politest of dogs tend to approach from the side, perhaps even at 90 degrees. They avoid direct eye contact. On the other hand, two dogs standing face-on, staring into each other's eyes, are trouble—big trouble—and I see it sometimes in dog-to-dog aggression cases. Dogs may greet head-on on occasion, but it's not polite, and it leads to tension and sometimes aggression" (McConnell 2002, 14–15).

14. The reference to the "spreading of legs" and sinful behavior evokes human eroticism (similar to the "becoming one" in Panizza's encounter) that is connected to the upright position and the importance of scent. In reference to Darwin, Sigmund Freud takes the development of the upright posture to be a move from scent-centered interaction to visual stimuli in the context of sexual attraction (2002, Chap. IV).

WORKS CITED

Alt, Peter-André. 2005. *Franz Kafka: Der ewige Sohn*. Munich: Beck.
Andics, Attila, Anna Gábor, Márta Gácsi, Tamás Faragó, Dóra Szabó, and Ádám Miklósi. 2016. Neural Mechanisms for Lexical Processing in Dogs. *Science* 353: 1030–1032.
Ben-Aderet, Tobey, Mario Gallego-Abenza, David Reby, and Nicolas Mathevon. 2017. Dog-Directed Speech: Why Do We Use It and Do Dogs Pay Attention to It? In *Proceedings of the Royal Society B* 284. Accessed January 28, 2017. https://doi.org/10.1098/rspb.2016.2429.
Berg, Nicolas. 2010. Forschungen eines Hundes. In *Kafka-Handbuch: Leben, Werk, Wirkung*, ed. Manfred Engel, and Bernd Auerochs, 330–336. Stuttgart: Metzler.
Bondeson, Jan. 2011. *Amazing Dogs: A Cabinet of Canine Curiosities*. Ithaca, NY: Cornell University Press.
Bowker, Danielle. 2014. Memes: 'A Linguistic Essay about Memes Wow.' *Danielle Bowker Blog*, September 24. Accessed February 3, 2017. https://dbowkerblog.wordpress.com/2014/09/24/memes-a-linguistic-essay-about-memes-wow/.
Brown, Laura. 2010. *Homeless Dogs and Melancholy Apes: Humans and Other Animals in the Modern Literary Imagination*. Ithaca, NY: Cornell University Press.
Burnham, Denis, Christine Kitamura, and Uté Vollmer-Conna. 2002. What's New, Pussycat? On Talking to Babies and Animals. *Science* 296: 1435.
Cooper, Jonathan, Clare Ashton, Sarah Bishop, and Robert John Young. 2003. Clever Hounds: Social Cognition in the Domestic Dog (Canis Familiaris). *Applied Animal Behaviour Science* 81 (2): 229–244.
Coren, Stanley. 2000. *How to Speak Dog: Mastering the Art of Dog-Human Communication*. New York: Simon & Schuster.
Driscoll, Kári. 2015. The Sticky Temptation of Poetry. *Journal of Literary Theory* 9 (2): 212–229.
Empson, William. 1989. *The Structure of Complex Words*. Cambridge, MA: Harvard University Press.
Freud, Sigmund. 2002. *Civilization and Its Discontents*, trans. Joan Riviere. London: Penguin.

Harel, Naama. 2013. Investigations of a Dog, by a Dog: Between Anthropocentrism and Canine-Centrism. In *Speaking for Animals: Animal Autobiographical Writing*, ed. Margo DeMello, 49–59. New York: Routledge.

Hearne, Vicky. 2007. *Adam's Task: Calling Animals by Name*. New York: Skyhorse.

Horowitz, Alexandra. 2009. *Inside of a Dog: What Dogs See, Smell, and Know*. New York: Scribner.

Kafka, Franz. 1988. Investigations of a Dog, trans. Willa and Edwin Muir. In *The Complete Stories*, ed. Nahum N. Glatzer, 310–346. New York: Schocken.

———. 2007. Researches of a Dog. In *Kafka's Selected Stories*, trans. and ed. Stanley Corngold, 132–160. New York: Norton.

Kaminski, Juliane, Josep Call, and Julia Fischer. 2004. Word Learning in a Domestic Dog: Evidence for "Fast Mapping." *Science* 304: 1682–1683.

Know Your Meme. A. Yes, This Is Dog. Accessed 14 October 2016. http://knowyourmeme.com/memes/yes-this-is-dog.

———. B. I Have No Idea What I'm Doing. Accessed 14 October 2016. http://knowyourmeme.com/memes/i-have-no-idea-what-i-m-doing.

———. C. LOLcats. Accessed 14 October 2016. http://knowyourmeme.com/memes/lolcats.

———. D. Moon Moon. Accessed 14 October 2016. http://knowyourmeme.com/memes/moon-moon.

———. E. Doge. Accessed 14 October 2016. http://knowyourmeme.com/memes/doge.

———. F. Doge: No Trimming, Plz. Accessed 14 October 2016. http://knowyourmeme.com/photos/581720-doge.

———. G. Stop It Son, You Are Doing Me a Frighten. Accessed 8 October 2017. http://knowyourmeme.com/memes/stop-it-son-you-are-doing-me-a-frighten.

Kohlhauer, Michael. 2002. Wenn Hunde erzählen: Miguel de Cervantes' "Coloquio de los perros" und die Tierliteratur. *Iberoromania* 56: 51–81.

Kuzniar, Alice. 2006. *Melancholia's Dog*. Chicago: University of Chicago Press.

Levinas, Emmanuel. 1990. The Name of a Dog, or Natural Rights, trans. Seán Hand. In *Difficult Freedom: Essays on Judaism*, 151–153. Baltimore: Johns Hopkins University Press.

Massumi, Brian. 2014. *What Animals Teach Us about Politics*. Durham, NC: Duke University Press.

McConnell, Patricia. 2002. *The Other End of the Leash: Why We Do What We Do Around Dogs*. New York: Random House.

McCulloch, Gretchen. 2014a. A Linguist Explains the Grammar of Doge. Wow. *The Toast*, February 6. Accessed January 28, 2017. http://the-toast.net/2014/02/06/linguist-explains-grammar-doge-wow/.

———. 2014b. Much Doge. So Linguistics. Wow. *All Things Linguistic Blog*. Accessed February 3, 2017. http://allthingslinguistic.com/post/75803057891/much-doge-so-linguistics-wow-i-have-written-a.

Moekel, Paula. 1920. *Mein Hund Rolf: Ein rechnender und buchstabierender Airedale-Terrier*. Stuttgart: R. Lutz.

Myers, Caitlin Rose. 2015. 'I'm Told I'm Famous on the Internet': Henri the Cat and the Critical Possibility of Anthropomorphism. *Humanimalia* 6 (2): 21–32.

Neumann, Gerhard. 1996. Der Blick des Anderen: Zum Motiv des Hundes und des Affen in der Literatur. *Jahrbuch der deutschen Schillergesellschaft* 40: 87–122.

Panizza, Oskar. 1977. Aus dem Tagebuch eines Hundes. In *Aus dem Tagebuch eines Hundes: ... auch Hunde sind keine Menschen*, ed. Martin Langbein, 145–244. Munich: Matthes & Seitz.

Pilley, John W. 2013. Border Collie Comprehends Sentences Containing a Prepositional Object, Verb and Direct Object. *Learning and Motivation* 44: 229–240.

Pilley, John W., and Alliston K. Reid. 2011. Border Collie Comprehends Object Names as Verbal Referents. *Behavioural Processes* 86: 184–195.

Pisorski, Rodolfo. 2015. Of Zoogrammatology as a Positive Literary Theory. *Journal of Literary Theory* 9 (2): 230–249.

Prawer, Siegbert. 1977. 'Ein poetischer Hund': E.T.A. Hoffmann's Nachrichten von den neuesten Schicksalen des Hundes Berganza and Its Antecedents in European Literature. In *Aspekte der Goethezeit*, ed. Stanley Corngold, Michael Curschmann, and Theodore Ziolkowski, 273–293. Göttingen: Vandenhoek und Ruprecht.

Ratcliffe, Victoria F., and David Reby. 2014. Orienting Asymmetries in Dogs' Responses to Different Communicatory Components of Human Speech. *Current Biology* 24: 2908–2912.

Uther, Maria, Monja Knoll, and Denis Burnham. 2007. Do You Speak E-NG-L-I-SH? A Comparison of Foreigner- and Infant-Directed Speech. *Speech Communication* 49: 2–7.

von den Berg, Britt. 2008. *Die "Neue Tierpsychologie" und ihre wissenschaftlichen Vertreter*. Berlin: Tenea.

Ziolkowski, Theodore. 1983. Talking Dogs: The Caninization of Literature. In *Varieties of Literary Thematics*, 86–122. Princeton: Princeton University Press.

"'Sire,' says the fox": The Zoopoetics and Zoopolitics of the Fable in Kleist's "On the Gradual Production of Thoughts whilst Speaking"

Sebastian Schönbeck

As a genre, the fable enjoys a relatively poor reputation within animal studies. Scholars doubt that the animals depicted in those texts, in which only animals act and speak in a reasonable way, refer to animals at all. Instead, they expect or assume that all those animals depicted in animal fables exclusively signify humans. In *The Animal That Therefore I Am*, for instance, Jacques Derrida calls the fable an "anthropomorphic taming," a genre that he wants to "avoid" because it "remains a discourse of man, on man, indeed on the animality of man, but for and in man" (Derrida 2008, 37). It seems that Derrida considers the animal fable to be a thoroughly anthropocentric genre. Looking closer at Derrida's text, it becomes doubtful that the deliberate avoidance of fables and literary animal agents in general was successful or even desired. It is in the same context that

S. Schönbeck
University of Würzburg, Würzburg, Germany

© The Author(s) 2018   81
K. Driscoll and E. Hoffmann (eds.), *What Is Zoopoetics?*,
Palgrave Studies in Animals and Literature,
https://doi.org/10.1007/978-3-319-64416-5_6

Derrida mentions "zoopoetics" to highlight that his own cat has nothing in common with all the literary cats from various literary histories and genres. Derrida incessantly repeats that his cat is neither a fabulous cat nor a cat from a fable. Whereas his cat may not be part of "Kafka's vast zoopoetics" (6), the genre of the fable most certainly is. As a part of "zoopoetics," fables are "something that nevertheless merits concern and attention here, endlessly and from a novel perspective" (ibid.).

In this chapter, I argue that Kleist's theory of the fable—as it is included in a nutshell in his essay "On the Gradual Production of Thoughts whilst Speaking" (1805/1806)[1]—provides such a "novel perspective," because it moves away from the traditional and simplistic idea that fables talk of animals but mean humans,[2] an idea that might be called a simple "disappearing animal trick" (McHugh 2009, 1). This trick is connected to the conception of a moralistic use of the fable of and for the human only. On the contrary, as Derrida suggests in his last seminar, fables can be considered in terms of the documentation and performance of power relations by means of an analogy that "designates for us the place of a question rather than that of an answer" (Derrida 2009, 14). To take the analogy of humans and animals in fables seriously, therefore, means reading the animals depicted in fables literally and not metaphorically. Reading literary animals literally requires setting aside their artificial character and willfully suspending the rhetoric of a specific text in which animals appear.

Derrida's understanding of fables implies a critique of the moralistic use of the fable of and for the human. Kleist's works provide a historical equivalent of Derrida's critique to the extent that they are characterized by the struggle with the anthropocentric concepts of education, morality, formation, reason, and mores that typify the French and German Enlightenment. I argue that Kleist's treatment of fables is instrumental in the critique of the ideas and values of the European Enlightenment. Kleist problematizes the meaning of literary animal agents because he does not believe in their moralistic value for the human anymore. He takes animals and their anthropomorphic characters seriously instead, and projects the behavior and the characteristics of animals onto humans. In "On the Gradual Production of Thoughts whilst Speaking," Kleist suggests that neither meditation nor reasonable dialogue lead to true and powerful thought. Rather, the speaker has to give himself up to the power of language—a language that is perhaps never exclusively individual or even human.

Sharing Kleist's skepticism about human sovereignty in terms of language, this chapter aims to move beyond a reading of fables that consists in deciphering one moral of and for the human toward a zoopoetic reading of fables that asks for a *multiple human-animal relation*, that is a "relation of production, or resemblance, or comparability in which identity and difference coexist" (Derrida 2009, 14).[3] Accordingly, I argue that the power relations shown in fables are never exclusively *human power relations*, but fundamentally also *animal power relations* and *human-animal power relations*. This chapter is thus concerned with one specific historical answer to the question "What is zoopoetics?" I argue that the example of the speech of the fox in Kleist's essay can be considered a paradigmatic figure of zoopoetics that calls for a zoopoetic reading.

The concept of zoopoetics outlines the historical, discursive, and metaphorical entanglement of poetics and zoology (or natural history). According to Kári Driscoll, zoopoetics is a notion that highlights "a way of looking at, and thinking about, how animality functions *within* language, especially within poetic or metaphorical language" (Driscoll 2015, 220, original emphasis). In this sense, zoopoetics is concerned with "the interplay of animality and language" in literature, so that the concept generates an additional value for both elements envisioned (*zōon and* poetics), for "the animal" *and* "language." As an object and a method (cf. Driscoll 2015, 212) "zoopoetics" implies two historical moments: firstly, the moment in which a literary animal studies scholar undertakes a study, and secondly, the moment in which the object the scholar is interested in was created. Aaron Moe heads in a similar direction when he describes "zoopoetics" as a "theory" that "recognizes that nonhuman animals (*zoion*) are makers (*poiesis*), and [that] they have agency in that making" (Moe 2013, 2). Moe calls poetry that has been created "in harmony with the gestures and vocalizations of nonhuman animals" a "multispecies event" (ibid.). Rather than conceiving of Driscoll's and Moe's definitions of zoopoetics as opposing or competing, I would like to argue that both approaches have in common that they first multiply the number of agents of creation, and, second, that both demand the entanglement of "the animal" and "literature," especially when it comes to creation or *poiesis*.

After a close reading of Kleist's version of the fable, I will contextualize the quotation of the speaking fox by tracing a discussion about the properties of the fox in Johann Jakob Breitinger's "Critical Poetics"

("Critische Dichtkunst," 1740), which contains the first extensive consideration of the fable in the poetics of the German Enlightenment. Breitinger discusses the problem of determining which of the fox's qualities are natural and which are artificial, and highlights the importance of these qualities for the poetics of the fable, asking whether it is legitimate to ascribe language and reason to foxes. The famous role of the fox in Breitinger's "Critical Poetics" underlines that the fox is a paradigmatic poetological figure. This detour via Breitinger sheds light on Kleist's reasons for choosing this particular speaking fox as an example and not some other speaking animal out of some other animal fable. Kleist's text is concerned with a specific quality of the fox: that he is able to produce a thought while speaking. As an apology of the king (the lion) the fox's speech also shows the poetic production of political power. By inventing his speech, Kleist's fox legitimizes the political power of the lion. That is to say: this zoopoetics is also a zoopolitics.

KLEIST AND THE FABLE (LA FONTAINE)

The narrator of Kleist's essay presents six examples to prove his thesis that the invention of thoughts often takes place during a speech and not before. The examples used all come from different contexts, situations, and periods. The first example describes a personal situation in which the narrator's sister helps him through her mere presence to develop his thought. For his second example, the narrator turns to French literature, specifically Molière and the positive influence of his maidservant. Hereupon, the text refers to the context of the French Revolution, to the famous Mirabeau who rebukes the master of ceremonies and refuses to follow his orders. The fourth example, to which I will return in a moment, is the fable "The Animals Ill with the Plague" by Jean de la Fontaine. The fifth consists in a public conversation during which a quiet person suddenly rises to speak, whereas the sixth and final example takes up the theme of education, describing a pupil during an examination.

It is striking that Kleist's text makes use of different metaphorical fields and of several historical facts and rhetorical techniques to prove the thesis that the invention of thoughts happens while speaking. After the historical example of Mirabeau and before the example of the fable, for instance, the narrator uses a simile (or parable) to explain what happened in the châtelet and how it is related to the Kleistian jar[4]: "We have here a remarkable congruence between the phenomena of the physical world and those of the moral world which, if we were to pursue it, would hold good in the subsidiary circumstances too. But I shall leave my comparison and return to the matter in hand" (Kleist 2004, 407).[5] At this point the argument consists of stating that the thesis holds true in the physical world as well as in the moral world. There is no preference or valuation within the chain of examples, neither between the physical or moral phenomena, nor between the "comparison" [*Gleichnis*] and the "matter in hand" [*Sache*] (1990, 537; 2004, 407). The fact that the fable follows upon the announcement of the "matter in hand" is surprising, as in the poetics of the Enlightenment, fables were considered similar to "parables" or *Gleichnisse* rather than matters of fact (cf. Dithmar 1974, 98). In Kleist's text, the distinction between the "parable" of the Kleistian jar, Mirabeau's speech, and the "matter in hand" that is La Fontaine's fable, is problematic. Further on in the text, the fable is called a "remarkable example" (Kleist 2004, 407). This is a definition of the fable that refers back to Aristotle's *Rhetoric*; he says there are two "variet[ies]" (Aristotle 1994, 1393a30) of examples (*parádeigmata*): fables and "illustrative parallels." Both are framed by "thinking out [an] analogy" (1394a5). He writes: "You will in fact frame them just as you frame illustrative parallels: all you require is the power of thinking out your analogy, a power developed by intellectual training" (ibid.). Applying this definition to Kleist's text, I argue that the narrator is "thinking out the analogy" of different objects such as "parables," "matters," "fables," and "examples," relating them to the thesis on the gradual production of thoughts that Kleist puts forward in his essay.

The notion of a "remarkable example" can itself be called paradigmatic, insofar as examples—according to Agamben—organize analogous relations of particulars rather than relations of particulars and universals (Agamben 2009, 19). Derrida, too, highlights the important role of the analogy when he considers the "beast" and the "sovereign" with regard to the "fable" (cf. Derrida 2009, 12). Derrida implicitly argues for a new understanding of fables that involves an understanding of analogy that "brings man close to the animal" (Derrida 2009, 14). I argue that Kleist's text makes use of the fable by means of such an analogy that brings the narrator close to the fox.

It is possible to describe this characteristic of the text in terms of the dual structure of language; a structure that can be described in different terms such as the relation between *res* and *verba*, *signifier* and *signified*, as well as literal and figurative. The German literary scholar Wolfram

Groddeck argues that the whole text reverses the five steps of the classical rhetorical structure of the creation of a speech, usually beginning with *inventio*, followed by *dispositio, elocutio, memoria*, and ending with *actio* (Groddeck 2003, 103). According to the thesis put forward in Kleist's text, I would like to argue that *inventio* and *actio* coincide. Moreover, *res* and *verba* likewise coincide. The coincidence becomes apparent when the text problematizes the relation between fact and fiction as well as the relation between literal and figurative speech, calling La Fontaine's fable a "remarkable example" of the "matter in hand" if not the "matter in hand" itself. Does the narrator in Kleist's text refer to the fable in a more literal way rather than in terms of an allegory that contains a moral? In the essay on the gradual production of thoughts, the fable of La Fontaine has no meaning; it is a fable without a moral (cf. Kleist 1990, 353).

The speech of the fox is one example for the central thesis, according to which a speaker should develop his thought and the power of this thought *in* the act of speaking and not *before*. The fox in question stems from La Fontaine's fable "The Animals Ill with the Plague" ("Les animaux malades de la peste"). The lion, king of the animals, invites all representatives to find out who is to blame for the plague, to find someone they can sacrifice to appease God's wrath. After the lion confesses that he has devoured some sheep and shepherds, the fox holds a speech in front of the remaining animals to convince them of the lion's and his own innocence. The fox in the fable is able to "think on his feet" and to persuade all other animals at the same time. At the end of the speech it seems to be established "that the donkey, the bloodthirsty donkey (devourer of grass and plants) is the most fitting sacrifice" (Kleist 2004, 407–408[6]; cf. La Fontaine 2007, 157–158).

When introducing the fable, the narrator asserts: "The fable is well known" [*Man kennt diese Fabel*] (Kleist 2004, 407). On the one hand, this underlines the popularity of the genre in general and points to the important role of La Fontaine's fables in France and in European poetics since La Motte, Breitinger, Hagedorn, and Lessing, among others. On the other hand, the awareness of the specific fable that the text quotes contrasts with the specific quotation technique that the text deploys:

"Sire," says the fox, wishing to ward the lightning off himself, "in your zeal and generosity, you have gone too far. What if you have done a sheep or two to death? Or a dog, a vile creature? And: quant au berger," he continues, for this is the chief point, "on peut dire," though he still does not know what, "qu'il méritoit tout mal," trusting to luck, and with that he has embroiled himself, "étant," a poor word, but one which buys him time, "de ces gens là," and only now does he hit upon the thought that gets him out of his difficulty, "qui sur les animaux se font un chimérique empire." (Kleist 2004, 407)[7]

Kleist's text contains two direct quotations: one from the speech by Mirabeau and the other from the fox. The latter is partly a direct quotation of the fable of La Fontaine. At first, Kleist translates the text he quotes: "Sire, dit le renard, vous êtes trop bon roi" (La Fontaine 1991, 250). Later, however, Kleist's text quotes the French original, but in a specific way: the text modifies, translates, paraphrases, and twists the original text.

I would like to highlight three differences between La Fontaine's and Kleist's versions. The first difference is that Kleist includes only the speech by the fox, whereas in La Fontaine's version there are three speeches: by the lion, the fox, and the donkey, respectively. Kleist paraphrases the lion's speech and omits the donkey's entirely. The second difference consists in the fact that Kleist's text cuts the speech of the fox into pieces and inserts comments and evaluations by the narrator. The third difference is that by choosing the speech of the fox, Kleist's text ignores the moral (epimythium) that is articulated at the end of La Fontaine's version: "Our courtiers judge us black or white: / The weak are always wrong; the strong are right" (La Fontaine 2007, 158).[8] The fact that Kleist truncates the speech of the donkey is surprising, because only in relation to the donkey does the specific rhetoric employed by the fox become legible. The text distinguishes between two modes of speaking: *clearly* and *cunningly*. The text ascribes the different properties (clarity and deception) to different animals: whereas the fox argues cunningly, the donkey argues clearly:

And I went nibbling through a swath of grass:
A tongue's width, little more, but still …
Ah, when they heard him, cries of "Kill him! Kill!"
Rang out against our scurvy, ragtag ass.
(ibid)[9]

At the same time, the text invokes the differentiation between the Cartesian idea of philosophical speech, which is clear and distinct, and the idea of rhetoric to deceive and thereby provoke a false judgment (cf. Kant 2007, 155). Whereas the donkey, therefore, appears as the "philosophical animal," the fox can be considered the "rhetorical animal": Kleist prefers the fox in this text and, thus, a deceptive and effective rhetoric.

The narrator's commentary to the words of the fox are interpretations insofar as they ascribe to them a special meaning that is not a moral meaning: the fox wants to distract his listeners, to "ward the lightning off himself." The fox's ability to survive by means of deceit or diverting attention appears in the text as a rhetorical device by which the fox convinces the other animals. At the same time, the narrator uses the example of the fox to convince the reader (the "you" of the first sentence) of the thesis of the gradual production of thoughts whilst speaking. The necessary condition of this diversion is the illusion of authenticity and clarity and the concealment of the illusionary character of the speech. The speech of the fox shows, similar to Derrida's idea of the fable, that power is an effect of the fable and of fabulation. Political power is dependent on the creation of the speaker or the narrator. At least two narrators are involved in this case: first, the intradiegetic narrator (the fox), second, the extradiegetic narrator of the essay. At the moment when the narrator switches from a German translation of the words of the fox to the French original, the extradiegetic narrator explains what he considers to be the "chief point" of the fox's speech with regard to the idea of political power. In the speech of the fox, the esteem of the political power of the lion appears in contrast to the "chimérique empire" (Kleist 2004, 407) of the shepherd.

All in one breath, the speech of the fox arranges, justifies, and makes plausible from the fox's perspective the relations between animals and humans and between the sovereign (lion) and his subjects (the other animals). The speech of the fox highlights the fictive, performative, and poetic character of political power (cf. Derrida 2009, 217–218). Moreover, it highlights the participation of at least two agents who make and who create these *multiple* power relations: the narrator and the fox. If a zoopoetic reading not only considers specific objects of study, but is itself also a method, the reader and interpreter of the fable become part of the power relations that the text develops. The reader also makes and creates the power relations inherent in the fable. To answer the question what kind of power relations are connected to the fox, it is fruitful to contextualize Kleist's quotation by tracing a discussion about the abilities and challenges of the fox in the fable poetics of Breitinger.

WHAT DOES THE FOX SAY? (BREITINGER)

The reason Kleist choose the fox's speech as an example lies within the poetics of the fable in the German and French Enlightenment. In this context, the fox serves as a prime example for discussing the plausibility of animal fables in general, and a fox issuing statements and making judgements in particular. In what follows, I trace the debate concerning the fox and correlate it to Buffon's natural history—first, to demonstrate that the fox in Kleist's essay can be understood as a zoopoetic animal and, second, to highlight Kleist's work with and against the German and French Enlightenment. Kleist takes up aspects of Enlightenment fable poetics and elaborates the inherent paradoxes and potentials to innovate the genre.

In the beginning of the chapter concerned with "wonderful fables" that features animals and plants acting and speaking in a rational way, Breitinger (1740, 188) discusses various animal fables, all of which deal with foxes. The first text that Breitinger analyzes is Aesop's fable no. XV, "The Fox and the Grapes," in which the fox, unable to reach some grapes hanging from a tree above, remarks: "Oh, you aren't even ripe yet! I don't need any sour grapes" (Aesop 2002, 125). Breitinger is particularly interested in the fox's dissimulation: the fox seeks the grapes, but pretends that they are still sour (Breitinger 1740, 235). The fox displays the same quality (to dissimulate) in the second fable Breitinger discusses, "The Fox and the Mask": "A fox happened to find a mask used for performing tragedies and, after turning it this way and that several times, he remarks, 'So full of beauty, so lacking in brains!'" (Aesop 2002, 253). Breitinger quotes Friedrich von Hagedorn's (1738, 86–87) translation of this fable and outlines the debate concerning the composition of fables: should the author let the fox articulate the judgment concerning humans lacking in brains or should that judgment rather be expressed by a human and not by the fox? This question initiates a complex discussion between literary critics such as La Motte, Hagedorn, Triller, Breitinger, and others. Whereas some of them argue like Breitinger that it is only consistent to ascribe animals the ability to judge because this ability follows from the ascription of reason and language, others head into the opposite direction, maintaining that it would be more appropriate for a human being to articulate the human's lack of brains. Breitinger outlines the discussion and asks whether the ascription of the ability to judge is in line with the laws of nature. Whereas, for most of the critics, this point hinges upon the similarities and differences of humans and animals in general, it is only Friedrich von Hagedorn who acknowledges the coherence between the plot and the specific properties of the fox. Hagedorn takes into account that the fox is an animal characterized by wit. He suggests that because of their wit, foxes do have the right to judge the human's lack of brains (cf. Hagedorn 1738, 87). The characterization of the fox by his wit or slyness is an anthropomorphism, because human properties are ascribed to the fox. The aforementioned critics discuss whether anthropomorphisms like this are plausible and probable.

To answer that question, it is possible to consult the natural history of the fox, as in Buffon's *Histoire Naturelle*. According to Buffon, the fox is cunning and merits his reputation. He describes the special mental abilities of the fox by detailing his hunting techniques that forgo brute force and pointing out his capability to build and furnish a den, which implies self-consciousness and even art (cf. Buffon 2007, 778–779):

> This difference [between the fox and other animals], though it appears even among men, has greater effects, and supposes more powerful causes, among the inferior animals. The single idea of a house, or settled place of abode, indicates a singular attention to self. The choice of situation, the art of making and rendering a house commodious, and of concealing the avenues to it, imply a superior degree of sentiment.[10] (Buffon 1812, 5:172)

Buffon explains that the actions of the fox require a "superior degree of sentiment." Thus, Buffon also makes use of emphatic anthropomorphisms to describe the specific behavior of the fox. Like the literary critics who must face the challenges of the fable, Buffon reflects the anthropomorphisms by highlighting the analogy between the behavior and the characteristic traits of humans on the one hand and of foxes on the other hand. The phrase, "though it appears even among men," suggests that wit is neither a genuine human nor a genuine animal trait, but one that can be ascribed to certain superior living beings who can pick a location, construct their 'house' or den in an artful way, and conceal "the avenues to it." Kleist chooses the fox because of his superior character, which resembles the character of certain superior humans.

Breitinger's "Critical Poetics," however, raises the question of whether it is possible to conceal the animals' natural lack: They do not have the ability to judge. Surprisingly, the answer is given by quoting a fable of La Fontaine's that—again—deals with foxes; and this time with foxes in comparison to donkeys. La Fontaine's translation of "Le renard et le buste" shows how to conceal the supposed "lack of nature":

> Nobles are often merely theatre masks.
> The vulgar masses, awed, bow low. The ass's
> Judgment is formed by what he sees: he asks
> No more; whereas the fox, probes, passes
> Before, behind, beside … all round. And when
> He finds them to be naught but show,
> Then does he utter once again
> A most appropriate bon mot;
> One he once said, if I recall,
> About a hero's bust wrought by some master,
> Larger than life, but hollow—quite—withal:
> "A handsome head; but brains? No, none at all."
> How many a noble is mere empty plaster!
> (La Fontaine 2007, 95)[11]

According to this fable, the superior beings are theatre masks. More important than this conclusion in the beginning of the fable is that their appearance is responsible for their bad reputation. The text distinguishes between two kinds of judgments: first the judgment of the donkey which is based on the perception of the exterior and, second, the judgment of the fox which is based on examination and reflection. This difference between the exterior apparition and reflection becomes multiplied in the fox's perception of the sculpture—a sculpture that is beautiful on the outside, but hollow on the inside. Following Breitinger, it is possible to conclude that the difference between a simple judgment and a reflective one is legible in La Fontaine's fable as the difference between the supposed stupidity of the donkey and the cunning of the fox; only the fox is able to figure out the masquerade. The fox is even able to reveal the stupidity of sovereignty and, thereby, he seems to be more sovereign in terms of his capacity to examine "à fond" and to judge. The discussion of literary critics concerning the fox's capabilities shows that the meaning of the cunning speech of the fox is yet unclear and constitutes an open question that allows for different answers. Kleist chooses the speech of the fox as an example because the fox's judgment is reflective and not "simple" like the donkey's.

When this conclusion is confronted with the new zoopoetic theory of fables summarized earlier, it is possible to consider the *multiplicity of power relations* connected to the speech of the fox. First of all, it is possible to read the fable as a statement about human politics, for instance the politics of Louis XIV. In this case the fox can be substituted with the poet who names Louis "a mask without brain." *The fabulist writes "through" the fox about humans and their politics.* Secondly, it is possible to read the fable as a statement about animal power relations. In this case, the judgment of the fox can be read as self-reflexive, as a statement of the fox about foxes. In this sense the fox says, "I have brains and the statue does not." The literary scholar asks how the fox's specific abilities are depicted. Hagedorn underlines that, because of his wit, the fox is able to pass judgment on human brains. As Buffon shows, the wit of the fox is crucial for the fox's survival, to protect himself from other animals. *The fabulist writes about foxes and their politics.* Thirdly, the text can be read with regard to human-animal power relations. The discussion of Breitinger, Hagedorn, and La Motte shows the political implications related to the fox's judgment. The fox, who reflects and judges humans and their art, appears as a disturbing factor within the "anthropopolitics" of the poetics of the Enlightenment (cf. Borgards 2013, 61). Nevertheless, it is possible to argue that the fox is able to judge the human brain because of the "rhetorical capacities" he shares with humans: for instance, his ability to act cunningly. For Breitinger, the fox in La Fontaine's fable is able to dissimulate the "lack of nature" that he probably cannot act and speak in a reasonable way. In other words: La Fontaine is able to conceal the "lack of nature" because the fox is able to speak cunningly. *The fabulist writes with the fox rather than about the fox and highlights the complex analogy between human and animal politics.* These three readings are possible because of an analogy between humans and foxes that cannot be described merely in terms of substitution. Kleist's essay and the quoted fable draw attention to the third conclusion because the shared rhetorical capacities of humans *and* foxes are underlined by bringing the fox closer to the narrator.

CUNNING (KLEIST)

The fox in Kleist's essay is thus a zoopoetic figure. Kleist's quoting of La Fontaine can be placed within the broader context of his treatment of fables. Kleist wrote two fables himself: "The Dogs and the Bird" (*"Die Hunde und der Vogel"*) (Kleist 1990, 353) and "The Fable without a Moral" (*"Die Fabel ohne Moral"*) (ibid.).[12] The title of the latter highlights a poetological dimension regarding fables, because the generic term "fable" also forms part of the title of the text. More important than the indicated subtraction of the moral from the fable is the conclusion of the text that surrenders in the face of the requirements of dealing with animals in the present case: riding a horse. In "The Fable without a Moral," a human is standing naked in front of a horse who refuses to be mounted. The human feels that if he had possessed the horse at the time when the animal was still "uneducated," he would have been able to lead him and they would both have felt at ease, but because the horse has been "educated" and taught "arts" of which the man, naked as he is, knows nothing, no such communion is possible. "The Fable without a Moral" thus unites the domestication of the horse with the question of education. In this sense, the term "uneducated" is a deliberate "anthropomorphism," because horses are not "educated" but rather "broken" and then "trained" (cf. Teupert 2017). Because the horse has been "taught" these "arts," it has become impossible for the man to meet the horse on an equal footing: "I would have to come to you in the hippodrome (and may God preserve me from that) in order for us to come to terms with each other" (Kleist 1990, 353).[13]

"The Fable without a Moral" can be read as a poetological text that posits an idea of the fable that differs from the usual conception of the genre in the poetics of the German Enlightenment. In the latter, fables are often reduced to hiding only one allegorical proposition and, therefore, make use of animals only to benefit the human (cf. Eichhorn 2013). The fable without a moral suggests that humans and animals ought to be able to communicate. At the same time, the narrator finds that this possible communication is disturbed (troubled). The disorder is related to a different development of the arts in the case of the human and in the case of the horse. At this point, Kleist deviates from the thesis put forward in Rousseau's *Discourse on the Origin of Inequality* (1755): the depravation of the human being during the process of civilization.

Rousseau argues that it would be necessary to go back to the "state of nature," but that "the more we accumulate new knowledge, the more we deprive ourselves" (1992, 11). In Kleist's fable without a moral, however, the human is imagined in his "state of nature," but finds himself in front of a horse with a saddle and harness; the horse surpasses him artificially. In this regard, the text becomes legible as a capitulation: a concession that it is no longer possible to write fables because to write a fable it would be necessary to establish communication between animals and humans and to enter the riding arena. Yet it is not human "knowledge"—as Rousseau has it—that is the reason for the disruption of communication between man and horse, but the lack of human art.

The art of the fox, be it in the text or in the poetics of the fable, or in the texts of natural history, as Buffon, Hagedorn, Breitinger, and Kleist describe it, is to act cunningly. What the fox does and says in the case of Kleist, is that he pretends to argue for the lion, whereas in fact he is arguing for himself. This pretense consists in concealing the artificial character and the actual meaning of his speech within the act of speaking. The dissimulation of the illusionary character of the fox's speech can be described in terms of what ancient rhetoric called "dissimulatio artis" (cf. Till 2009, 1034–42), as it is described, for instance, by Quintilian when he considers forensic speech (*genus iudicale*). He argues that in front of a judge it is necessary to show neither the art of the composition nor the ornate style of the speech. The "dissimulatio artis" highlights that a speech artificially produces a nature of a second degree, a second nature that is animated by its latent techniques. The fox's cunning consists in hiding his cunning speech or action before the judge who decides whether an action is legal or illegal. Especially when it comes to the statement of facts by the defendant, it is necessary to avoid anything that seems artificial:

> It is therefore specially important in this part of our speech to avoid anything suggestive of artful design, for the judge is never more on his guard than at this stage. Nothing must seem fictitious, nought betray anxiety; everything must seem to spring from the case itself rather than the art of the orator. (Quintilian 1921, 119)

For Quintilian, it is necessary for a defendant to dissimulate the "artful design" of his speech to convince the judge. The defendant proves his rhetorical power in front of the legal authority by means of cunning and demonstrates that fabulation is part of the jurisdiction. The same goes for the fox in the fable quoted in Kleist's "On the Gradual Production of Thoughts whilst Speaking." The fox hides his interest in "conducting the lightning off himself" and pretends to speak sincerely; this pretense leads to the conclusion that neither the lion nor the fox is a proper sacrifice.

With regard to the *multiple power relations* connected to the fox in the poetics of Breitinger, it becomes obvious that Kleist's text participates in the same discussion. The main difference between both approaches is that, on the one hand, Breitinger is writing a poetic treatise in which he elucidates how fabulists should write fables, whereas Kleist, on the other hand, is writing an essay or telling a story in which a narrator elucidates the thesis that the creation of thoughts (and of political power) takes place within the process of speaking. The power relations are produced while the fox's speech is being made (*poiesis*). The *multiple power relations* in Kleist's text can be categorized—just like those in Breitinger's poetics. First of all, Kleist's text can be interpreted with regard to human power relations. The animals depicted would be replaced by humans: the lion is Louis XIV, the fox is the poet, and the ass is representative of the people. *The text uses the fox in order to talk about humans and their politics.* Secondly, the text also documents the superiority of the fox within the animal kingdom. The fox is a survival artist because of his abilities to act and speak cunningly. *The text is about foxes and their politics.* Thirdly, and with regard to human-animal power relations, the speech of the fox consolidates the sovereignty of the lion and justifies his killing of several "shepherds," referring to the "chéme-rique empire" of humans and their rule over animals. The sovereignty of the lion becomes legitimized by the delegitimization and the inversion of the human-animal power relations. Finally, the extradiegetic narrator develops the idea of the "gradual production" while writing or narrating the text by means of cunning rhetoric. The fox's strategy of "dissimulatio artis" also pertains to him. *Together with the fox, the narrator acquires the power to persuade, narrating with the fox—not about the fox—and high-lighting the complex analogy between human and animal politics.*

Zoopoetics refers to certain objects of study and to a specific reading technique. The aim of this chapter was to read fabular foxes literally. I have proposed two alternative readings that differ from to the common substitution of the animals in fables with humans: first, a reading that focuses on the animals depicted in fables and, second, a reading that focuses on human-animal relations in fables.

The fox becomes legible as a paradigmatic object of zoopoetics that is characterized by various zoopolitical implications. By means of his cunning rhetoric, the narrator dissimulates the fact that his speech is cunning. As an animal, it is necessary for the fox to dissimulate his interests to survive and to turn everything to his own advantage (*"tourne tout à son profit"*) (Buffon 2007, 779). The actions and the speech of the fox, as well as the foxy narrator, oscillate between authenticity and deceit, between being natural and being artificial.

But is the fox also a paradigmatic figure for zoopoetics as a method? Or should we as readers aim to resemble donkeys rather than foxes? For a scholar in literary animal studies, it is sometimes tempting and even necessary to find the "real" animal within a literary text and, therefore, to dissimulate its artificial, linguistic character. In this sense, it is possible to conclude that whenever we try to hide or to ignore the literary character of textual animals, we necessarily engage in dissimulation and obfuscation, cunning like the fox.

Notes

1. The reception of Kleist's essay has been long and varied, but scholars have usually avoided the "question of the animal." Scholars have argued that the text shows the poetological relevance of different discourses and topics such as physics, aesthetics, rhetoric (Groddeck 2003), communication (Itoda 1991; Klinger 2014), cultural anthropology (Neumann 1994) and contingency (Wellbery 1992). Other scholars have focused on the role of the relationship between France and Germany including the French Revolution (Rohrwasser 1993) in the text and considered it as exemplary for the importance of French literature in Kleist's writing in general (Schlüter 1987; Moser 2000; Hülk 2000).
2. Also Kári Driscoll and Harun Maye problematize the simplistic idea that fables talk of animals but mean humans (cf. Driscoll 2015, 213–214; Maye 2016, 39).
3. Kleist's contemporary, Jacob Grimm, makes a similar argument in his introduction to "Reinhart Fuchs" ["Reynard the Fox"] when he outlines the idea that fables, and especially animal fables, document the former history of coexistence or cohabitation of both humans and animals and their shared properties of action and language (Grimm 1974, iv–vi).
4. The designation Kleistian Jar is a synonym for Leyden Jar or condenser. In a number of experiments, Heinrich von Kleist's distant relative Ewald von Kleist tried to collect and to accumulate electricity in a jar with the help of liquid alcohol.

5. "Dies ist eine merkwürdige Übereinstimmung zwischen den Erscheinungen der physischen und moralischen Welt, welche sich, wenn man sie verfolgen wollte, auch noch in den Nebenumständen bewähren würde. Doch ich verlasse mein Gleichnis und kehre zur Sache zurück" (Kleist 1990, 537).

6. "Und jetzt beweist er, daß der Esel, der blutdürstige! (der alle Kräuter auffrißt) das zweckmäßigste Opfer sei, worauf alle über ihn herfallen und ihn zerreißen" (Kleist 1990, 538).

7. "'Sire', sagt der Fuchs, der das Ungewitter von sich ableiten will, 'sie sind zu großmütig. Ihr edler Eifer führt sie zu weit. Was ist es, ein Schaf erwürgen? Oder einen Hund, diese nichtswürdige Bestie? Und: quant au berger', fährt er fort, den dies ist der Hauptpunkt: 'on peut dire'; obschon er noch nicht weiß was? 'qu'il méritoit tout mal'; auf gut Glück; und somit ist er verwickelt; 'étant'; eine schlechte Phrase, die ihm aber Zeit verschafft: 'de ces gens là', und nun erst findet er den Gedanken, der ihn aus der Not reißt: 'qui sur les animaux se font un chimérique empire'" (Kleist 1990, 538).

8. "Selon que vous serez puissant ou misérable, / Les jugements de cour vous rendront blanc ou noir" (La Fontaine 1991, 250).

9. "Je tondis de ce pré la largeur de ma langue. / Je n'en avais nul droit, puisqu'il faut parler net" (ibid.).

10. "Cette différence [sc. between the fox and other animals], qui se fait sentir même parmi les hommes, a de bien plus grands effets, et suppose de bien plus grandes causes parmi les animaux. L'idée seule du domicile présuppose une attention singulière sur soi-même; ensuite le choix du lieu, l'art de faire son manoir, de le rendre commode, d'en dérober l'entrée, sont autant d'indices d'un sentiment supérieur" (Buffon 2007, 778–779).

11. "Les Grands, pour la plupart, sont masques de théâtre; / Leur apparence impose au vulgaire idolâtre. / L'Âne n'en sait juger que par ce qu'il en voit. / Le Renard au contraire à fond les examine, / Les tourne de tout sens; et quand il s'aperçoit / Que leur fait n'est que bonne mine, / Il leur applique un mot qu'un Buste de héros / Lui fit dire fort à propos. / C'était un Buste creux, et plus grand que nature. / Le Renard, en louant l'effort de la sculpture: / Belle tête, dit-il, mais de cervelle point. / Combien de grands Seigneurs sont Bustes en ce point!" (La Fontaine 1991, 161).

12. Furthermore, Kleist translated and modified one fable by La Fontaine: "Die beiden Tauben. Eine Fabel nach Lafontaine" ["The Two Pigeons: A Fable after La Fontaine"] (Kleist 1990, 409–411).

13. "und ich müßte zu dir in die Reitbahn hinein (wovor mich doch Gott bewahre) wenn wir uns verständigen wollten" (Kleist 1990, 353).

WORKS CITED

Aesop. 2002. *Fables*, trans. Laura Gibbs. New York: Oxford University Press.

Agamben, Giorgio. 2009. *The Signature of All Things: On Method*, trans. Luca D'Isanto and Kevin Attell. New York: Zone Books.

Aristotle. 1994. Rhetoric, trans. W. Rhys Roberts. In *The Complete Works of Aristotle. The Revised Oxford Translation*, vol. 2, ed. Jonathan Barnes, 2152–2169. Princeton: Princeton University Press.

Borgards, Roland. 2013. 'Das Thierreich'. Anthropologie und Zoologie bei Barthold Heinrich Brockes. *Zeitschrift für Germanistik* 23 (1): 47–62.

Breitinger, Johann Jakob. 1740. *Critische Dichtkunst worinnen die poetische Mahlerey in Absicht auf die Erfindung im Grunde untersuchet und mit Beyspielen aus den berühmtesten Alten und Neuem erläutert wird*. 2 vols. Zürich: Conrad Drell und Comp.

Buffon, George-Louis Leclerc, Comte de. 1812. *Natural History, General and Particular. The History of Man and Quadrupeds*. Translated, with notes and observations by William Smellie, ed. William Wood. 20 vols. London: Cadell and Davis.

———. 2007. *Œuvres*, ed. Stéphane Schmitt, Paris: Gallimard.

Derrida, Jacques. 2008. *The Animal That Therefore I Am*, trans. David Wills, ed. Marie-Louise Mallet. New York: Fordham University Press.

———. 2009. *The Beast & the Sovereign, Volume One*, trans. Geoffrey Bennington, ed. Michel Lisse, Marie-Louise Mallet, and Ginette Michaud. Chicago: University of Chicago Press.

Dithmar, Reinhard. 1974. *Die Fabel. Geschichte, Struktur, Didaktik*. Paderborn: Schnönigh.

Driscoll, Kári. 2015. The Sticky Temptation of Poetry. *Journal for Literary Theory* 9 (2): 212–229.

Eichhorn, Kristin. 2013. *Die Kunst des moralischen Dichtens: Positionen der aufklärerischen Fabelpoetik im 18*. Ergon: Jahrhundert. Würzburg.

Grimm, Jacob. 1974. *Reinhart Fuchs*. Hildesheim: Georg Olms.

Groddeck, Wolfram. 2003. Die Inversion der Rhetorik und das Wissen der Sprache. Zu Heinrich von Kleists Aufsatz 'Über die allmähliche Verfertigung der Gedanken beim Reden'. In *Kleist Lesen*, ed. Nikolaus Müller-Scholl and Marianne Schuller, 101–114. Bielefeld: Transcript.

Hagedorn, Friedrich von. 1738. *Versuch in poetischen Fabeln und Erzehlungen*. Hamburg: Conrad König.

Haverkamp, Anselm. 2002. *Figura Cryptica. Theorie der literarischen Latenz*. Suhrkamp: Frankfurt am Main.

Hülk, Walburga. 2000. Natur und Fremdheit bei Rousseau und Kleist. *Kleist-Jahrbuch*: 33–45.

Itoda, Soichiro. 1991. Die Funktion des Paradoxons in Heinrich von Kleists Aufsatz 'Über die allmähliche Verfertigung der Gedanken beim Reden.' *Kleist-Jahrbuch.* 218–228.

Kant, Immanuel. 2007. *Critique of Judgement*, trans. James Creed Meredith, ed. Nicholas Walker. New York: Oxford University Press.

Kleist, Heinrich von. 2004. *Selected Works*, trans. and ed. David Constantine. Indianapolis: Hackett.

———. 1990. *Sämtliche Werke und Briefe, vol. 3: Erzählungen, Anekdoten, Briefe*, ed. Ilse-Marie Barth, Klaus Müller-Salget, Stefan Ormanns, and Hinrich C. Seeba. Frankfurt am Main: Deutscher Klassiker Verlag.

Klinger, Florian. 2014. Kleist phatisch-dramatisch. In *Kleist Revisited*, ed. Hans Ulrich Gumbrecht and Frederike Knüpling, 103–110. München: Fink.

La Fontaine, Jean de. 1991. *Œuvres complètes*, ed. Jean-Pierre Collinet, Paris: Gallimard.

———. 2007. *The Complete Fables*, trans. Norman Shapiro. Champaign: University of Illinois Press.

La Motte, Antoine Houdar de. 1719. *Fables Nouvelles. Avec un Discours sur la Fable*. Paris: Gregoire Dupuis.

Maye, Harun. 2016. Tiere und Metapher. In *Tiere. Kulturwissenschaftliches Handbuch*, ed. Roland Borgards, 37–45. Stuttgart: Metzler.

McHugh, Susan. 2009. *Animal Farm*'s Lessons for Literary (and) Animal Studies. *Humanimalia* 1 (1): 24–39.

Moe, Aaron M. 2013. Toward Zoopoetics: Rethinking Whitman's 'Original Energy'. *Walt Whitman Quarterly Review* 31 (1): 1–17.

Moser, Christian. 2000. Angewandte Kontingenz. Fallgeschichten bei Kleist und Montaigne. *Kleist-Jahrbuch.* 33–45.

Neumann, Gerhard. 1994. Das Stocken der Sprache und das Straucheln des Körpers. Umrisse von Kleists kultureller Anthropologie. In *Kriegsfall – Rechtsfall – Sündenfall*, ed. Gerhard Neumann, 13–30. Freiburg: Rombach.

Quintilian, Marcus Fabius. 1921. *Institutio Oratoriae*, trans. Harold Edgeworth Butler. Cambridge, MA: Harvard University Press.

Rohrwasser, Michael. 1993. Eine Bombenpost: Über die allmähliche Verfertigung der Gedanken beim Schreiben. In *Heinrich von Kleist*, ed. Heinz Ludwig Arnold, 151–162. Munich: Text + Kritik.

Rousseau, Jean-Jacques. 1992. *Discourse on the Origin of Inequality*, trans. Donald A. Cress, ed. James Miller. Indianapolis: Hackett.

Schlüter, Gisela. 1987. Kleist und Montaigne. *Arcadia* 22: 129–151.

Teupert, Jonas. 2017. Dressieren – Führen – Erziehen. Überlegungen zu Gewalt- und Machtverhältnissen in zwei Fabeln von Kleist. In *Unarten. Kleist und das Gesetz der Gattung*, ed. Andrea Allerkamp, Matthias Preuss, and Sebastian Schönbeck. Bielefeld: Transcript.

Till, Dietmar. 2009. Verbergen der Kunst (lat. dissimulatio artis). In *Historisches Wörterbuch der Rhetorik*, vol. 9, ed. Gert Ueding, 1034–1042, Tübingen: Niemeyer.

Wellbery, David E. 1992. Contingency. In *Neverending Stories: Toward a Critical Narratology*, ed. Ann Fehn, Ingeborg Hoesterey, and Maria Tatar, 237–257. Princeton: Princeton University Press.

PART II

Bodies

The Light That Therefore I Give (to): Paleonymy and Animal Supplementarity in Clarice Lispector's *The Apple in the Dark*

Rodolfo Piskorski

Clarice Lispector's fourth novel, *The Apple in the Dark* (*A Maçã no Escuro*, 1961), tells the enigmatic story of Martim, a man we encounter in flight from the police after having committed a serious crime. This crime has jettisoned him from the law, so that he finds himself outside sociality, morality, and even language. The novel explores this by tracing his trajectory in "evolutionary" stages, from a meaningless, shapeless darkness to rudimentary stages of consciousness until he recovers language and thought. In that trajectory, Martim enters and leaves various realms of animality as he moves from an unthinking, almost nonliving thing to what he himself calls a man or a "hero." From a zoopoetical perspective, it would appear that one of her most famous novels, *The Passion According to G.H.* (1964)—in which a middle-class housewife has a crisis of subjectivity after killing and eating a cockroach—would be the most relevant. However, it is telling that the translator of the 1985

R. Piskorski
Cardiff University, Cardiff, UK

© The Author(s) 2018
K. Driscoll and E. Hoffmann (Eds.), *What Is Zoopoetics?*,
Palgrave Studies in Animals and Literature,
https://doi.org/10.1007/978-3-319-64416-5_7

English language edition of *The Apple in the Dark*, Gregory Rabassa, argues that the later, cockroach-focused book works most aptly as a long footnote to her 1961 novel (Lispector 1985, xii).

Therefore, I wish to look into the Derridean zoopoetics of *The Apple in the Dark*—and, consequently, into Lispector's own zoopoetics as articulated in this early, long work. Mainly, I argue that one must read her zoopoetics textually, and not literally. That means refraining from reading her texts for animal representations and, instead, locating how she enmeshes animality in literary representation itself. Her prose has been repeatedly described as unusual and syntactically innovative, but a close analysis of this unusualness seems to be lacking. One of her most famous readers, Hélène Cixous, explored Lispector's fiction as an instance of "écriture feminine," but her close readings are frustrated by her limited knowledge of Portuguese (cf. Arrojo 1999). This is a serious shortcoming, for I argue that the zoopoetics of *The Apple in the Dark* must be read in the textuality of (Brazilian) Portuguese idiomaticity. As the title reveals, light and darkness are important themes in the novel, but the extent to which they are intertwined with Lispector's zoopoetics is located only in the intricacies of Portuguese. Specifically, I shall focus on how light and darkness are enmeshed in the idiomatic expressions describing the (animal, mammalian) act of giving birth, and how the two possible Portuguese expressions for giving birth suggested by the novel point to an essential undecidability at the heart of the question of animality for Lispector. I argue that this undecidability, and the system of *dilemmas* it produces, are products of a repression of an "earlier," "originary" element I term *arche-animality*, akin to Derrida's arche-writing. If Derrida coined the "old name"—or *paleonym*—arche-writing in order to circle the condition of language that would emerge "before" the distinction between speech and writing, I hope to show that Lispector's novel explores an arche-animality which, in fact, furnishes the traditional concepts of animality—and its other, humanity—as it confusingly works within competing ontological systems. I argue that the novel's preoccupation with the succession of days and nights—the play of light and dark—gets intertwined with the image of evolution and a chaining of generations by means of the Portuguese expression for "giving birth." This reveals that the supplementarity at work between the stages of evolution from nature to culture, and which furnishes the novel's zoopoetics, is a figure of the arche-animal.

At the start of the novel, Martim is fleeing from a hotel late at night fearing detection, and wanders during nighttime and daytime until he reaches a farm where two women live. They allow him to work there for room and board and their three lives are woven together in strange ways, not least because of Martim's own path of self-(re)discovery. Martim disregards them in sexist disdain and, thus, believes himself safe, but Vitória, the owner of the farm, senses this disdain and turns him over to the police. The novel ends with Martim allowing the police to take him away in resigned humiliation. Earl Fitz connects the overall Lispectorian project—which he sees as foreshadowing poststructuralism—to the theological overtones of the apple in the title of this novel. Even if the symbolism of the biblical apple as Fitz formulates it can readily be accepted, a closer reading of the novel shows that the "darkness" that envelops it is far from being easily interpreted. It might surround the apple so as to keep it hidden from us, but it might, according to the novel, also mean that the apple can in fact be *grasped*, before or instead of being seen. Either lost in darkness or so close at hand that it need not be lit, the apple's relationship to light stands at the core of a flickering hesitation that structures the whole novel, and this undecidability reverts back to a prior, grammatological instability regarding the status of animality, which I hope to uncover in the Portuguese idiomaticity of "giving birth." Or rather, this hesitation inhabits the very direction of the question: Is its truth to be found by reverting back or by moving forward? Are animals the backdrop from which humanity emerges, or are they the first bodily supplement to metaphysico-spiritual humanity? Do humans supplement animality, or does humanity supplement animals?

I argue that, in *The Apple in the Dark*, Lispector works through these questions by revealing the extent to which it is animality itself—or, more precisely, what I call the *arche*-animal—which performs the work of supplementarity that makes possible these articulations, in whichever direction they appear to advance. I start by discussing the poetics of light and dark as evidenced by the title as the clef in which the arche-animal is written into the novel. Then I point out how arche-animality relates to Derridean supplementarity. I move on to analyze the Portuguese idioms employed in the novel to describe giving birth as they theorize the undecidability of supplementary arche-animality. I show that Derrida plays with French idioms in *Of Grammatology* that similarly display ambiguities in the relation between nature and culture in his discussion of auto- and hetero-affection. Finally, I suggest that Lispector's zoopoetics are focused on the arche-animal rather than animals, insofar as she portrays animality as a procedure.

ESCURIDADE AND ARCHE-ANIMALITY

In his preface, Gregory Rabassa stresses the multilayered character of the novel, composed as it is of stages which complement or overturn the other (Rabassa 1985, xv). Thus, Martim is said to go "from rock to plants to vermin to cattle to children and finally to contact with other humans, whom he had abandoned before," in a progression which Rabassa terms "the evolutionary scale" (xiv), readable—as the beginning of the novel—both in biblical and in Darwinian terms.

He also stresses the importance of the title, stating that it "is a kind of symbol of all that goes to make up the final theme of the book" (xv). Because I share Rabassa's opinion regarding the importance of the title, I shall refer to the novel's exploration of the play of light and dark as its *escuridade*. In this neologism, I combine the word *escuro* ("dark") from the title, with the noun *claridade* ("clarity"), which is recurrent throughout the novel. *Escuro*, like the English "dark," is more often than not an adjective, which can function as a noun when preceded by an article: *o escuro* ("the dark"). The noun proper, just as in "dark-ness," would have a suffix attached—*escur-idão*. Thus, *escur-idade*, despite gesturing toward "clarity," consists, in fact, of the "wrong" suffix being attached to the noun/adjective *escuro*. This is meant to underscore the fact that, in the play of light and dark throughout Martim's journey, darkness is bound to "win," as it not only appears as one of the elements of the dichotomy, but it also installs the very *différance* which structures the difference between light and darkness. Just as writing in Derrida names the originary element (arche-writing), which, in fact, engenders the difference between itself and speech, shades of light and dark are always already products of darkness. In other words, darkness is not only one of the elements of the pair, it is also a structuring component with shades that make possible the articulation between "levels" of darkness. Also, I hope that it reveals the work of *paleonymy* involved in revealing the differing/deferring elements which structure the dichotomies they subsequently appear to take part in. If the difference between speech and writing is produced by an arche-writing, then before there can be a play of *escuro* and *claridade*, there is an arche-darkness—*escuridade*.

Leonard Lawlor has discussed this Derridean recourse to old names (paleonymy) as the "second phase" of deconstruction, after the initial moment of overturning the classical hierarchy (e.g. speech/writing, human/animal). The second phase "reinscribes the previously inferior term as the 'origin' or 'resource' of the hierarchy itself," so that this term "becomes what Derrida calls an 'old name' or a 'paleonym.'" Lawlor sees these terms as "the experience of a process of differentiation that is also repetition" (Lawlor 2007, 30). He proceeds to explain some Derridean examples, starting from *Dissemination*'s pharmakon as it "refers to the resource called the *logos*, language, but language prior to the division between living voice and dead writing" (ibid.). Similarly, I propose the paleonym arche-animal to refer to the "resource" of the distinction between human and animal, and to the interface between animal embodiment and human spirituality. "Before" the distinction between human and animal as the metaphysical distinction between spirit and body, there must be a sort of *pure* difference, a pure inscriptional space where the differentiation between body and soul might be possible. A chain of other possible names emerges for this "old" concept, besides that of an inscriptional space: animation, articulation, difference. No concept of the human as bearer of a soul and/or capable of language seems possible without the animalistic notion of animation, or of species difference itself, as that which secures the borders of language and establishes the laws of referentiality and figuration (i.e., animation of signifiers, etc.). The metaphysical, vulgar concept of the animal is, thus, revealed to be a modification of this pure difference.

In order to grasp an animality which would be located "before" both the human and the "vulgar" animal, it is useful to track Derrida's procedure when outlining the arche-writing lurking "behind" both writing and speech. Geoffrey Bennington frames it as "show[ing] that the generally admitted relations between speech and writing [...] must draw their possibility from an earlier root: we call this root 'writing' or 'arche-writing' because the current concept of writing names obliquely some of its components" (Bennington 1993, 60). In *Of Grammatology*, which contains the most thorough discussion of the term, Derrida argues that the ordinary sense of writing—as notation for speech—is itself a "dissimulation" of arche-writing, produced by (and in the name of) a speech which represses arche-writing and puts in its place a thoroughly obedient concept (Derrida 2016, 61). And the parallels between writing and animality (and hence between arche-writing and the arche-animal) are confirmed when Derrida expresses his continuing interest in the "the animality of writing" (2008, 52).

Elsewhere (Piskorski 2015), I have argued that the practice of paleonymy is crucial for the study of zoopoetics because of the methodological problems it triggers. The conflict, in analytical approaches, between formalism and paraphrase is especially acute for zoopoetics because it mirrors the tension between body and soul which is at play when one tries to theorize animal embodiment. I concluded there that a way out of the paralyzing dichotomies of metaphysical embodiment is to circle the very origin of the dichotomy in the shape of the arche-animal. Similarly, this paleonymic leap can then be reproduced methodologically by making the arche-animal the object of study of zoopoetics.

ESCURIDADE AND SUPPLEMENTARITY

Escuridade, too, is a paleonym for the alternation between clarity and darkness, and is in itself a figure of supplementation, but this alternation is tied up with a different—albeit related—instance of supplementation from the very start of the novel. The novel is divided into three parts: "How a Man Is Made" (eleven chapters), "The Birth of the Hero" (nine chapters), and "The Apple in the Dark" (seven chapters). The very beginning of chapter one of part one describes the darkness of "a night as dark as night can get when a person sleeps" (Lispector 1985, 1.i.3),[1] which is then contrasted with a daytime image:

> By day, however, the countryside was different, and the crickets, vibrating hollow and hard, left the entire expanse open, shadowless. [...] [A]nd like a point drawn upon the point itself, the voice of the cricket was the very body of the cricket, and it told nothing. (1.i.4)

The last chapter of "How a Man Is Made" presents a different image, which together with the cricket figure serves to frame the first part and establish precisely "how a man is made":

> As he faced the extension of enormous and empty land, with a suffocated effort Martim was painfully approaching—with the difficulty of someone who is never going to arrive—he was approaching something that a man on foot would humbly call the desire of a man, but which a man on horseback could not resist the temptation to call the mission of a man. And the birth of that strange eagerness was provoked, now as it had been when he first walked upon the slope, by the vision of an enormous world which seems to be asking a question. And which seemed to call [*clamar*] for a new god, who, understanding, would in that way complete [*concluísse*] the work of the other God. Confused there on a jumpy horse, jumpy himself,

in just a second of looking Martim had emerged totally and as a man. (1.xi.116–117)

Between the cricket's voice and its body—but also between God and god, a case of supplementary addition is displayed. They represent the two possible meanings of the supplement according to Derrida: an unnecessary addition to something whole, or an essential part that comes to complete something unfinished. The addition of voice to the cricket is wholly external and accidental, to the point that it changes nothing: It can neither improve nor undermine the wholeness of its body. On the other hand, Martim as a supplementary "god" is the emissary whose task is to "complete [God's] work." The work of God is incomplete without external help—which in the end is no longer external for becoming an essential part of the work.

The trajectory of hominization—of how a man is made—goes from a stage of nonsupplementary (of the supplement erased for being external) to a point of "essential" supplementation. From the undifferentiated world of animality emerges the human who can, apparently, both *be* a supplement and also *manipulate* it. Martim as "god" completes "God," but he must also *act* in order to finish His work, so that the human is both the object and subject of supplementation.

Hominization is framed as the history of spacing. The daylit expanse opened by the vibrating cricket represents, nevertheless, the plenitude of self-presence that neutralizes all distance into accessible proximity. In contrast, the "extension of enormous and empty land" faced by Martim during his epiphany is irreducibly distant, despite his clear desire of conquering and understanding it. That is, Martim's hominization conforms to the traditional picture of the human as that which *is an instance of* the maximum distancing from the background of nature, but also that which is able to *perceive* that distance, only to then believe itself capable—because of this ability—of neutralizing all this spacing by the power of *logos*.

These paradoxes are at the heart of the contradiction ingrained in humanism's view of the animal. Animality is that which is life-infused and closest to nature, but also that which is most inanimate, embodying writing, technology, and prosthetics by *being* embodiment itself. These paradoxes are famously explored by Derrida in *Of Grammatology*. He writes that, in Rousseau's thought,

[t]he difference between the glance [used in gestural language] and the voice [needed for true, human language] is the difference between animality and humanity. Transgressing space, mastering the outside, placing souls in communication, voice transcends natural animality. That is to say a certain death signified by space. Exteriority is inanimate. The arts of space carry death within themselves and *animality* remains the *inanimate* face of *life*. (Derrida 2016, 213)

There is a radical difference, "at the same interior and exterior," that cleaves every possible meaning of life, nature, animality, or humanity. That will mean that "the animal who [...] has no relationship to death is on the side of death," whereas speech (or *logos*, reason, etc.) "is *living* speech even while it institutes a relation to death, and so on." Human speech "is more *natural* to man but more foreign to a nature which is in itself dead *nature* [still life]" (2016, 213).

That is why, after the continuous supplementation of stages in an evolution of the supplement—in which the human world becomes more and more marked by supplementary relations—the human can "return to nature" by neutralizing the very spacing that marks that humanity. Speech, language, signification—the very things that, by supplementing reality and standing in for real things, take the human out of nature—dream of their own spiritual power of eliminating the very supplementary space between thing and sign which makes signification possible. The break from nature which both necessitates and engenders language is undone by the belief that (human) signification can make the leap back and close the distance between reality and sign. Nature is, thus, that *from* which (archeo) and *to* which (teleo) the human supplementary march *should* advance.

Thus, reaching the stage of nonsupplementary[2] is both feared and desired, an ambiguity which is essential to Martim's oscillations regarding his crime and his progress. After having his first thought after his crime returned him to a simple stage of mere life, Martim instantly revolts against what he sees as "the insidious return of a vice"; his whole project—at least as he now sees it—was to leave humanity behind and, thus, never "think" again, to which he succumbs soon after his rebirth. Martim is clearly disappointed with the widespread functioning of the supplement: "Thinking," for him, is ineluctably tied to conceptual signification as grounded in signifying. He attempts to fight it off, though, demonstrating Derrida's argument that the supplement, while feared, is

also employed as protection against itself or against the seductive danger
of nonsupplementary:

> He needed to defend what, with such enormous courage, he had con-
> quered two weeks before. With such enormous courage, that man had
> finally stopped being intelligent.
>   Or had he ever really been intelligent? [...]
>   "The fact is," he then thought, using great care as he tried that
> defensive trick, "the fact is that I was only imitating intelligence just as
> I could swim like a fish without being one!" Then man moved about
> contentedly: "I was imitating, of course!" [...] The fact is, he concluded
> with great interest, he had only imitated intelligence, with that essential
> lack of respect which makes a person imitate. And along with him, mil-
> lions of men were copying with great effort the idea of a man, next to
> thousands of women who were attentively copying the idea of a woman
> and thousands of people of good will were copying with superhuman
> effort their own face [*cara*] and the idea of existing; not to mention the
> anguished concentration with which acts of good or evil were imitated—
> with a daily caution so as not to slip toward an act that is true, and there-
> fore incomparable, and therefore inimitable, and therefore disconcerting.
> (1.ii.25)

Martim produces a full-fledged—if acutely traditional—theory of representation. For him, humans live out their lives according to the supplement, imitating and referencing what they believe is transcendental
reality. They constantly refer to that which they purport to wish to reach,
but Martim is aware that people know that the full presence of reality
would be lethal, and must therefore be kept at bay by means of the supplement. For Derrida,

> [a] terrifying menace, the supplement is also the first and surest protection;
> against that very menace. [...] [For] presence is at the same time desired
> and feared. [...] Enjoyment [*jouissance*] *itself*, without symbol or supple-
> tory, that which would accord us (to) [*nous accorderait (à)*] pure presence
> itself, if such a thing were possible, would be only another name for death.
> (Derrida 2016, 168, last interpolation mine)

In this sense, Martim's identity as "god" cannot be read only as the
positive supplement that completes God's work. If his mission and
desire of "completing God's work" stands for the obedient side of the

supplementary sign-function that respects the interdict, he also transgresses it by offering up the difference that interrupts the uniqueness of capitalized "God," so as to inaugurate the plurality of lowercase "gods." Eden serves only as a prologue that justifies the human condition as it is experienced by fallen man: exposure to supplementarity and mortality. The double functioning of the supplement—obedience and transgression—figures as cognate to the "double nature" of humanity: the human is materialized in an animal body but is also endowed with divine patronage and gifts (having been made in His image, having a soul, speaking, etc.).

Therefore, I establish that the novel's poetics of light and dark is the key in which the logic of the supplement—as *escuridade*—is inscribed. This logic, and the enchainment of supplements, emerges both as an obstacle in Martim's quest for a nonsupplementary language, and as crucial to reading the novel's arche-animality as it is intimately connected to this play.

After the deep darkness with which the novel opens, variations of light are used throughout the text as a way of charting Martim's relationship to the stages he is going through and the level of *mediation* he experiences. *Escuridade* encodes the supplementary articulation between elements—such as original and copy, or thing and word—and between stages in a progressive line. Usually, light represents the immediate world of accessible things and transparent truth—a form of transcendence. Darkness, on the other hand, usually means the textural density of a world with intervals and gaps. *Escuridade*, therefore, signifies both the difference between proximity and distance, and the distinction between free-flowing and intermittent. This is animalized in several moments in which the extension and openness of light is contrasted to animals' supposed independence from light for knowing their environment; Vitória qualifies "animals" as "the animals out of which the dark is made" (3.iii.245). In a crucial passage, Martim observes:

> The maximum clarity had given into our inhabited darkness. [...] As if with that submission [*vergar-se*] of the clarity [...] before the darkness there had finally come about the union of the plants, of the cows, and of the man that he had begun to be. Each time that day turned into night, the man's dominion would become renewed, and a step forward would be taken, blindly. (2.i.130)

Clarity submits (*verga-se*, literally "bends itself") to darkness, and that is the only way through which a union can be made between stages in his development. Only by accepting the interruption of nighttime darkness can clarity move forward and bind together—by illuminating—the coming stages in this human evolution. By means of the cyclical, pendular movement between day and night, Martim can move forward, each alternation signifying one step ahead. Darkness, thus, *articulates*: it is that which both separates elements in their differentiating specificities, but also keeps them together.

THE LIGHT THAT THEREFORE I GIVE (TO)

The extent to which Lispector reveals the work of what I term *escuridade* as a function of arche-animality will be crucial to my argument regarding the Derridean zoopoetics of the novel. As mentioned previously, Martim's journey is caught up with the question of otherness. Initially, alterity is shunned in the same gesture with which he rejects common language, which he terms "the language of others." Later on in his progress, however, Martim realizes that, to accede fully to humanity, he must *create* otherness. Because he experiences his stages as moments of creation, he concludes he must create (i.e., give birth) to other humans so that he can be fully human: "concentrating very hard on the birth [*parto*] of others, in a task that only he could carry out, Martim was there trying to be one with those who will be born" (3.vii.335–336).

Hélène Cixous reads this passage as a "scene […] of masculine birth," where "the metaphor and the bodily labor" of giving birth "cannot not be borrowed from the real other, here the woman" (Cixous 1990, 61). However, the entire passage is also readily connected to *escuridade* because it consists of Martim's reflections on lighting a bonfire; his ultimate direct manipulation of light, after chapters fascinated by it, intoxicates him. In one of the few long dialogue passages of the novel, Vitória speaks of the only time she loved, which was when admiring a young man lighting a bonfire. A few days later, she asks Martim to light one while she observes. Interpellated by her into the bonfire-lighting young man's position, Martim feels both uncomfortable and victorious. Light extinguishes all doubt and all distances, and Martim has created it himself, as a man—a proper, heroic one—should.

This is part of a clear sequence of events that transpire in the third and last part of the novel, which shares its name with the book's title.

Chapter three could be considered an alternative, when a torrential downpour interrupts the suspenseful drought that had plagued the farm during the two previous parts, releasing tension for all three main characters. Martim spends most of the night in the heart of the woods, terrified of his loneliness, finally and painfully aware that his self-making project was a lie, that he deceived himself into believing he could create a perfect language capable of grasping transparent truth. Chapter five, after the long dialogue between Vitória and Martin in chapter four, is only a few pages long, and it paints a picture of calm now that all three characters have found some sort of closure. Surprisingly, Martim feels strangely victorious, despite his terrifying conclusion in the woods that he had failed. The chapter starts:

> And as if everything had come to an end before its appointed time, and as if everybody had got whatever it was they had wanted from the man [Martim]—they suddenly left him alone. The air was soft and full, and in the morning the cow gave birth to a calf [*bezerro*]. (3.v.309)

Victorious light is confirmed:

> There followed a period of great calm. Life revealed obvious progress the way one suddenly perceives a child has grown. [...] And the few days that followed mounted up without incident, like one single day.
> They were clear and tall days, woven into the air by the birds. [...] And in spite of the distance, the clear air brought the mountain within the range of a shout.
> [...] And in the cowshed, after the birth of the calf, serenity reigned.
> [...] Martim, in spite of himself, joined in with the light and went over to the winning side. (3.v.309–310)

Sexual difference seems to short-circuit Martim's most acute and productive insights—after having accepted, in the woods, the inescapable reality of "the dark" which envelops "the apple," Martim succumbs to the illusory power of light to reveal all of reality. This is connected both to Vitória's monologue, which seems to Martim to confirm his sexist assumptions about her, and to the theme of giving birth. "Giving birth," in *The Apple in the Dark*, is irreducibly related both to the impersonality (and otherness) contained within the notion of animal reproduction, and to *escuridade*.

Martim's first developmental stage in the farm—his kinship with the plants—is prefaced in terms of light: "Clarity, coming after stages and stages [*etapas*] of silence, became reduced there to mere visibility, which is the most that eyes need" (1.vi.79). At this stage, Martim revels in the mere visibility of his plot of land which for him signifies the primitive life of plants and, even, rats—not the darkness that surrounded the meaningless sleep which opens the novel, but neither the meaning-giving light that recognizes distance only to undermine it in infinite illumination: only a sort of hazy visibility that gets life going. In contrast to this, Martim's entrance in his next, cow phase is marked by the different luminosity associated with the cows:

> [H]is new and confused steps led him one morning out of his reign in the plot into the half-light of the cowshed where cows were more difficult than plants.
> [...] The light of the cowshed was different from the light outside to the point that at the door some vague threshold was established. (1.viii.93–94)

The cow stage is interesting as it not only introduces Martim to the realm of higher animals, but it also encodes in the novel the meanings of sexual difference and reproduction. And the cow passages all make clear the deep connection between reproduction and *escuridade*: "as if from out of that shapeless entanglement little by little one more form were being concretely prepared. [...] Cows were made there" (1.viii.94).

Further on, the passage from the light of the morning of plants into the "half-light" of the cowshed endows both reproduction and *escuridade* with the evolutionary scale motif, the gradual addition of cumulative stages or steps that bridge nature and culture. That there could be stages at all, *The Apple in the Dark* implies, that time and space can be textured according to *spacing*, one needs darkness and the differentiating capacity it brings to a world of diffuse light. Distance, difference, and spacing are part of a chain which, together with language, the sign, and the supplement, *seems* to happen accidentally to undivided presence:

> [A]ll that was needed was a step backwards, and he would have found himself in the full fragrance of morning which is a thing already perfected in

the smallest leaves and smallest stones, a finished work without fissures—
and at which a person can look without any danger because there is no
place to enter and lose oneself. [...]
[The cows] began to moo slowly and moved their feet without even
looking at him—bypassing, as animals do, the necessity of seeing in order
to know, as if they had already crossed the infinite extension of their own
subjectivity to the point of reaching the other side: the perfect objectivity
that no longer need be demonstrated. (1.viii.95)

Martim's birthing of otherness is connected to the previous cow passages
in its focus on impersonality. He seems to conclude that being the most
human means being the least personal, like a cow who has extinguished
all her subjectivity, so that he can be *all* humans:

A few hours before, beside the bonfire, he had attained an impersonality
inside of himself: he had been so profoundly himself that he had become
the "himself" of any other person, the way a cow is a cow of all cows. [...]
[H]e had just attained the impersonality with which a man, falling, another
rises up. The impersonality of dying while others are born. (3.vii.335)

(Animal) reproduction had already been flagged in the cowshed passage
as intimately related to *escuridade*:

The cowshed was a warm and good place which pulsated like a thick vein.
It was by [*à base de*] that thick vein that men and beasts [*bichos*] had children. [...] It was through [*à base de*] a cowshed that *time is indefinitely
replaced by time*. (1.viii.97, my emphasis)

Time is created at the base of a pulsating vein, by the means of which life
can articulate stages by linking generation to generation. The chaining
of time as the continuing movement of supplementarity structures the
impersonality that Martim seeks, which is none other than the impersonality brought about by animal mortality. Death makes all living things
impersonal to the extent that they must merge with the chaining of
countless generations. This mortality is the foremost experience of time
as articulation, as discreet stages which interrupt an otherwise steady,
undifferentiated time of an eternal "now."
    This is made most acute in the chapter describing the feeling of vic-
torious calm after Vitória's monologue. As stated previously, the first

paragraph of the chapter informs us that "in the morning the cow gave birth to a calf" (3.v.309). The relevance of this sentence is lost in translation. The original reads "de manhã a vaca deu à luz um bezerro" (Lispector 1999, 3.v.287), which literally translates as "in the morning the cow gave to the light a (male) calf." As in Italian and Spanish, the commonplace expression in Portuguese for "giving birth" directly references light. "Give to the light" would be cognate with expressions in which the mother is said to "bring [the child] forth" into the world (of light). However, it would be correct to affirm that *dar à luz* is not the only form of the Portuguese expression used to describe giving birth; it is simply one variety, the high-register one, prescribed by normative grammar; different editions of the novel contain different varieties. The other construction, although considered incorrect and, thus, informal, is "dar a luz," without the grave accent.[3] Making use of the preposition *a* ("to"), *dar a luz a um bezerro* literally translates to "give the light to a calf." The distinction between the two forms hinges on which is the direct object of the sentence and which is the indirect object. In *dar à luz um bezerro*, the calf is the direct object of the act of giving, and he is being given *to* the light, the indirect object. In *dar a luz a um bezerro*, the light is the direct object which is being given *to* the darkness-dwelling indirect object, the calf. The confusion between the two forms probably stems from the fact that, in Brazil, *a* and *à* are pronounced the same.[4]

Earlier editions of *The Apple in the Dark* did, indeed, contain in this passage, the "incorrect" informal variety of the expression. As a rule, more recent editions of Lispector novels in Brazil are not prone to correct her language, giving her free rein to explore and flaunt normative rules as she sees fit. Until recently, Lispector's current Brazilian publisher, Rocco, had appended an introductory note to all her novels, explaining their editorial policy regarding possible contradicting versions of the same Lispector text. The publisher, as justification for its strict adherence to the first published edition as the "true originals,"[5] presented a quote by the author stating that she carefully rewrote and edited her manuscripts while she typed them out but then never revised her text after she sent it to the publisher – a quote that also frames any deviation from the norm as intentional.

The ambiguity between the two forms speaks of an irreducible flicker between two different ways of relating light and reproduction. Is the "light" something that can be manipulated by a subject and, thus, given to the next generation, added to a stratum so as to constitute the next evolutionary step? Or are subjects, conversely, passively added to the light as that which will obscure it? Are subjects foreground objects that can occlude the light, or are they visited by it so as to be outshone? In a certain sense, this asks the very question of subjectivity and, thus, prohibits the framing of the discussion in terms of subjects—especially because the novel provides this discussion in the clef of cows, who/ which, we are informed, have reached postsubjectivity. Only the free manipulation of light would constitute sovereign subjectivity, while being instrumental *to* the light equates to being objectified. Rather than the actions of a subject, the flickering grave accent (*a* vs. *à*) interrogates the mechanics of subject creation. In the living being's relationship to death as that which chops up life's flow of time, "giving the light" does admittedly come across as acceptance of mortality, but only insofar as death—as darkness—separates stages so as to take the light to a more advanced one. In other words, mortality is accepted simply because it is the only way of being able to "pass on the torch," and assumes the truth of life as light. Conversely, "giving to the light" sees in mortality a more radical finitude rooted in embodiment, whose darkness would indeed be the truth of life as living in a body. Giving offspring over to the light would register as approaching the "light at the end of the tunnel" at the end of one's life, a light which by definition cannot be reached while living and, thus, must be left to the next generation. "Giving the light" assumes a primordial light being interrupted by the dark, while "giving to the light" supposes an original darkness kept only alive by the "spark" of movement which death brings about.

Human *logos*—or light in *The Apple in the Dark*—equals absolute self-presence and the complete illumination of all the space of the world, an illumination that in fact neutralizes the world *as* space. Like speech, the world drenched in light in *The Apple in the Dark* has only one dimension, it is a linear extension through time and, thus, can be wholly comprehended instantaneously. Darkness introduces space and distance, making a series of discrete, different chunks of the luminous whole. Dialectically, this darkness is pure negation. It only *is* to the extent that it *is not* and that it can interrupt light. The play of light and dark, or the succession of days and nights, is revealed to be grounded on an *escuridade* that is in fact the very possibility of articulating light and dark, day and night. One night can separate two days—and, thus, make them two—only on the condition that there exists articulation and supplementation. Martim's quest and project—committing a crime so as to be driven from society and returned to square one—seems to attempt to run back along the chain of days and nights, of supplemented and supplementer, to encounter the originary presence that had first to be supplemented. But rather than that, he finds that everything actually "begins" with supplementation itself and, thus, does not really begin. The dark "spark" that sets the chain of supplements in motion can only be an instance of what Derrida calls an "inscribed origin" (Kates 2005, 185).

If "the animal"—as embodiment—has been described as the first technological supplement to (and corruption of) luminous, spiritual humanity, it is also reasonable to picture humanity coming *after* animality, coming about *by the means of* and *in the form of* the addition of light to the darkness of animal density. Human nature, in ontotheological terms, is primordial: the first spark, which then becomes corrupted by its descent into the materiality of the world, its incarnation into animal corporeality. Crucially, that is also true in phenomenology. Parallel to that, however, and in the same tradition, humanity is also what emerges, as an improvement, from the background of natural animality, abandoning the dark realm of instinct and unreason.[6]

I argue that these two competing claims are, in fact, both products of the repression of arche-animality. In the novel, arche-animality is shown to be engendered by the supplementary alternation of days and nights, but this kind of supplementary substitution is in turn held up as responsible for the very process of signification in which a sign stands in for something else. In the movement by which culture seemingly supplements nature—only to turn back to it as when Martim reverts to the dawn of time—the work of the sign as a supplement to a real, natural world is established. And *The Apple in the Dark* theorizes that it is animal embodiment and death, the enchainment of time by means of reproduction and the sequence of generations, that give rise to this articulatory, supplementary work responsible for signification. In this way, the novel itself makes a zoopoetic claim.

I Am Given (Myself?): *Donner le Change*

The vacillation between the two varieties of the expression *dar* (*à*) *luz* maps out onto the flickering of another *a* with a grave accent in the Derrida passage quoted. He argues that "presence is at the same time desired and feared," hence the double functioning of the supplement as that which approximates us to presence while also protecting us from it. For Rousseau, it was a question of rerouting his pleasure from the direct access to sexual experience to masturbation, as a compensatory stand-in for the presence of sexual enjoyment, which Derrida describes as "Enjoyment [*jouissance*] *itself*, without symbol or suppletory, that which would accord us (to) [*nous accorderait (à)*] pure presence itself" (Derrida 2016, 168). His explanation suggests two symmetrically opposed options: either presence is delivered to us, or we are delivered to it. This is the same undecidability which is at the heart of the issue of "giving (to) the light" and, as Derrida makes clear, ultimately describes a concept of death. After all, the full presence of pleasure itself "would be only another name for death," hence the fear and the need for the supplement. If supplements mediate the relationships that we, as subjects, entertain with presence, one would think that bypassing supplementation would grant us presence as an object to be attained. However, in a certain sense the fullness of presence could never be an object: The human subject would need to be the object which is then given over to presence or, in other words, to death. As Derrida has pointed out, life is another name for auto-affection (180), and that which touches itself is not one and is not self-present.

Both *dar (à) luz* and *la jouissance elle-même [...] qui nous accorderait (à) la presence pure* interrogate what it means to be *given*—whether one is given *something* or is given *to* it (light/presence), communion with which would stop the work of *escuridade*/supplementarity and, thus, equal death. Interestingly, Derrida introduces the idiomaticity of French in order to stress this point. We learn that Rousseau believes he is *misleading* his own desires by rerouting them into himself instead of prostitutes. Fearing "habitation with women"—pleasure *itself*—Rousseau conjures up their presence by means of the apparent self-presence of masturbation. This restitution of presence by means of symbols is experienced as *immediate*, despite being itself a form of mediation. This is the case "because as experience, as consciousness or conscience, [this symbolic restitution] *passes over passage through the world*. The toucher is touched, auto-affection gives itself as pure autarchy" (2016, 167). However, Derrida demonstrates that this restitution is illusory, insofar as it depends on the supplementary structure of auto-affection. Rousseau himself is, thus, sidetracked or deceived by the supplement:

But what is no longer deferred is also absolutely deferred. The presence that is thus delivered to us in the present is a chimera. Auto-affection is a pure speculation. The sign, the image, the representation, which come to supplement the absent presence are the illusions that sidetrack [*donnent le change*] us. (2016, 167, translator's interpolation)

Derrida foregrounds the French idiom *donner le change* as mapping the functioning of the supplement as the latter promises to procure an absent presence by means of the (false) self-presence of auto-affection:

> *Donner le change* [literally "giving change"]: in whatever sense it is under-stood, this expression well describes the recourse to the supplement admirably. In order to explain his "disgust" for "common prostitutes," Rousseau tells us: [...] "I had not lost the pernicious habit of sidetracking [*donner le change*] my needs". (2016, 167–168, translator's interpolations)

In their article "What Gives (*Donner le change*)," Ravindranathan and Traisnel discuss Derrida's use of this idiom. They point out that "in hunting parlance, *donner le change* was originally used to refer to the substitution by which a chased animal, most often a deer, would escape by offering up another of its species in its place" (Ravindranathan and Traisnel 2016, 146). However, in modern-day French, the expression means "simply *to deceive* or *to mislead*, to pass one thing for another," often used pronominally and reflexively (or auto-affectionately, as it were) as *se donner le change*, "to convince oneself of an untruth" (2016, 147). Therefore, Rousseau believes it possible to mislead or deceive his own desires into accepting self-eroticism instead of intercourse, but the symbolic restitution performed by auto-affection is only an illusion brought about by denial. Like the deer which can give the *change* by giving the hunter the slip and offering up another as if it were the self-same, the supplement gives Rousseau the *change* by offering an image of him-self in auto-affection as if it were truly himself. When something gives you the *change*, one could say that:

> the enjoyment [*jouissance*] of the *thing itself* is thus worked over, in its act and in its essence, by frustration. [...] Promising itself there as it hides there, giving itself as it displaces itself, is something that cannot even be rigorously called presence. [...] The supplement is maddening because it is neither presence nor absence. (Derrida 2016, 168)

After all, what does it mean to ask whether the deer who has given the *change* is present when it is able to give the change "by inscribing a difference for which there is no mark of concept" (Ravindranathan and Traisnel 2016, 147)? For Ravindranathan and Traisnel, the Derridean supplement as *donner le change* inscribes the possibility of an animal subject, an animal able both *to give* and to give *another as itself.* In this scene of giving by an animal of its own likeness, there is a challenge to our "current economy of signification […] in which the animal disappears, or appears merely *as (a) given*" (2016, 147).

The belief that animals are simply *given* or *a given* implies that they are part of nature, conceived as the inert background against which human intentionality plays and which it fashions. The given would be that which is immediately ready to hand, as the apple shrouded in darkness promising the direct intimacy of the touch. And, of course, auto-affection as suggested by masturbation is the ready to hand *par excellence.* And, like masturbation, the direct access to the animal as a given is complicated by the law of supplementarity, the moment the animal slips away from its status as a given raw material onto the confusion of the giving/given brought about by passing another as oneself. The animal presence sought in pursuit is thought to be reachable by means of the self-presence of the pursuing subject (as engendered by auto-affection), but the very mediation betrayed by auto-affection is also revealed in the interchangeability between the deer and its *change*: if I know that *I* who is following *am I* only by means of an auto-affection, which I is touched and which is touching? Which one gives and which one is given?[7] Which one is using the other so as to "pass one thing for another," such as money, and, thus, to engender presence? Similarly, which deer am I following? Is/are the deer merely matter given to be fashioned, lit under the subject's eye, or is/are it/they, conversely, the shadowy trickster with the presence of mind to elude us?

APING, THE ARCHE-ANIMALITY

Hence, *dar (à) luz* is the pivot around which all the other undecidables in the novel turn. As discussed previously, the title may refer either to a pessimistic view of human linguistic existence (we are always lost in dark, the apple always out of reach), or to a triumphant affirmation of the vast knowledge we have at hand (if we abandon language and reason, we can actually access the apple directly).

Perhaps the most important aspect of the epiphanic passage in the woods is that it contains one of the two references to apples in the dark. However, it is firmly inserted in the masculinist framework which seduces Martim into bravado and overconfidence. It outlines only one of the meanings of the title:

> [I]t was silly not to understand. "You don't understand only if you don't want to!" he thought boldly. [...] Martim, very satisfied, had that attitude. As if now, stretching out his hand in the dark and picking up an apple, he recognized on fingers that love had made so clumsy that it was an apple. Martim no longer asked for the name of things. It was enough for him to recognize them in the dark. And rejoice, clumsily.
>
> And afterwards? Afterwards, when he went out into the light, he would see the things his hand had felt before [*pressentidas com a mão*], and he would see those things with their false names. Yes, but he would already have known them in the dark like a man who has slept with a woman.[8] (Lispector 1985, 3.vi.319)

However, this bravado is finally undermined by his terrified reflections in the wood, and then the narrator informs us exactly what Martim's real journey was:

> And the real journey had been this: that one day he had left his house of man and his city of man seeking, through adventure, precisely that thing that he was now experiencing in the dark, seeking the great humiliation, and along with himself, with ferocious pleasure, he was humiliating a whole human race. (3.iii.234)

Beyond the hesitation regarding his project of rebirth, breaking free both from the spiritual quest for infinite knowledge and the material regrounding into one's animality—in other words, beyond *dar a luz* and *dar à luz*—there exists through this "great humiliation" a more primordial articulation that gives rises to these possibilities: *escuridade* itself. The primariness of *escuridade* is not, of course, structured as an origin, otherwise it would be a safe transcendental root onto which Martim could hold. It is only ever an inscribed origin, the nonorigin which is originary *différance*.

And the novel intimately bonds *escuridade* and arche-animality when Martim recognizes in fury the *primariness* of the *secondarity* of symbolicity, representation, and supplementarity. Moments after confessing his (attempted) murder, Martim tries to explain himself to God. He argues that he *elected* to suffer so that he could become the symbol of suffering to which other people could refer. "Suffering," as a concept, would only be conceivable in reference to that which would be the "symbol of suffering"—absolute, ideal suffering, the most suffering of all:

> But—he rebelled immediately then, justifying himself to God—someone had to sacrifice himself and bring unconsoled suffering to its ultimate term and then become the symbol of suffering! someone had to sacrifice himself, I wanted to symbolize my own suffering! I sacrificed myself! I wanted the symbol because the symbol is the true reality and our life is symbolic of the symbol, just as we ape [*macaqueamos*] our own nature and try to copy ourselves! now I understand imitation: it's a sacrifice! I sacrificed myself! he said to God, reminding Him that even He had sacrificed a son and that we also had the right to imitate Him, we had to renew the mystery because reality is getting lost! (3.iii.238–239)

This dense passage addresses most of the issues of the novel, and presents clearly an arche-animality (*macaquear*, "to ape") which is other than a simple animal representation (e.g. *macaco*, "ape" or "monkey"). Human nature, that from which the human emerges and which should not coincide with animal nature, can only exist through a structure of referencing and imitation, articulated by an animal—as arche-animal. This arche-animal emerges as a procedure by means of which the human can imitate the very thing which is fact created by this imitation: here copying is originary.

In *The Open*, Giorgio Agamben puts forth what he calls the anthropological machine as the way through which the human understands itself as nonanimal, crucially, in it the arche-animality of aping figures as related to, but separate from, the ape as a "vulgar" animal. He posits that the anthropological machine "is an optical machine constructed of a series of mirrors in which man, looking at himself, sees his own image always already deformed in the features of an ape" (2004, 27). The whole of the machine, however, despite containing an ape, itself functions as a form of aping: "In medieval iconography, the ape holds a mirror in which the man who sins must recognise himself as *simia dei* [ape of God]" (ibid.). Just as the sinner must ape God and follow in Jesus's ways, the human must choose to follow the image of humanness which is only suggested by the anthropological machine. If in the mirror of the machine the man sees an ape, he probably misses the fact that the whole machine is probably being held by an arche-ape.

Macaquear, an arche-animal, is, thus, another instance of paleonymy in the novel, alongside *escuridade* and the flickering itself between *dar a luz* and *dar à luz*, which Martim finally recognizes and accepts during his epiphany: "that man knew that he had to believe only in light [*claridade*] and in darkness [*escuridão*]" (Lispector 1985, 3.iii.240). By putting forth aping as the supplementary element that articulates human and animal, nature and culture, represented and representation, Lispector underscores the arche-animality which is always already at play in the supplementarity of light and dark.

NOTES

1. All further references are to this edition and are given as an Arabic numeral representing one of the three parts, a Roman numeral for the chapter number, and a page number. Rabassa's published translation has been mostly modified in order to match the original more closely.

2. Crucial for our reading of the zoopoetics of supplementarity in Lispector is Derrida's argument that "animality […] represents here the still living myth of fixity, of symbolic incapacity, of nonsupplementary. If we consider the *concept* of animality not in its content of understanding or misunderstanding but in the *function* reserved for it, we shall see that it must locate a moment of *life* which knows nothing of symbol, substitution, lack and supplementary addition, etc." (2016, 263). For that reason, it is important to stress that the desire for the presence of Nature must in fact be limited by an *almost*. The space between the supplementary symbol that strives to grasp the presence of Nature and Nature itself must not disappear: "nature is the ground, the inferior step: it must be crossed, exceeded, but also rejoined. We must return to it, but without annulling the difference. This difference must be *almost nil*, separating the imitation from what it imitates. Through the voice [vowel] one must transgress animal, savage, mute, infant or crying nature; by singing transgress or modify the voice. But the song must imitate cries and laments" (2016, 214, emphasis in original).

3. The grave accent over the *a* in the standard expression marks the germination of the preposition "to" (*a*) and the article "the" (*a*), in what is known in Portuguese as *crasis*: thus, **a a luz* is rendered as *à luz*.

4. "In the case of [the preposition] *a* plus the feminine article *a*, contraction of the geminate vowels was definitive. […] As European Portuguese

typically has a vowel of open quality of a contraction of this type, the agglutinated form [a] is there opposed to [ə] for either the preposition or the article alone. In Brazil, on the other hand, neither the central vowel nor the mid vowels are ever open when in unstressed position, but there is, in compensation, a secondary stress on the agglutinated preposition plus article form, which therefore is open. There is a slight difference, however, because secondary stress is possible, and indeed frequent, even on the simple preposition. This results, of course, in the loss of the phonological distinction between the latter and the agglutinated form" (Câmara Jr. 1972, 156–157). "In European Portuguese, [...] [the] vowel /a/ is always realized as [ɐ] in unstressed position" (Mateus and d'Andrade 2000, 18). "In BP [Brazilian Portuguese], the unstressed vowel [ɐ] only occurs in word-final position" (Mateus and d'Andrade 2000, 134). It is worth noting that the slightly raised version of /a/ is sometimes transcribed either as [ə] or [ɐ]. Therefore, in Portugal, deu à luz ("gave birth") is pronounced/ˌdewaˈluʃ/, whereas deu a luz is /ˌdewɐˈluʃ/. In Brazil, both forms are pronounced /ˌdewaˈlujs/.

5. Rocco's webpage for *The Apple in the Dark* states that the current (1998) edition of the novel "went through a rigorous textual revision [...] based on the first edition" (2014, my translation). Curiously, the first edition does indeed contain the incorrect, colloquial "dar a luz" (without the accent), which Rocco have indeed corrected in the current edition despite their disclaimer to the contrary. As it is, one cannot know whether Lispector originally wrote the informal variety or whether the first edition might have changed her 'correct' use of the expression to the informal one that they published.

6. It is well known that Derrida in "The Animal that Therefore I Am (More to Follow)" inscribes identity, subjectivity, the "I am" (*je suis*) or the *ergo sum* within the act of pursuit, of the "I follow" (*je suis*) (2008). I *am* only to the extent that I *follow* and pursue something or someone (*je suis donc je suis*, I follow therefore I am), so that the pursued element emerges as primary. I am/follow an animal because humanity comes after animality so as to supersede and improve it, or so the humanist and/or evolutionary story goes. But, as we saw, the idea of the animal embodiment of the soul suggests a primacy of the thinking subject—if I follow the animal, things start with the *I*. Crucially, the connection between the verbs "to follow" and "to be" in French only exists in the first person singular.

7. The sentence I coined in a previous footnote describing the necessity of following to being—*je suis donc je suis*—displays the same undecidability. It can mean both "I follow therefore I am" and "I am therefore I follow," with the latter establishing the primacy of the I—I can follow only to the extent that *I am an I*. In this sentence, it is not clear which

version of phrase *je suis* follows which, as the phrase "gives the *change*" as it exchanges itself with its double within the sentence unnoticeably.

8. It is interesting to note that Martim's confidence in being able to bypass language to achieve presence is coded in terms of having an object "ready to hand." Like Rousseau, his self-reliant recourse to that which is at hand is undertaken, in a certain sense, as a substitute for or analogous to "sleeping with a woman." The syntax of the last sentence in the quoted passage is ambiguous: either he "would have already know [things]" intimately and directly the same way a man knows a woman intimately when he sleeps with her, or his knowing things by the means of the hand is being presented as just as good as knowing them in the light so that he would be indistinguishable from a "real man" who has lain with a woman, as if making recourse to the substitutes at hand were no different from the real thing. In more than one way, his self-reliance comes across as masturbatory.

WORKS CITED

Agamben, Giorgio. 2004. *The Open: Man and Animal*, trans. by Kevin Attel. Stanford: Stanford University Press.

Arrojo, Rosemary. 1999. Interpretation as Possessive Love: Hélène Cixous, Clarice Lispector, and the Ambivalence of Fidelity. In *Postcolonial Translation: Theory and Practice*, ed. Susan Bassnett and Harish Trivedi, 141–161. London: Routledge.

Bennington, Geoffrey. 1993. Derridabase. In *Jacques Derrida*, ed. Geoffrey Bennington and Jacques Derrida, 3–316. Chicago: University of Chicago Press.

Câmara Jr, Joaquim Mattoso. 1972. *The Portuguese Language*, trans. Anthony J. Naro. Chicago: University of Chicago Press.

Cixous, Hélène. 1990. *The Apple in the Dark*: The Temptation of Understanding. In *Reading with Clarice Lispector*, ed. and trans. Verena Andermatt Conley, 60–97. Minneapolis: University of Minnesota Press.

Derrida, Jacques. 2008. *The Animal That Therefore I Am*, trans. David Wills and ed. Marie-Louise Mallet. New York: Fordham University Press.

———. 2016. *Of Grammatology*, trans. Gayatri Chakravorty Spivak, introduction by Judith Butler. Baltimore: John Hopkins University Press.

Fitz, Earl E. 2001. *Sexuality and Being in the Poststructuralist Universe of Clarice Lispector: The Différance of Desire*, 9. Austin: University of Texas Press.

Kates, Joshua. 2005. *Essential History: Jacques Derrida and the Development of Deconstruction*. Evanston, IL: Northwestern University Press.

Lawlor, Leonard. 2007. *This Is Not Sufficient: An Essay on Animality and Human Nature in Derrida*. New York: Columbia University Press.

Lispector, Clarice. 1985. *The Apple in the Dark*, trans. Gregory Rabassa. London: Virago.

———. 1999. *A maçã no escuro*. Rio de Janeiro: Rocco.

Mateus, Maria Helena, and Ernesto d'Andrade. 2000. *The Phonology of Portuguese*. Oxford: Oxford University Press.

Piskorski, Rodolfo. 2015. Of Zoogrammatology as a Positive Literary Theory. *Journal of Literary Theory* 9: 230–249.

Rabassa, Gregory. 1985. *Introduction to The Apple in the Dark*, ed. Clarice Lispector, ix–xvi. London: Virago.

Ravindranathan, Thangam, and Antoine Traisnel. 2016. What Gives (*Donner le change*). *SubStance* 45: 143–160.

Rocco. 2014. A Maçã no Escuro. Accessed February 7, 2017. http://www.rocco.com.br/index.php/livro?cod=2213.

"Constituents of a Chaos": Whale Bodies and the Zoopoetics of *Moby-Dick*

Michaela Castellanos

In Herman Melville's *Moby-Dick* (2007 [1851]), the whale body figures prominently as an exasperatingly difficult-to-grasp organism. A "system-ized exhibition of the whale is his broad genera," the narrator Ishmael notes, amounts to nothing less than "the classification of the constitu-ents of a chaos" (Melville 2007, 133). Ishmael pokes fun at reputable scientists, the "lights of zoology and anatomy," for knowing so little of the whale and admitting that an "impenetrable veil" covers their "knowl-edge of the cetacea" (ibid.). For Ishmael, matters are, in fact, quite sim-ple: "a whale is *a spouting fish with a horizontal tail*. There you have him" (135, original emphasis). Whales are, of course, not fish but mam-mals, and this was already an established notion at the time *Moby-Dick* was written. Ishmael even explicitly acknowledges this by remarking that Linnaeus, in his *System of Nature*, declared whales separate from the fish because they have warm blood, lungs, movable eyelids, and hollow ears, with males having penises for reproduction and females having teats for nursing like other animals that live on land (ibid.).[1]

M. Castellanos
Mid Sweden University, Sundsvall, Sweden

© The Author(s) 2018
K. Driscoll and E. Hoffmann (eds.), *What Is Zoopoetics?*,
Palgrave Studies in Animals and Literature,
https://doi.org/10.1007/978-3-319-64416-5_8

129

Nonetheless, the idea that whales should be mammals was not yet fully accepted, as we can also see from the fact that a New York court settled the question of whether whales were mammals or fish in 1818. A "cacophonous conversation about the order of nature" (Burnett 2007, 195) dominated the United States in the first half of the nineteenth-century, and it was full of passionate disagreements over taxonomic classification and its potentially unsettling implications about the place of man in the order of nature. *Moby-Dick*'s explicit engagement with the question "What is a Whale?"[2] thus imports a contentious discourse into the novel. Some of the uncertainties and anxieties surrounding this issue, I argue in this chapter, register in *Moby-Dick*'s literary animals, the "animals created by words" (Borgards 2015, 155).

Because whales played a crucial role in this divisive discourse, literary representations of whales in *Moby-Dick* do specific cultural work that can be better understood if we move beyond reading them as metaphors representing something other than whales, as has long been standard practice in literary studies.[3] Some scholars have begun to do just that and, approaching *Moby-Dick* from animal studies and ecocritical perspectives, are finding ways to read the novel's literary animals as animals.[4] For example, over the last few decades, there has been considerable scholarly interest in reading Melville's classic in the context of natural history.[5] To avoid ahistorical readings, textual analyses must historicize the prevailing attitudes toward particular animals, Philip Armstrong points out (2005, 97).[6] Armstrong discerns two competing structures of feeling in *Moby-Dick*: "humanized fellow-feeling and the calculus of market value and profit" (2004a, 1040). The cultural and historical contexts of the novel further suggest that *Moby-Dick*'s literary whales register, and at the same time communicate, that the notion of human exceptionalism had come under threat. *Moby-Dick* is full of textual tensions because it mobilizes the period's contradictory and sometimes incompatible approaches to classifying animals within a comprehensive system. The implications of this endeavor for human (self-) understanding are negotiated in the novel's complex interplays between different types of literary animals.

A ZOOPOETIC CETOLOGY

Moby-Dick registers the deep-seated anxieties about bodies and how to interpret them that pervaded American culture in the first half of the nineteenth century. For Aaron Moe, language and animality are co-constitutive insofar as the material animal body creates the impulse to grasp it in language. Moe defines *zoopoetics* as "the process of discovering innovative breakthroughs in form through an attentiveness to another species' bodily *poiesis*" (Moe 2014, 10, original emphasis). This definition acknowledges animal agency in the poetic process, but the poetic process itself is somewhat reductively characterized as a rather straightforward translation from animal body to human language. In *Moby-Dick*, language and animality are intertwined in a more complicated way: Ishmael ruminates excessively about his inability to capture the essence of the whale in words, and he grapples not only with the difficulties of parsing the whale's body in language but also with the impossibility of fully describing its myriad cultural meanings. This makes Kári Driscoll's understanding of zoopoetics as the inseparable intertwinement of animality and language (2015, 223) more useful for approaching the novel. If "poetics in general" treats "language as both the medium and the message," Driscoll writes, "zoopoetics is concerned not only with the constitution of the animal in and through language, but also the constitution of language in relation and in opposition to the figure of the animal" (ibid.). In *Moby-Dick*, language self-reflexively gestures toward the whale without ever fully comprehending it, and it is precisely in this gesturing—which marks the *impossibility* of straightforward translation—that language and animality become co-constitutive.

Ishmael's self-description, as it were, as a whale author outlines his endeavour as a zoopoetic one. The narrator's excessive descriptions aimed at approximating the whale in the chapter entitled "Cetology" do not have a complete and neat taxonomy as their *telos*; the classificatory system Ishmael presents instead satirizes the classifying endeavour of the natural sciences by suggesting that whales should be divided "into three primary books (subdivisible into chapters)," and accordingly named "[t]he Folio whale, the Octavo whale, and the Duodecimo whale" after books of a particular size (Melville 2007, 136). Ishmael here plays on the purported correspondence between the superficial characteristics of material objects such as size and the information supposedly contained on their inside, and this mock-cetology expresses suspicion toward a science that sought to make definitive claims about the true nature of things based on exterior appearances. Language constitutes the human and nonhuman animals in the novel, and language is the site on which the contingencies and consequences of taxonomic classification are explored. In a well-known chapter on *Moby-Dick* in *Melville's Anatomies*, literary scholar Samuel Otter interprets Ishmael's cetology as a critical comment on physiognomy (a practice in which inferences about a person's character are drawn from observing his or her facial features) and phrenology (the comparative study of skulls, which, among other things, was used to ascribe less-than-human status to Africans). The interactions between whales and African, Native American, and Pacific Islander characters in *Moby-Dick* are indeed the vehicles through which this critique of pseudosciences is routed, and Otter reads the whale body simultaneously as a material organism and as a representation of the animalized human body in his analysis. Yet the literary whales in the novel simultaneously import meanings associated with the whale body in the nineteenth century, a time in which the whale body was very much a site of epistemological contestation and biopolitical control. In *Animal Capital*, Nicole Shukin extends Michel Foucault's argument that "society's control over individuals was accomplished not only through consciousness or ideology, but also in the body and with the body" (Foucault 2000, 137) to animal bodies (Shukin 2009, 8), and Colleen Boggs argues in the same vein that "the 'anatomopolitics' of the modern state does not limit its reach to human bodies but also exercises power over animal bodies" (2013, 11). For Boggs, literary representations of animals in nineteenth-century American literature "form the nexus where biopolitical relationships get worked out" (ibid., 13). Moe's notion of "another species' bodily *poeisis*" can thus be productively extended by conceptualizing the body as a site on which discourses collide and on which biopolitical forces act. Read through a zoopoetic lens, *Moby-Dick* negotiates the contingencies of the categories human and animal simultaneously.

Moby-Dick was written and published in the Golden Age of American whaling when whale bodies had become a driving force of the national economy.[7] The increased economic value of the whale body affected a change in its cultural meanings as well. The industrialization of whaling, in other words, impacted the ways in which whales function as *animal capital*. Shukin uses the term animal capital to underscore that "animal signs and the carnal traffic in animal substances" (2009, 7) cannot be separated from one another. In the same way, the notion of zoopoetics is grounded in a conceptualization of the material and the semiotic as co-constitutive. Zoopoetics reconceives language as emergent from a creative, more-than-human process and poetics as not exclusively human while acknowledging that rendering animals in language involves power relations that are inherently askew. Ishmael's cetology is a decidedly zoopoetic endeavor: by engaging ostensibly with the various other taxonomies into which the whale could have been placed in the period and by eventually placing it into a bookish cetology, the narrator stages the whale body as the site of epistemological contestation.

A CETOLOGICAL ZOOPOETICS

As historian of science D. Graham Burnett points out, the cultural resistance to the reclassification of whales complicates "the narrative that considers the late eighteenth and early nineteenth century the 'golden age' of the classificatory sciences" (2007, 194). While scientists certainly considered systematic classification "a proper order in which things had names and places in schematic hierarchies that were themselves [...] reflections of the nature of things," laymen worried that it displaced other types of knowledge, such as the knowledges communicated in vernacular natural histories, folk taxonomies, and biblical accounts of creation (ibid., 86).

The idea that humans enjoyed a special place outside of a systematic scheme that could comprehend the animal kingdoms was threatened by problematic organisms like whales. Some types of animals could not be accommodated in the accepted classifying systems of the time and, as I will explain in more detail later, furthermore upset laymen taxonomies such as the biblical one, which distinguished between beasts, birds, and fish. This prompted Linnaeus to devise a new category by the name of *mammifers* which could accommodate anomalous organisms. Because the physical traits shared by animals in this group were also shared with humans, it became increasingly more difficult to maintain that humans were not animals (Burnett 2007). The literary representations of whales in *Moby-Dick* are a repository for anxieties resulting from this threat to human self-understanding.

Like whales in the middle of the nineteenth century, the literary whales in *Moby-Dick* elude unambiguous classification. They take many shapes in the novel, appearing as living animals, dead animals, consumer products derived from whale bodies (such as blubber and spermaceti oil), and artifacts made from whale teeth and baleen, but also as characters in stories and images in paintings. This diverse range of representations brings the distinction between *diegetic animals*, those literary animals that appear as living beings in story-world, and *semiotic animals*, those that appear only by name in the diegesis to denote someone or something other than an animal (Borgards 2012, 89, my translation), to its limits. Many of *Moby-Dick*'s whales operate simultaneously in both modes and therefore share a conceptual unwieldiness with whales in the controversial discourse on the order of nature. Frustrating the desire for a conclusive answer to the question of their ontology, they emphasize the tensions between the logics that undergirded the prevalent options for classification.

Tensions concerning who wielded the definitional power over the whale body are a central concern in the chapter entitled "A Bower in the Arsacides." Here, before presenting his opinions on the topic of cetacean anatomy, the whaler Ishmael first concedes that the reader might react with incredulity to his claim to be an expert in such matters. In a mock argument between the narrator and an imaginary person who presents a series of objections to Ishmael's authority, several possible ways to classify the anomalous whale organism are pitted against one another.

> But how now, Ishmael? How is it that you, a mere oarsman in the fishery, pretend to know about the subterranean parts of the whale? Did erudite Stubb, mounted upon your capstan, deliver lectures on the anatomy of the Cetacea; and by help of the windlass, hold up a *specimen rib* for exhibition? Explain thyself, Ishmael. Can you land a *full-grown whale* on your deck for examination, as a cook dishes *roast-pig*? Surely not. A veritable witness have you hitherto been, Ishmael; but have a care how you seize the privilege of discoursing upon the joists and beams; the rafters; ridge-pole, sleepers, and underpinnings, making up the framework of leviathan; and belike of the *tallow*-vats, *dairy*-rooms, *butteries, cheeseries* in his bowels is Jonah's alone. (Melville 2007, 395, my emphases)

First, the objector challenges the whaler's authority for the simple fact that whalers are not scientists. Stubb, Ishmael's crewmate, is characterized as a mere layman by the *absence* of the specimen rib, which metonymically represents the whale as an object of scientific knowledge. Conversely, the specimen rib suggests that the scientist ought to be considered the proper whale authority. The specimen rib (not present but invoked in the diegesis) thus transfers negative qualities onto Stubb, an individualized whaler, while transferring positive qualities onto a generalized scientist (who is neither present in the diegesis nor in the embedded story-world). In the embedded story-world created by the rhetorical question, the specimen rib appears as a diegetic animal—if not as a living animal then, nevertheless, as part of a once-alive animal—and there represents the scientific knowledge of scientists, who drew abstract conclusions about whale anatomy from animal bones and used such bones to visualize scientific principles. The semiotic currency of the specimen rib thus helps establish the scientist, not the whaler, as the true authority.

Because the rib also denotes a piece of whale cadaver, however, it simultaneously undermines the scientist's authority. Scientists were mocked for rarely venturing out onto the open ocean to observe whales' behavior in their natural habitat and only studied dead whales.[8] When the trial *Maurice v. Judd* sought to settle the legal question of whether whales were fish or not in 1818, the testimonies of whalers were given more credit than scientists' opinions, because the former's direct experience with the whale body and whale behavior made them credible authorities on the subject of whales while the latter's abstract knowledge met much resistance.[9]

Through its complexity, this literary whale brings literary taxonomy to its limit and makes a clear distinction between semiotic and diegetic animal impossible. It draws on the signifying power of the material organism as well as on the social and cultural context in which it is ascribed meaning. Reducing the dead animal body to a particular function, namely illustrating scientific knowledge, the specimen rib is barely legible as an animal representation at all. By pointing to something other than to the animal, this metaphor achieves a similar effect as a physical rendering of the whale body: it reduces the animal to an object of human *telos*. Yet as the rib's signifying power rests on a tension between diegetic absence and presence, it invites the reader to oscillate between literal and figurative interpretation.[10] It is precisely this instability that makes the specimen rib an animal representation in Boggs's sense. For Boggs, the term *animal representation* acknowledges a tension inherent in the term representation, which is used as a "more generic term for depiction in the context of literature" but has a more specific meaning in a political context, where it "suggests the ability to be recognized by a subject in the political system and to participate in it" (2013, 19). The fact that animals are represented in the literary sense but "cannot have representation" in the political sense, Boggs argues, achieves "a representation of animals' *exclusion* from representation" (ibid., my emphasis). On the basis of such representation, the "terms of animals' exclusion become legible" and are opened up to critique (ibid., 20). If we read the rib as an animal representation in this sense, it simultaneously represents the material whale organism; a body of whale knowledge; the authority to claim knowledge of the whale body and to interpret it; and the animal life eclipsed in the process. The specimen rib then also stands in for a life unable to represent itself, a life without moral or legal standing.

The fact that it is, of all bones, the rib that represents scientific authority humorously references the fact that the difficult endeavor of classifying whale bodies ultimately threatened to displace Man. The rib invokes the biblical creation myth, according to which God first created Adam and then created Eve from Adam's rib. According to the same creation myth, man was utterly distinct from animals because he was created in God's image. The book of Genesis set out the order of nature by separating all animals into three kingdoms: beasts, birds, and fish. Those animals that crept on land were beasts, those that flew in the air were birds, and those that swam in the water were fish (Burnett 2007, 21). It therefore seemed preposterous to think that whales could be anything but fish. What else could they be, as they neither lived in the air nor on land? Those clinging to a biblical understanding of nature had trouble with the idea that whales were in any way exceptional, as man was the only creature with a place outside of the natural order. Science offended sensibilities by implicitly suggesting that the biblical taxonomy should be abandoned, and even more so by suggesting a very troubling new category. The category *mammifers* is based on features such as teats for nursing, and this implicitly suggested that humans might be placed into this category as well. By humorously suggesting that man was created from the rib of the whale, the specimen rib also alludes to the devastating implications of whale anatomy on the biblical understanding of man.

In a second objection, Ishmael's imaginary interlocutor then challenges how complete a whaler's understanding of cetacean anatomy could be. Ishmael's authority is called into question because a "full-grown" whale is impossible to behold in its entirety. Ishmael concedes that neither a scientist nor a whaler can fully comprehend the anatomy of an adult whale, but counters that he once "[broke] the seal and read [...] all the contents of [a] young cub" (Melville 2007, 395). The verb "reading" here semantically entangles the whale with books, knowledge, the Bible, written language, science, and the transgression of boundaries, and, taken together, all of these connotations characterize the dissection of the whale calf as sacrilegious. The way in which the violation of the whale body is described as an attempt to extract knowledge contained on its inside constitutes a veiled allusion to the apocalypse, which is initiated by the breaking of the seven seals in the book of Revelation. The implication here is that cetacean anatomy is a forbidden fruit that, once tasted, will usher in a new era that profoundly changes the world.

The biblical notion that man was granted dominion over all animals aligned neatly with the taxonomies of the market, and this is implied in a simile that compares possessing knowledge of whale anatomy to serving a roasted pig. The two organisms, whale calf and pig, are similar in size and small enough to behold in their entirety, but the simile also draws on the connotations associated with the pig, which was unambiguously classified as a beast, making the consumption of its meat morally unproblematic. The objector seems to ask whether a whaler can firmly place the whale into one of the biblical categories. Ishmael's declaration that the whale is a fish is inextricably linked to the idea that fish were created specifically to sustain man. This logic underpins the biblical taxonomy and justifies the commodification of whales. The whale calf made of words, like the specimen rib, evokes a diegetic whale that semiotically represents a body of whale knowledge; in this literary whale, the material and semiotic properties of whales are intertwined. Both of these literary animals are receptacles of the conflict-laden discourse on whales of the period. Animal agency is an integral element of the poetic process from which they emerge.

The third objection continues to develop the idea that the whale is created for the benefit of man. The metaphors tallow-vats, dairy-rooms, butteries, and cheeseries describe the interior of the whale body as places in which animal products are stored. Like pigs, dairy animals fell clearly under the dominion of man. On the one hand, the butteries and cheeseries bring the monstrous whale body into the realm of the familiar and the controlled. On the other hand, they fail to do so completely because they also problematize the interdependence of biblical and artisan taxonomies. Metaphors involving products derived from farm animals' bodies function on the semiotic level but are inseparable from how animal products function as capital in the storyworld. Through Boggs's concept of animal representation, we can also see the tallow-vats, butteries, and cheeseries as metonymic representations of living beings and the exclusion of these beings from representation. The language in this passage is zoopoetic because it corresponds to the way in which commodification precludes the representation of animal life. The metaphors' *telos* is anthropocentric, but at the same time, animal meaning cannot be totally subsumed and controlled.

These metaphors further create a semantic link between mammalian traits and the commodification of bodies. This link implies that the animalization of bodies is facilitated by an intersection of religious and economic interests. The similarities between human and whale bodies caused moral concern about turning them into consumer products, as I will explore in the next section, which was a direct outcome of their unclear status in the Biblical taxonomy. Animals such as cows and sheep, too, gave birth to live young and nursed, but they could be exploited without scruples because they clearly fell under the dominion of man. The literary whale in this passage—Jonah's whale in the rendition of an objector imagined by the narrator—thus embodies a threat to human self-understanding and opens up the logics of animal exploitation to closer scrutiny. The intertext of the book of Jonah in the Bible further suggests that the whale body was purposefully designed to shelter and provide for the prophet. The whale body in this example serves as an object of religious knowledge, and this religious knowledge is inseparable from the economic uses to which the animal body may be put. Like other whales in *Moby-Dick*, this literary whale records the commodification of historical whales by the whaling industry and at the same time points out that rendering animals in language also commodifies them: Whales created by words store meanings.

Nevertheless, the unwieldiness of *Moby-Dick*'s literary whales leaves a space in which animals' exclusion from representation becomes legible. The zoopoetic language in this passage also allows for a reading in which the tallow-vats, butteries, and cheeseries represent a material whale body and its biological functions, such as fat storage and digestion. Crafted in poetic language, the mock objections construct the whale body as the site on which scientific, religious, and economic logics interact: These logics converge, collide, or become indistinguishable from one another. This makes the whale representations incongruent, and this in turn makes it difficult to ascribe them a single, specific *telos*.

ENTANGLED FUNGIBILITY, FUNGIBLE ENTANGLEMENT

As Ishmael's cetological explorations perform the implications of the period's taxonomies and the connections between them, *Moby-Dick* probes the contingencies and consequences of classifying whales. In the novel's language, animality and metaphoricity become entangled and fungible. This has implications for representations of animals as well as for representations of humans. When whales are represented in human form in the novel, this often has a humorous and sentimentalizing effect and reflects two historical attitudes toward whales that competed with one another: a sense of "humanized fellow-feeling" and an appreciation of their bodies as a driving force of the American economy (Armstrong 2004a, 1040). The chapter entitled "The Grand Armada" first emphasizes physical similarities between whales and humans and then frames the whale body as a resource to be harvested. This, Armstrong argues, produces sympathy for the hunted whales. When a harpooned whale drags one of the *Pequod*'s whaling boats through a large group of frantically fleeing sperm whales, it stops in the calm center where the female whales and their young seem to have been purposefully sheltered. In this "innermost fold" (Melville 2007, 345), the whalers discover a female that has evidently just given birth:

> As when the stricken whale, that from the tub has reeled out hundreds of fathoms of rope; as, after deep sounding, he floats up again, and shows the slackened curling line buoyantly rising and spiraling towards the air; so now Starbuck saw long coils of the umbilical cord of Madame Leviathan, by which the young cub seemed still tethered to his dam. Not seldom in the vicissitudes of the chase, this natural line, with the maternal end loose, becomes entangled so that the cub is thereby trapped. We saw young leviathan amours in the deep.* (346)

Words such as "Madame Leviathan" and "dam" encourage empathy with the animal; additionally, the description of the female and newborn whales as "small tame cows and calves" and "the women and children of this routed host" (345) characterizes them as more vulnerable and in need of protection. The image of an umbilical cord, the fetus's life support until its birth, underscores this image of vulnerability. When the umbilical cord is compared to a harpoon line, a dissonant simile results from the very different connotations of these two objects. Dissonance is amplified in the footnote to this passage, which reads as follows:

> *The sperm whale, as with all other species of the Leviathan, but unlike most other fish, breeds indifferently at all seasons; after a gestation which may probably be set down at nine months, producing but one at a time; though in some few known instances giving birth to an Esau and Jacob.

[...] When by chance these precious parts in a nursing whale are cut by the hunter's lance, the mother's pouring milk and blood rivallingly discolor the sea for rods. The milk is very sweet and rich; it has been tasted by man; it might do well with strawberries. When overflowing with mutual esteem, the whales salute *more hominum*. (346)

Here, the female whale is referred to as "mother," and the occasional occurrence of twin birth in whales is indicated with the help of a metaphor involving Jacob and Esau. Considering the implications of cetology on the biblical order of nature, I suggest that these metaphors would also have evoked a considerable level of discomfort in addition to sympathy. While the appeal to motherhood might have evoked a positive sense of fellow feeling, at least some readers of the period would have also reacted with repulsion. The footnote suggests that the gestation period of sperm whales might be nine months, and this suggests an equivalence between whales and humans that many would have considered provocative.

In the same vein, whale milk is equated with human breast milk in this footnote, and this undermines the biblical classifying logic, indicating that whales confused any clear division between humans and animals; at the same time, it is equated with dairy products, which upholds the taxonomy. The implicit comparison of nursing whales to white middle class mothers in particular would have been perceived as offensive (Burnett 2007, 14),[11] and the thought that whale milk should be consumed by anyone other than the newborn whale appears especially inappropriate. Because of the undeterminable nature of the whale, whale milk, unlike that of dairy animals, was not be consumed without hesitation. At the time of the novel's publication, the suggestion to serve whale milk with strawberries would have appeared even more jarring than it does today. Moreover, the insinuation that whales "salute" or kiss *more hominem*, or in the manner of humans, a thinly veiled description of whales having sexual intercourse face to face, explicitly discusses animal sexuality in human terms, which surely offended many a reader.

The umbilical cord merits special attention as it complicates the analogy between humans and whales further. Like the specimen rib, the whale calf, and Jonah's whale, the umbilical cord created by words in this passage entangles multiple meanings and metonymically represents the vulnerable whale body and animal life more generally. In sharp contrast, the harpoon line, a material tool in whaling, represents a threat to this life and the taking of animal life more generally. The umbilical cord metonymically links whales with all mammals, and thereby suggests that man and whale belong to the same category; yet the harpoon line represents the dividing line between human and animal, which remains in place irrespective of any shared physical traits and fellow feeling. At first semantically entangled in a simile that emphasizes their visual similarities, the umbilical cord and harpoon line later become entangled on the diegetic level: In the image of a trapped newborn whale caught up in a deadly chase, the umbilical cord metonymically represents a vulnerable newborn life unable to defend itself, and this image certainly encourages empathy toward the animal. To interpret the imagery in this scene as crude anthropomorphism, however, would disregard the way in which this entanglement performs against itself. In the context of the quoted passage and its footnote, fellow feeling does not exclusively evoke pity but also a deep-rooted suspicion of animality and a desire to reinstate hierarchy via a clear boundary between human and animal. In *Moby-Dick*'s zoopoetic language, whale and human may be described in terms of another, and the flow of meaning is not unidirectional. When animals are described as humans, the formers' incomprehensible nature colors this rendering; when humans are described as animals, both categories become less monolithic.

In the chapter entitled "The Monkey-Rope," the image of an umbilical cord imports another important facet of the contentious classificatory discourse. The umbilical cord is one of several fungible images with which the narrator describes a rope connecting Ishmael and Queequeg. The name of this rope, "monkey rope," calls to mind how science was instrumentalized in claims that the bodies of nonwhites were more like animal bodies than human bodies. Phrenology sought to provide empirical grounds for excluding racialized Others from the category of the human, while a divisive rhetoric of animality discursively suspended the racialized body between human and animal. The literary umbilical cord in the following passage complicates and counteracts such a rhetorical exclusion. After a successful whale hunt, Queequeg begins to process the body of a dead whale tied to the side of the whaleship. While standing on the slippery carcass, Ishmael secures him from the ship's deck with a rope.

You have seen Italian organ boys holding a dancing-ape by a *long cord*. Just so, from the ship's steep side, did I hold Queequeg down there in the sea, by what is technically called in the fishery a *monkey-rope*, attached to a strong strip of canvas belted round his waist. It was a humorously perilous business for both of us. For, before we proceed further, it must be said that the *monkey-rope* was fast at both ends; fast to Queequeg's broad canvas belt, and fast to my narrow leather one. So that for better or for worse, we two, for the time, were *wedded*; and should poor Queequeg sink to rise no more, then both usage and honor demanded, that instead of cutting the cord, it should drag me down in his wake. So, then, an *elongated Siamese ligature* united us. Queequeg was my own inseparable twin brother; nor could I any way get rid of the dangerous *liabilities* which the *hempen bond* entailed. (Melville 2007, 288–289, my emphasis)

Like the whale bodies, human bodies, umbilical cords, and harpoon lines in the passages I discussed previously, the objects at stake in this example also complicate any sharp distinction between diegetic and semiotic objects. These lines made of words act as metaphors for the relationship between Ishmael and Queequeg. As Ishmael ventures into an explanation of the figurative meanings of the rope that joins the two characters in the diegesis, he first compares it to a leash; then to marital ties; to a shared umbilical cord; and, finally, to the shared risk the men take by participating in whaling. Because the term monkey rope imports the connotations associated with the animal from which it takes its name, Queequeg is inevitably animalized by the first metaphor. The narrator then lavishes other connotations onto the rope which imply that the relationship between the two men is a more complex and decidedly equal one.

In this passage, the rope has three incongruent meaning: the unequal power balance between an animal and its owner, the commitment made by a married couple, a life-sustaining connection, and a jointly taken risk. The image of a shared umbilical cord suggests that Ishmael and Queequeg are biologically identical, and this rhetorically elevates the harpooner to fully human status. The zoopoetic language of this passage thwarts a unidirectional transfer of animality, and the fluidity of the literary representation again emphasizes that the category "human" has pragmatic contingencies. The conflation of the monkey rope with an umbilical cord represents the connection between whaling and equality. Ishmael's asserts that this cord would not even be cut if both men went overboard; if Queequeg perishes, so does Ishmael. Even if the harpooneer is considered less than human by others because of his race, on the sea, his occupation as a whaler makes him equal. Historically, the "ideological system put in place by the white race to exert political control over others; to amass wealth by appropriating other people's land, resources, and labour; and to enjoy privileges and prestige"—proved not as adaptable to the context of whaling (Shoemaker 2015, 5). On board whaling ships, the lived experience of race often proved an exception to the rule, as, for example, the high status attained by Native American whalers among their crews, documented by Nancy Shoemaker, shows. Like the harpoon line and umbilical cord in "The Grand Armada," the monkey rope imports the contentious discourse of zoological classification and its implications for the conceptualization of the human. *Moby-Dick*'s literary animals are a body of language on which the pervasive uneasiness about whale bodies and human self-understanding are worked out.

When historicized attitudes toward whales are brought to bear on the novel and *Moby-Dick* is contextualized with history of science, the cultural work accomplished by its literary animals comes into sharper focus. Language performs the impossibility of comprehending and communicating any true essence; it upsets the quest after a veritable animal or human nature. As a result, taxonomies, their functions, limits, and contingencies gain greater prominence. While whales were far removed from the everyday lives of most Americans, the embodied experience of whalers, commerce in whale products, and the scientific interests associated with whaling brought these uncanny animals uncomfortably close. Impossible to accommodate in lay taxonomies, whales challenged the notion that humans were utterly distinct from animals even before Darwin's *On the Origin of Species* (1859) made this idea inescapable. *Moby-Dick*'s whales, I have argued here, are a receptacle for the power struggles, inadequacies, and implications of systemic classification that still loomed large in the first half of the nineteenth century. Ishamel's zoopoetic cetology sets the tone for all encounters with literary animals throughout the novel. Simultaneously expressing and frustrating a desire to come to terms with whales and what they mean, Ishmael's cetology emerges from and reflects a specifically cetacean poetics.

NOTES

1. Linnaeus initially classified whales as fish in the first edition of *Systema Naturae* but moved them to the mammals in the tenth edition published in 1758, which is cited in *Moby-Dick*.
2. See Hub Zwart's chapter of the same title for a reading of *Moby-Dick* as a case study in comparative epistemology (2008, 77–98).
3. Susan McHugh remarks that the reading practices common in literary studies make animals disappear by directing critical attention elsewhere. Likening such practices to a magician who puts a rabbit into his hat, she calls this the "disappearing animal trick": "Now you see the animal. Now you don't" (2009, 24).
4. For a critique of reading practices that either ignore animals in literary texts or treat them exclusively as metaphors, see e.g. Simons (2002), Armstrong (2008), McHugh (2009), and Copeland (2012). Armstrong (2008, 101) and Copeland (2012, 91) specifically discuss that the whales in *Moby-Dick* are rarely read as animals.
5. For a recent overview of the historical trajectory of *Moby-Dick* scholarship, see Brian Yother's chapter "The Critic and the Whale" in the edited volume *Moby-Dick: Critical Insights* (2014). Yother dates critical attention to the natural environment, the human body, and race in *Moby-Dick* to the 1980s (2014, 54–55 and 21, respectively). Jonathan A. Cook, in a chapter in the same volume, offers an exploration of *Moby-Dick* in the context of natural history writing, a common pastime for laymen in the period. Cook pays attention to Melville's creative adaptation of the genre's conventions. The influence of visual arts and visual interpretation on *Moby-Dick*, according to Yothers, came into the focus of literary critics in the 1990s (2014, 54); it has more recently been pursued by Felix Lüttge (2016), who analyzes Melville's juxtaposition of whalers' and naturalists' knowledge in the novel's iconography. Lüttge's focus is on how the whale in the novel is constituted as an object of knowledge in relation to travelogues, whaling logbooks, and oceanographic maps.
6. Armstrong emphasizes that "historical differences between the world of the text and the world of that of the critic" can easily be elided or distorted if the critical method does not "fit with the poetic it explores" (2004, 21). For a criticism of approaches to *Moby-Dick* in which literary animals are read "as animals" without historicizing the prevalent attitudes of the era, see 2004b and 2005. Ecocritical readings of *Moby-Dick* by Elisabeth Schulz and Robert Zoellner are used as foils to make this point about ahistorical reading in the former, whereas Zoellner's reading is criticized for reinstating the very human/nature dichotomy it critiques in the latter.

7. Mark Bousquet locates the Golden Age of American whaling between the end of the War of 1812 and 1860. He describes three distinct phases of American whaling: drift whaling, or salvaging stranded cadavers, before 1650; shore-based whaling until the beginning of the eighteenth century; and open ocean whaling until 1860 (254). When whales no longer had to be pursued in rowboats and returned to the shore for processing, American whaling ships turned thousands of whales into consumer products every year during their globe-spanning, multiyear voyages.

8. Scientific knowledge was often dismissed as too abstract and philosophical. Burnett (2007, 44–94) and Zwart (2008, 81–85) emphasize that whalers and laymen doubted scientists' expertise on whales, because it did not extend to encounters with live animals.

9. See Burnett (2007) for an extensive interpretation of the trial *Maurice v. Judd* from a historian of science's perspective. The trial came about after Samuel Judd, a spermaceti merchant, refused to pay a mandatory whale oil inspection fee to inspector James Maurice. Judd argued that he was under no legal obligation to pay for an inspection of fish oil, if whales were in fact not fish, like scientists suggested. In the end, the court did rule that whales were mammals, not because scientific expertise was deemed credible, however, but "because of the behind-the-scenes legislative lobbying by a clique of oil merchants" (2007, 214).

10. My argument here rests on Boggs's contention that literary representations of animals always "raise the question of whether the animal is to be taken literally or figuratively" and thereby "confront readers with the complex terrain of epistemology and ontology, of representation and symbolization" (Boggs 2013, 33).

11. Burnett notes that "the implications of a system that puts bats and whales together in the same category with a young (white) woman with a baby at her breast—that essential feature of the *mammifers*—received probing and nervous scrutiny in the court" during the trial *Maurice v. Judd* (2007, 14, original emphasis).

WORKS CITED

Armstrong, Philip. 2004a. 'Leviathan Is a Skein of Networks': Translations of Nature and Culture in *Moby-Dick*. *ELH* 71 (4): 1039–1063.
———. 2004b. *Moby-Dick* and Compassion. *Society & Animals* 12 (1): 19–37.
———. 2005. What Animals Mean, in *Moby-Dick*, for Example. *Textual Practice* 19 (1): 93–111.
———. 2008. *What Animals Mean in the Fiction of Modernity*. London: Routledge.

Boggs, Colleen Glenney. 2013. *Animalia Americana: Animal Representations and Biopolitical Subjectivity*. New York: Columbia University Press.

Borgards, Roland. 2012. Tiere in der Literatur. In *Das Tier an Sich*, ed. Herwig Grimm and Carola Otterstedt, 87–118. Göttingen: Vandenhoeck & Ruprecht.

———. 2015. Introduction: Cultural and Literary Animal Studies. *Journal of Literary Theory* 9 (2): 155–160.

Bousquet, Mark. 2012. The Cruel Harpoon and the Honorable Lamp: The Awakening of an Environmental Consciousness in Henry Theodore Cheever's *The Whale and His Captors*. *Interdisciplinary Studies in Literature and Environment* 19 (2): 253–273.

Buell, Lawrence. 2001. *Writing for an Endangered World: Literature, Culture, and Environment in the U.S. and Beyond*. Cambridge, MA: Harvard University Press.

Burnett, D. Graham. 2007. *Trying Leviathan: The Nineteenth-Century New York Court Case That Put the Whale on Trial and Challenged the Order of Nature*. Princeton: Princeton University Press.

Cook, Jonathan A. 2014. *Moby-Dick* and Nineteenth Century Natural History. In *Moby-Dick: Critical Insights*, ed. Robert C. Evans, 191–208. Salem: Salem Press.

Copeland, Marion W. 2012. Literary Animal Studies in 2012: Where We Are, Where We Are Going. *Anthrozoös: A Multidisciplinary Journal of the Interactions of People & Animals* 25 (1): 91–105.

Driscoll, Kári. 2015. The Sticky Temptation of Poetry. *Journal of Literary Theory* 9 (2): 212–229.

Foucault, Michel. 2000. The Birth of Social Medicine. In *Power: Essential Works of Foucault 1954–1984*, vol. 3, trans. Robert Hurley and ed. James D. Faubion, 134–156. New York: New Press.

Lüttge, Felix. 2016. Weniger schlechte Bilder. Walfängerwissen in Naturgeschichte, Ozeonographie und Literatur im 19. Jahrhundert. *Berichte zur Wissenschaftsgeschichte* 39 (2): 127–142.

McHugh, Susan. 2009. *Animal Farm*'s Lessons for Literary (and) Animal Studies. *Humanimalia* 1 (10): 1–16.

Melville, Herman. 2007. *Moby-Dick*, ed. John Bryant and Haskell Springer. New York: Pearson Longman.

Moe, Aaron M. 2014. *Zoopoetics: Animals and the Making of Poetry*. Lanham, MD: Lexington Books.

Otter, Samuel. 1999. *Melville's Anatomies*. Berkeley: University of California Press.

Schultz, Elizabeth. 2010. Melville's Environmental Vision in *Moby-Dick*. *Interdisciplinary Studies in Literature and Environment* 7 (1): 97–113.

Shoemaker, Nancy. 2015. *Native American Whalemen and the World: Indigenous Encounters and the Contingency of Race*. Chapel Hill: University of North Carolina Press.

Shukin, Nicole. 2009. *Animal Capital: Rendering Life in Biopolitical Times*. Minneapolis: University of Minnesota Press.

Simons, John. 2002. *Animal Rights and the Politics of Literary Representation*. Basingstoke: Palgrave.

Yothers, Brian. 2014. The Critic and the Whale. In *Moby-Dick: Critical Insights*, ed. Robert C. Evans, 42–62. Salem: Salem Press.

Zoellner, Robert. 1973. *The Salt-Sea Mastodon: A Reading of Moby-Dick*. Berkeley: University of California Press.

Zwart, Hub. 2008. *Understanding Nature: Case Studies in Comparative Epistemology*. Dordrecht: Springer.

Queering the Interspecies Encounter: Yoko Tawada's *Memoirs of a Polar Bear*

Eva Hoffmann

In her novel *Memoirs of a Polar Bear* (2016, German original, *Etüden im Schnee*, 2014), Yoko Tawada conceptualizes human-animal relationships as a complex web of entanglement that brings both the bodily intimacy between individuals of different species and our global interconnectedness on an ecologically endangered planet to the foreground. In the novel, Tawada engages with the motifs of transnationalism and interculturalism that are familiar in her other works: the protagonists of this multigenerational narrative migrate from Soviet Russia to the German Democratic Republic, illegally crossing geographical and ideological borders, until finally arriving in the present-day reunified Germany. But she also transgresses borders between species, telling the story from multiple perspectives, including three generations of polar bears, whose lives—and at times physical bodies—are intricately intertwined with the human narrator. Like other works by Tawada, such as "Canned Foreign" ("*Das Fremde aus der Dose*") or *Where Europe Begins* (*Wo Europa anfängt*), *Memoirs of a Polar Bear* deploys the perspective of "the outsider" to

E. Hoffmann
Whitman College, Walla Walla, WA, USA

© The Author(s) 2018

K. Driscoll and E. Hoffmann (eds.), *What Is Zoopoetics?*,
Palgrave Studies in Animals and Literature,
https://doi.org/10.1007/978-3-319-64416-5_9

break the spell of habit: whether participating in a conference on energy politics or writing her autobiography, the polar bear's perspective evokes a sense of wonder, which leads the reader to question her own cultural conventions. However, resisting the essentialism that underpins categories of "animal" and "human," *Memoirs of a Polar Bear* also points to regulated sets of reiterated behaviors at work in the process of identity formation, shifting the notion of performativity from the discourse of gender and sexuality to the realm of species membership, and drawing attention to the complexities involved in the attempts to divide constructs of nature and culture.

Moreover, by making the intimate and erotic entanglement between bear and human the provenance for new narratives that open different ways of communication and deep forms of understanding between species, Tawada's novel resists a purely metaphorical reading of the polar bear as just another cultural outsider or stranger. Her specific approach to zoopoetics, rather, takes the desire between individuals across species borders as points of departure from which joint narratives emerge. These narratives present identity as fluid, defy the linearity of time and the logic of space, and run counter to heteropatriarchal systems that prioritize procreation over pleasure and heteronormative family structures over free kinship affiliation and affect. In other words, *Memoirs of a Polar Bear* queers zoopoetics by envisioning kinship formations between humans and other animals and by marking this desire both as productive for the poetic text and as a site where the critique of sexual violence intersects with speciesism and discourses on animal rights.

In this chapter, I illustrate how Tawada's zoopoetic writing engages animal figures in various ways: through intertextual and extratextual references—the novel alludes not only to a plethora of texts, legends, and shamanistic tales, from Franz Kafka's "A Report to an Academy" to the prevalence of bears in the mythology of many indigenous ethnic groups and religions,[1] but also draws on the popular history in the German Democratic Republic and postreunification Germany—*Memoirs of a Polar Bear* illustrates how human and nonhuman animals share and shape historical spaces, times, and narratives in conjunction with each other. The polar bear Tosca and her animal trainer Barbara were historical protagonists in the rise and demise of the German Democratic Republic's *Staatszirkus*, while Tosca's son Knut—the narrator of the last part of the novel—became arguably the most famous animal ever to inhabit a German zoo.

The intertextual references that the novel invokes, however, also draw attention to the performativity of textual animals. As Tawada's polar bears emerge through citations of other textual authorities, such as Heidegger and Descartes, the power of discourse, in the words of Judith Butler, to "produce that which it names" (Butler 1993, 17) comes to the forefront. I argue that the novel displays animality as another identity category that is produced by and performed through a humanistic discourse that poses animals as the "Other" and that intersects with the construction of race, gender, and sexuality. I read the intimate encounters between Tosca and Barbara in the second part of the novel as a queering of this discourse and illustrate how *Memoirs of a Polar Bear* reconceptualizes traditional relationships between circus animal and human trainer: rather than a relation of threat and vulnerability that needs to be contained by mastery and domination, Tosca enters an intimate relationship with her trainer Barbara that allows for a queer reading of the interspecies encounter. Moreover, *Memoirs of a Polar Bear* rejects the prevalence of "maternal instincts" and subverts the hegemonic logic of heterosexual procreation by placing emphasis on the practices of "making kin" (Haraway 2016, 4) across species lines. I argue that in the liminal spaces coshaped by human and bear, narratives emerge that follow what Judith Halberstam understands under queerness as "non-normative logics and organizations of community, sexual identity, embodiment, and activity in space and time" (Halbertstam 2005, 6) and that bring the notion of interspecies desire into the process of *poiesis*.

While traditional literary criticism often ignores the specific literariness of animals in texts, queer theory remains skeptical toward theories and practices of posthumanism that seem to operate under a general notion of "the human." In that regard, queer theory shares the concerns of decolonial thinkers, such as Sylvia Wynter, who argues that posthumanism all too often "secures our present ethnoclass (i.e., Western bourgeois) conception of the human, Man, [as that] which overrepresents itself as if it were the human itself" (Wynter 2003, 317). As part of the posthumanistic project, critical animal studies, therefore, also run the risk of perpetuating an epistemological framework of what Wynter calls "Man" with a capital "M." I suggest that Tawada's zoopoetic writing in *Memoirs of a Polar Bear* illustrates the need to understand "the animal" as a category that always intersects with constructions of gender, sexuality, and race in fundamental ways. A reading that is attentive to queer zoopoetics—meaning not only the specific role of animals in the production of the text, but also the sexual implications of such a comaking and the desire and affect that motivates it—liberates the animal from its metaphorical service and provides animality as a fundamental category that intersects with and underlies the construction of other human identity groups.

ANIMALITY AND PERFORMATIVITY

Rather than determining animals as ontologically different from humans, *Memoirs of a Polar Bear* displays animality as a category of identity that emerges through reiterated sets of behaviors. In doing so, Tawada shifts this notion of identity from the discourse of gender and sexuality to questions of humanity and animality. Drawing on observations on gender and sexuality, Judith Butler argues that any identity category is performed, rather than being the result of a stable and preconditioned entity or origin: "There is no I that precedes the gender that it is said to perform" (Butler 2004, 358). Replacing the notion of an original with practices of learned, repetitious behaviors—performances in Butler's understanding of the term—these performances shape the self and bring it to the forefront through discourse. Butler concludes that it is not only gender, but any identity is "always drag" (361)—a mimetic and hyperbolic effect that tries to conceal the missing origin (1993, 23). This notion of identity as "copy of a copy" with no underlying original (2004, 362), however, unfolds its subversive power in the process of self-repetition. Because the copy is never identical with what it tries to mimic, a "disruptive promise" (364) emerges in the process of identity performance. Discourse, Butler argues, drawing on Foucault's *History of Sexuality*, is, therefore, both the instrument and effect of power that shapes the self, *and* a point of resistance and a starting point for opposing strategies (354) as it opens possible sites of resistance against a compulsively heterosexual framework.

In *Memoirs of a Polar Bear*, Tawada displays an "animal self" that is in Butler's words "always already disrupted by that Other" (364): an Other that the self incorporates and that enables the very possibility of identity. The novel begins with the account of a nameless polar bear—the reader will later learn that she is the mother and grandmother of the two subsequent animal narrators—who attends a conference on the significance of bicycles for the national economy. The animal turns out to be well versed in the manners and habits necessary to navigate the professional codex—to the point where she leads the conversation. Her eloquent yet strangely anachronistic prognosis of a future society in which people ride their bikes to do laundry in the river captivates her audience, and allows for a temporary subversion of power relations between masculine and feminine, cultural "insider" and "outsider," human and animal:

> The first beat was the session's leader's restrained "Go ahead." The second beat was the word "I," which I slammed down on the table in front of me. On the third beat, all listeners swallowed, and on the fourth I took a daring step, clearly enunciating the words "think." To give it some swing, I naturally stressed the second and fourth beats.
> I had no intention of dancing, but my hips began waggling back and forth on the chair. The chair immediately chimed in, contributing cheerful creaks. Each stressed syllable was like a tambourine underscoring the rhythms of my speech. As if bewitched, the audience listened, forgetting their duties, their vanity, themselves. The men's lips hung limply open, their teeth gleaming a creamy white, and from the tips of their tongues dripped something like liquefied carnality in saliva form. (Tawada 2016, 6)

The polar bear's speech is spectacular, visual, and imitative—it is both performative *and* exposes the conference and academic discourse as a performance that she as a former circus animal masters to perfection. She uses her training in the arena, effectively manipulating the situation to her advantage, but she also gets carried away by her own performance. As the rhythm of her speech takes hold of her body, the bear cannot help but start to dance, a connection established through the process of conditioning. But it is not only the animal's body responding in a predetermined way: by emphasizing the physical reaction of her male audience in what reads like a playful commentary on Pavlov's experiments, Tawada questions precisely the distinction between man's ability to respond and the uncontrollable reaction to stimuli of the animal as "machine." In *Memoirs of a Polar Bear*, the animal looks at the human, who is simultaneously looking at the animal. The polar bear sees bodily fluids, "liquefied carnality," the ejaculation as an uncontrollable physical reaction to an enticing stimulus. Both categories—humanity and animality—are disrupted by its respective Other, and her gaze exposes the discursive practices at work in the construction of identity.

Transferring the notions of destabilizing identity categories from the discourse on gender and sexuality to a humanistic discourse, Tawada's

novel unsettles compulsively anthropocentric frameworks and makes
the case for more fluid and permeable boundaries between humans and
other animals. Her animal figures are less a mimetic copy of an actual
polar bear than a performative act that reveals practices of repetitions,
and mimes under which identities are performed. In *Memoirs of a Polar
Bear*, animality interrupts simplistic analogies. Like queer theory, which
understands the notion of heterosexuality as a compulsive and learned
set of behaviors rather than a "natural" inclination that is essential to
one's identity, Tawada's zoopoetics complicates the boundaries between
human and other animals and questions concepts of essentialism behind
these categories. By drawing attention to the mechanisms at work in the
formation of identity, Tawada unmasks what Wynter calls the "epistemological framework" of "Man" as the "male gaze" that dominates perception and representation of Otherness in a heteropatriarchal culture. She
illustrates how the latter is constructed through intersecting identity categories that necessitate the inclusion of animality in the analysis of how
Otherness is constructed. At the same time, Tawada's novel offers points
of resistance that emerge precisely from the insight of identity as performance. In that context, Tawada especially emphasizes the role of writing
and the right of self-representation to reclaim discourse. Her zoopoetic
approach, therefore, intersects with queer theory and decolonial theory
as it not only exposes the power structures at work in discursive identity
formation but also marks the latter as a point of departure from where
these categories can be reclaimed and rewritten.

ANIMALITY AND INTERSECTIONALITY

Not only does the polar bear perform identity in a certain way, however;
the novel also draws attention to the ways textual animals are performed.
Through these intertextual references, Tawada's animal figures become
legible as what Mel Y. Chen calls "zones of attraction for racial, sexual,
or abled otherness, often simultaneously" (Chen 2012, 102). The textual animals are the site of a discursive mapping, in which other identity
categories—such as woman and foreigner—intersect. Reading animality as a site of intersection with other identity categories shaped by constructions of race, gender, and sexuality complicates a solely metaphorical
understanding of 'the animal' and draws attention to the complex ways
in which animal signifiers are bound up with human cultural, political,
and social meanings (101). Tawada's polar bear is, therefore, not just a

cipher for "the foreigner," but the site where animalities, racialities, and sexualities interplay. Thinkers of critical animal studies, such as Donna Haraway (2016), Carol J. Adams (1990), Claire J. Kim (2015), and others have argued for the necessity of intersectional analysis that understands animality as another axis in the formation of identity categories all along. Yet, zoopoetic approaches also need to be attentive to how animality functions in the production of racialized, gendered, and sexualized identities within language and the literary text. Through alluding to the tradition of literary animals and the practicing of Othering at work in the production of animality, Tawada's novel draws attention to how the dominant discourse evokes animals to bolster "human" self-conception. Moreover, *Memoirs of a Polar Bear* also illustrates the violence inherent in these practices that exceeds the treatment of actual animals and includes marginalized groups traditionally associated with animals (such as women or indigenous groups).

Alluding to the long history in literature and philosophy that excludes nonhuman animals from the production of language and meaning, the polar bear utters the very words intended to distinguish humans from other animals in the Cartesian tradition: "I think." This lineage of thought culminates in Martin Heidegger's claim that animals have no hand, further suggesting that they are incapable of "grasping" the "thing itself" in its abstract meaning. In other words, animals are—according to Heidegger—incapable of rational thinking and, hence, also deprived of language.[2] Tawada draws attention to this anthropocentric framework by explicitly emphasizing the fact that her bear does indeed have a hand: "A number of hands were thrust in my direction: a swollen hand, a bony hand, a thin hand, hand, hand, hand, hand, hand. I shook hands like a politician, giving each of these unfamiliar hands a self-important squeeze" (Tawada 2016, 55). These allusions to other texts make the objectification of actual animals in the history of literature and philosophy visible, and draw attention to similar mechanisms at work in the recolonization of groups often identified with or located near "the illiterate animal": the native, the woman, the cultural or linguistic outsider.

For Tawada's polar bear, the violence of cultural progress—"progress" defined by the "Enlightened Man"—prevails, echoing the experience of postcolonial repression many of Tawada's protagonists share. Like Kafka's famous ape Red Peter in "A Report to an Academy," the bear reflects on the genealogy of her cultural process, describing both the origin of culture as inaccessible and the inherent violence of the civilizing process in a similar way: "There had been a phase before my childhood began, one in which no clock ever ticked [...] I want to find out what happened to me before childhood" (30). However, after having read Red Peter's report with great interest, Tawada's bear dismisses the ape's assumption that his is a success story: "But if you'd asked me, I'd lose no time telling you that I don't consider it progress to walk on two legs" (62). The polar bear shares the experiences of forced assimilation with many of Tawada's human protagonists. As Susan Anderson puts it: "The pressure they feel to overcome their foreignness and conform to the culture in which they are immersed is often represented as an alluring, penetrating masculine force or figure" (Anderson 2010, 57). In *Memoirs of a Polar Bear* this dominating masculine force is not only embodied through the bear's male animal trainer, who "teaches" the bear to walk on two feet by burning her front legs with hot irons, but is also—once emancipated from the circus arena—perpetuated through her publisher. Ignoring her intentions to write in German and her attempts to overcome the difficulties of learning this language, her publisher expects the polar bear to write in her own language, with the prospect of her text being translated by the publishing house:

> "I thought we communicated quite clearly that you are to write in your own language, since we have a fantastic translator."
> "My own language? I don't know which language that is. Probably one of the North Pole languages."
> "I see, a joke. Russian is one of the most magnificent literary languages in the world."
> "Somehow I don't seem to know Russian anymore." (Tawada 2016, 57)

Claiming that she does not know how to speak or write in her own native language, the polar bear resists being fixed in her identity as the "foreigner" and reclaims her right for self-representation on her own terms. By drawing attention to the trauma involved in learning both how to walk on two legs—which involved the practice of burning her front paws—and to write, she lays bare the implicit violence behind the logocentric discourse that operates under the assumption of universal truth while marginalizing and silencing subjects based on their identity. The polar bear thwarts her publisher's attempts to reinscribe her foreignness—a risk that Butler sees at work in any identity politics that constructs what it claims to represent (Butler 2004, 354), and a pressure with which Yoko Tawada as a Japanese writer who writes and publishes her work in German is only too familiar, as she has often discussed in interviews and essays.[3]

Tawada envisions the bear as female, as foreigner, and as writer. Her animal figures are sites of what Chen calls "interplay," where identity categories intersect, are constructed, and become legible through and with animality:

> Recentering on animality (or the animals who face humans) tugs at the ontological cohesion of "the human" […] it is then that entities as variant as disability, womanhood, sexuality, emotion, the vegetal, and the inanimate become more salient, more palpable as having been rendered proximate to the human, though they have always subtended the human by propping it up. (Chen 2012, 98)

As Chen suggests, animality complicates notions of sexuality, race, and ability. Rather than working as a metaphor or analogy for the Other, animality is at the heart of the construction of this Otherness. Understanding animality as integral to intersectional approaches, however, makes animal studies not only a fundamental category in rethinking gender, sexuality, race, and (dis)ability, but also the potential site of resistance that can disturb these hegemonic constructions of identity. In other words, animality can function as queer by making visible and disrupting the hierarchies associated with identity groups and by making alternative forms of life legible that fall outside of binaries such as humanity and animality, man and woman, culture and nature. By drawing attention to the process of performativity at work in constructing gendered, sexual, and racialized identities that intersect fundamentally with notions of animality, and by understanding interspecies encounters as sites of affect and desire, Tawada's animal figures open the possibility for a queer resistance within the text.

QUEER ZOOPOETICS

Tawada's zoopoetic approach imagines language as a subversive tool that defies logocentrism and serves as a site of resistance. In *Memoirs of a Polar Bear*, language and new narratives emerge from affective and corporeal relationships between individuals of different species. Rather than the instrument and effect of power, language becomes a starting point from which identity can be constructed and understood as fluid and nonstable. Scholars of queer theory, such as Judith Butler (1993, 2004), Elizabeth Freeman (2010), Lee Edelman (2004), and Judith Halberstam (2005) have emphasized the significance of understanding the queer subject position precisely under these terms, which also requires keeping the term "queer" flexible (see also Browne and Nash 2010, 1). In a similar way, Tawada's zoopoetics responds to the notion that discourse as an instrument of power forcefully shapes bodies with a nonviolent and liberating practice that allows precisely for this flexibility and carves out the space for self-affirmation. In *Memoirs of a Polar Bear*, she envisions language as a practice of embodiment that allows for mobility of the subject once it abandons "making sense" in a traditional understanding of the word: "My bicycle is my language," the bear declares (Tawada 2016, 18). Tawada's animal narrator affirms the subversive power of what Deleuze and Guattari (1986, 19) call a "minor literature," in which the subject becomes "a nomad and an immigrant and a gypsy" in relation to her own language by opposing "a purely intensive usage of language to all symbolic or even significant usages of it" (ibid.). Once the belief in the universality of the signifier is surmounted, literature follows the "direction of deterritorialization" (ibid.) that questions the very notion of "originality" that underpins essentialist notions of identity and upon which logocentrism rests. Indeed, Tawada's polar bear experiences a similar effect when writing her autobiography:

> I have to admit it: my life changed because I'd made myself an author. Or to be precise, it wasn't exactly me who did that, I was made an author by the sentences I'd written, and that wasn't even the end of the story: each result gave birth to the next, and I found myself being transported to a place I hadn't known existed [...] Where was the ball of authorship rolling? (Tawada 2016, 30)

Resisting the assumption of an original, native language, the bear's attempts to learn German seem at first to be thwarted by her animalistic appetite: "I devoured [a short story] like salmon, forgetting all about grammar" (63). Yet, by literally incorporating the book, the bear inscribes sensual traces of the foreign language into her body, finding her own way to appropriate the foreign language: "Now language remained at my side, touching soft spots within me" (16). The complex image of the bear devouring the story like salmon playfully inverts notions of literal versus metaphorical meaning. On the one hand, she only figuratively devours the story *like* salmon. On the other hand, however, bears do not devour salmon figuratively, but rather literally, which turns this sentence into a complex literal-metaphorical/material-semiotic entanglement.

Memoirs of a Polar Bear imagines language as a visceral, embodied process. It illustrates how the utilization of a "foreign: language can release "revolutionary forces" (Deleuze and Guattari 1986, 19) in any literature, resisting the participation in the perpetual colonization of language that enables the ongoing oppression of subjects within the hegemonic power structure. The alleged disadvantage of writing in a "foreign" language becomes a creative force that undermines the fixation of subject positions and calls the notion of a stable identity into question. Observing the work of interpreters at an international congress, Tawada explains in "Erzähler ohne Seelen" ("Storytellers without Souls"):

> The human body, too, contains many booths in which translations are made. I suspect that these are all translations for which no original exists. There are people, though, who assume that everyone is given an original text at birth. They call the place in which these texts are stored a soul. (Tawada 2002, 12)

By engaging this notion of language as an embodied and fluid form of expression rather than an inherent and stable quality, Tawada's zoopoetics takes both the linguistic construction of animality (and, by extension, other identity groups) into account and the lived experience of exclusion, marginalization, and oppression that results from these categorizations. By foregrounding the animal's body, the text resists a reading of its animal figures as "empty signifiers" of a "sheer culturalism," as Nicole Shukin (2009, 26) puts it. Suggesting a critical practice of "rendering" animals that "provides a trope for a cultural-materialist analysis that navigates a fine line between reductively material and reductively cultural approaches" (ibid.), Shukin seeks to produce counterhegemonic relationships and effects within a discursive mode of production (28). Like Butler's notion of performativity, rendering, therefore, becomes a site of resistance within the mimetic act of "making a copy" (20) while taking the historical and material contingencies of the actual animals into account. In that regard, it presents a counterbalance to Chen's argument of "animal play"—in which animality serves as a site of intersecting identities, but remains itself an empty signifier—by making the animal both a figure of intersection *and* by situating the actual animal within the specific time and place from which it emerges. Shukin's notion of rendering, in other words, takes the actual animal into account as well as the complex entanglement between textual and "real" animal.

In a similar way, Tawada's zoopoetics presents the polar bear both as the site of intersection of identity groups that are constructed and legible through and with conceptions of animality, while, on the other hand, presenting the polar bear as an actual and specific animal. As a species, the polar bear is threatened by extinction on a globally endangered planet. Rather than representing the bear as an iconographic and nameless image for global warming, however, Tawada introduces the reader to three very specific polar bears, endowed with a name and a personal biography. *Memoirs of a Polar Bear* liberates the animals not only from serving as a metaphor for human experiences but also by foregrounding their individuality and emphasizing the intersubjective relationships that yield to new narratives.

Tawada's text invokes the specific body of the polar bear and emphasizes visceral aspects of language and communication. Like queer theory and feminist theory, which understand the body as "intelligible only through its encounters with other bodies" (Freeman 2010, 11), *Memoirs of a Polar Bear* envisions the animal body as closely intertwined with the human's and reconceptualizes the human-animal relationship as a queer kinship. The intimacy with which Barbara and Tosca entangle their tongues for their "Kiss of Death" performance in the arena and their bodies in their dreamlike encounters at night is motivated by desire and affect, which defies the heteronormative order that privileges procreation and conceptualizes kinship exclusively under the logic of the heterosexual and patriarchal family structure. Their signature performance during which Tosca "steals" a sugar cube from the tip of Barbara's tongue soon becomes a source of pleasure that encompasses erotic and libidinal components: "After learning from her how to stop time with a kiss, I never again had the opportunity to enjoy a similar encounter with another member of my sex," Barbara recalls (Tawada 2016, 154). Tosca's own account of the performance portrays what Jennifer Cooke calls "scenes of intimacy" which employ techniques that can deeply affect the reader (Cooke 2013, 3). In *Memoirs of a Polar Bear*, the intimate scene between animal and human may prompt an emotional response that enhances empathy for nonhuman animals and queers heteronormative assumptions about "proper" objects of love, desire, and kinship in the reader:

> I stand on two legs, my back slightly rounded, my shoulders relaxed. The tiny, adorable human woman standing before me smells sweet as honey. Very slowly, I move my face toward her blue eyes, she places a sugar cube on her short little tongue and holds up her mouth to me. I see the sugar gleaming in the cave of her mouth. Its colors reminds me of snow, and I am filled with longing for the far-off North Pole. Then I insert my tongue efficiently but cautiously between the blood-red human lips and extract the radiant lump of sugar. (Tawada 2016, 156)

Tosca prioritizes her affiliation with Barbara and the sense of responsibility for her friendship to her over the "natural bonds" she is expected to form with her biological son Knut:

> I don't belong to the family of cats, who are so overprotective of their newborns [...] I entrusted Knut's care to another animal. [...] But all that is history. I don't wish to write about the life of my son as if I could take credit for it. Among the mothers of Homo sapiens, there are some who treat their sons like capital. My task, on the other hand, is to narrate the magnificent life story of my friend Barbara, who otherwise would long since have vanished in Knut's shadows. (164)

The kinship between Barbara and Tosca, both traumatized by the experience of physical and emotional violence integral to the heteropatriarchal society, develops from a deep and mutual understanding: Barbara hints at the sexual violence she experienced during and after World War II, whereas Tosca's body is still mutilated by the "training" she underwent as a circus bear. By declaring that she will write her memoirs—not about the past, but rather about what is ahead in her future (69), the animal narrator disrupts the reader's understanding of autobiographic writing as following a linear logic. The polar bear writes her way backward, toward both the beginning and the ending of suffering, foregrounding the healing aspect of forming traumatic experiences into narratives and queering the notion of time as linear: "[T]he starting line [is] my goal. The place where the pain began is where it will end" (10).

Tawada marks the affective and libidinal interspecies relationship as a site of resistance against the logocentric and heteronormative patriarchal structure. The liminal space constructed by animal and human serves as a point of departure from which both can articulate their past trauma. Contrary to her mother, the nameless first-person narrator who conversed effortlessly with humans and other animals around her in the novel's first part, Tosca and Barbara can only communicate during their intimate and dreamlike encounters at night:

> I'd entered a realm where it was forbidden to set foot. And there, in dark-ness, the grammars of many languages lost their color, they melted and combined, then froze again, they drifted in the ocean and joined the drift-ing floes of ice. I sat on the same iceberg as Tosca and understood every word she said to me. Beside us floated a second iceberg with an Inuk and a snow hare on it, immersed in conversation. (98)

As borders between languages dissolve, boundaries of the self are also transgressed. Playfully engaging with the mythology of some Native American groups that a bear's soul can flow into a human body through a kiss,[4] Tosca gets a glimpse into Barbara's soul:

> A human soul is turned out to be less romantic than I'd imagined. It was made up primarily of languages—not just ordinary, comprehensible lan-guages, but also many broken shards of language, the shadows of lan-guages, and images that couldn't turn into words. (163)

It is only within the shared space between human and animal that the shards become (meaningful) words. The emerging narratives are asso-ciative and intersubjective, which makes it, at times, impossible for the reader to determine if bear or human is recounting her experiences. These intimate moments defy traditional understanding of time and space, and follow a non-normative, queer logic. They also make the desire between human and other animals integral to zoopoetics. As anthropologist and cultural theorist Roger Lancaster argues, desire is always already at work in the process of *poiesis*: "This desire is on the side of poetry, in the original and literal sense of the word: *poiesis*, 'pro-duction,' as in the making of things and the world. Not an object at all, desire is what makes objects possible" (Lancaster 2003, 266).

Tawada's zoopoetics affirms the queer moments that unfold between individuals of different species and makes this affect and desire produc-tive for new narratives. At the same time, her zoopoetic approach dis-plays how identity categories inherently intersect in their discursive construction and fundamentally rely on and shape notions of animality. A reading that ignores the intersections and the ways the text brings these to the forefront runs the risk of understanding the polar bear purely as a metaphor or analogy for the "foreigner." These interpretations dominate the reading practices of Tawada's œuvre and tend to miss the fundamental critique of binaries and the imagination of language and identity as fluidity that permeates her work (see, for example, the metamorphosis in her novel *The Bath*). In that regard, Tawada takes a zoopoetic approach to language and literature even in her works without nonhuman animals as protagonists and narrators. Only a reading that combines theoretical approaches and is informed by queer theory, zoopoetics, and decolonial theory, as well as by the various ways these identity categories intersect, can avoid reductionist understandings of her texts that reinforce binaries between what is perceived as Other and what as one's Own.

Memoirs of a Polar Bear opens ways for the reader to understand language as an intersubjective and interspecies event that can be a site of resistance against logocentric notions and hegemonic power structures between human and animal, native and foreign, man and woman, and offers modes of belonging beyond the affiliation with our own species or kind. Zoopoetic practices of reading need to be attentive to the various dynamics between humans and other animals that enter and shape the poetic text. Queer theory—and its methodological framework, which seeks to destabilize forms of identities that rely on the notion of fixated binaries and its imagination of community organizations, kinships, and desires beyond heteronormative structures—shares fundamental questions and concerns with zoopoetics. But queer theory also needs to take animality into account and analyze the various ways in which it intersects with and shapes the construction of other identity categories. Only if the two disciplines work closely together can they challenge the prevalent epistemological framework of "Man," and be receptive to alternative modes of writing, being, and belonging.

NOTES

1. See, for example, practices of bear worship by North Eurasian and North American indigenous ethnic groups and religions, such as Nivkh, Sami, or Ainu (Ramet 1996, 173).
2. In *What is Called Thinking?* Heidegger argues that "only a being [*Wesen*] that can speak, that is think, can have a hand and can be handy

in achieving works of handicraft" (2002, 18). In *Parmenides*, he further discusses this idea: "The hand, along with the word, is the essential mark of the human [...] no animal has a hand, and a hand never originates from a paw or a claw or a talon" (1992, 118).

3. See, for example, "Writing in Two Languages" (Interview with Monica Totten, 1999).

4. See, for example, the figure of the bear shaman in Wintu mythology (Trevelyan 84).

WORKS CITED

Adams, Carol J. 1990. *The Sexual Politics of Meat: A Feminist-Vegetarian Critical Theory*. New York: Bloomsbury.

Anderson, Susan. 2010. Meaning and Difference in Yoko Tawada's German Prose. *Seminar: A Journal of Germanic Studies* 46 (1): 50–70.

Brown, Kath, and Catherine J. Nash. 2010. Queer Methods and Methodologies: An Introduction. In *Queer Methods and Methodologies: Intersecting Queer Theories and Social Science Research*, ed. Kath Brown and Catherine J. Nash, 1–24. Burlington: Ashgate.

Butler, Judith. 1993. Critically Queer. *GLQ: A Journal of Lesbian and Gay Studies* 1: 17–32.

———. 2004. Imitation and Gender Insubordination. In *Queer Cultures*, ed. Deborah Carlin and Jennifer DiGrazia, 354–367. Upper Saddle River: Pearson.

Chen, Mel Y. 2012. *Animacies: Biopolitics, Racial Mattering, and Queer Affect*. Durham, NC: Duke University Press.

Cooke, Jennifer. 2013. Making a Scene: Towards an Anatomy of Contemporary Literary Intimacies. In *Scenes of Intimacy: Reading, Writing and Theorizing Contemporary Literature*, ed. Jennifer Cooke, 3–21. New York: Bloomsbury.

Deleuze, Gilles, and Félix Guattari. 1986. *Kafka: Toward a Minor Literature*, trans. Dana Polan. Foreword by Réda Bensmaïa. Minneapolis: University of Minnesota Press.

Derrida, Jacques. 2008. *The Animal That Therefore I Am*, trans. David Wills and ed. Marie-Louise Mallet. New York: Fordham University Press.

Edelman, Lee. 2004. *No Future: Queer Theory and the Death Drive*. Durham, NC: Duke University Press.

Freeman, Elizabeth. 2010. *Time Binds: Queer Temporalities, Queer Histories*. Durham, NC: Duke University Press.

Halberstam, Judith. 2005. *In a Queer Time and Place: Transgender Bodies, Subcultural Lives*. New York: New York University Press.

Haraway, Donna J. 2016. *Staying with the Trouble: Making Kin in the Chthulucene*. Durham, NC: Duke University Press.

Heidegger, Martin. 1968. *What is Called Thinking?* trans. Steven H. Propp. New York: Harper Torchbooks.

———. 1992. *Parmenides*, trans. André Schuwer and Richard Rojcewicz. Bloomington: Indiana University Press.

Kim, Claire Jean. 2015. *Dangerous Crossings: Race, Species, and Nature in a Multicultural Age*. Cambridge, MA: Cambridge University Press.

Lancaster, Roger N. 2003. *Trouble with Nature: Sex in Science and Popular Culture*. Berkeley: University of California Press.

Ramet, Sabrina Petra. 1996. *Gender Reversals and Gender Cultures: Anthropological and Historical Perspectives*. New York: Routledge.

Shukin, Nicole. 2009. *Animal Capital: Rendering Life in Biopolitical Times*. Minneapolis: University of Minnesota Press.

Tawada, Yoko. 2000. Zukunft ohne Herkunft. In *Zukunft? Zukunft! Tübinger Poetik Vorlesungen*, ed. Jürgen Wertheimer, 55–72. Tübingen: Verlag Claudia Gehrke.

———. 2002. Storytellers without Souls. In *Where Europe Begins*, trans. Susan Bernofsky and Yumi Selden, 101–114. New York: New Directions.

———. 2014. *Etüden im Schnee*. Tübingen: Claudia Gehrke Verlag.

———. 2016. *Memoirs of a Polar Bear*, trans. Susan Bernofsky. New York: New Directions.

Totten, Monica, and Yoko Tawada. 1999. Writing in Two Languages: A Conversation with Yoko Tawada. *Harvard Review* 17: 93–100.

Trevelyan, Amelia M. 2004. *Miskwabik, Metal of Ritual: Metallurgy in Precontact Eastern North America*. Lexington: University Press of Kentucky.

Wynter, Sylvia. 2003. Unsettling the Coloniality of Being/Power/Truth/Freedom: Towards the Human, after Man, Its Overrepresentation—An Argument. *CR: The New Centennial Review* 3 (3): 257–337.

Myth, Absence, Haunting: Toward a Zoopoetics of Extinction

Paul Sheehan

And some in dreams assuréd were.
Of the Spirit that plagued us so;
Nine fathom deep he had followed us.
From the land of mist and snow.
—Coleridge, "The Rime of the Ancient Mariner" (1969, 191)

The shooting of the albatross, in the first part of Coleridge's famous poem (189), has long since broken free of its narrative moorings and assumed a determinately metapoetic significance. The animal itself, a large oceanic bird comprising about twenty-one species, is now equated with its symbolic shadow. Which is to say, as a result of the poem—and in keeping with the mandates of appropriation—the word "albatross" stands for something other than a bird: a "source of frustration, obstruction, or guilt, from which it is difficult to rid oneself; a burden, an encumbrance; a hindrance," in the Oxford English Dictionary's definition.[1] Forced to become a metaphorical substitute, the actual, material animal is occluded; in effect, it disappears. But it is not so much the

P. Sheehan
Macquarie University, Sydney, Australia

167

material embodiment of the bird that is the issue here as the latter's sudden eradication, and the consequences that ensue: guilt, anguish, and regret. Animals, in this way, are "swallowed up" by language, absorbed into its predetermined anthropocentric directives. Accordingly, they act as screens for projecting human concerns, or mirrors for reflecting back human meanings; or they figure as symbols of mysterious otherness, prompting fearful human impotence and the compulsive reassertion of agency (through such acts as the killing of a harmless seabird).

In the case of the albatross, this act of appropriation constitutes a double disappearance. Even as the bird has been transfigured into an abstract noun, a prosaic signifier of haunted regret and oppressive guilt, it has also come to stand for *endangerment*, for its potential extinction as a species. In fact, albatross colonies in the Pacific region have been under threat of extinction since Coleridge's time, prey to such local practices as feather hunting and egg collection (van Dooren 2015, n.p.). Today, the World Conservation Union estimates that eighty-three per cent of albatross species are "threatened," the highest proportion of any bird family, largely as a result of longline fishing practices (see Safina 2002, 189–192). "The Ancient Mariner"'s ill-considered *acte gratuit*, which Coleridge brought to life at the end of the eighteenth century is, thus, indicative of wider-scale albatross disappearance, even if the causes of that decline have changed over time.

The question that underlies this chapter concerns extinction, starting from the strictly ecological sense of the term, in which species undergo a downturn from endangerment to nonexistence. There is, however, a cluster of cognate terms that demands a more philosophical—indeed, a more zoopoetic—consideration of this downturn. Death, disappearance, absence, haunting and, on the widest scale, the void: these are the terms that will enable a proper examination of (species) extinction to be undertaken and will bring to the fore the ensuing literary-philosophical implications. Extinction has always been a question of (literary) language and philosophy, which shapes our understanding of it in at least three different ways. In the first place, both literature and philosophy are concerned with (secular) notions of prophecy and/or prediction, whether as speculative narratives or thought experiments. Second, both seek to plot the limits of the human in relation to its (nonhuman) others, ascertaining the role of species in natural and cultural environments. And third, each attempts to understand the bases of life that underpin growth and decay, recuperation and loss, emergence and ending.

For us today, the question of extinction is also shaped by history—naturalistic history, as I demonstrate in the next section, but also by world history, stemming from the key traumatic event of the last century. As a paradigm of human-engineered extinction—even a failed one, targeted at a specific ethnic group—the *Shoah* casts a long and forbidding shadow over the postwar decades. Adorno's (1983, 34) infamous maxim that writing poetry after Auschwitz is "barbaric" could be modified into a less absolute, ecocritical dictum that there are, rather, diminished resources and semantic uncertainties "after Auschwitz." This might be seen as a further way in which literature and philosophy engage with the question of extinction. More than just a subject to be thematized, expiration or dissolution is also articulable through formal or stylistic constraint.

To return to my starting point: Coleridge's "The Ancient Mariner" is also a mourner, lamenting his wanton, capricious killing of the albatross; he is haunted by it, unable to shake the cloud of emptiness and defeat that has overtaken his life. Both "mourning" and "haunting" point to zoopoetics as a mode of reading, a way of seeing broader implications in the questions that concern animal endangerment and extinction. By restoring to the albatross its status as a particular species with a particular history—an actual bird, not just a metaphorical substitute—zoopoetics illuminates the mutability of the literary animal. In other words, language can also restore and reaffirm what language has taken away. Mourning, haunting, and elegizing are vital components of zoopoetic restoration when the matter of extinction arises. These components also come into play in a second mode, one that centers on artistic creation rather than critical (re)reading: poetry that is *intrinsically* zoopoetic, composed to foreground directly the bonds between animality and language, and to recognize that a poetry of extinction must take into account the volatile and potentially friable resources of poetic language itself.

To question traditional poetic resources means to reexamine the role of myth, which has always had a fraught relationship with the "literary animal," as an enduring agent of appropriation. Treating animals as mythical creatures is one of the most effective and indubitable ways of suppressing their "animality" in favor of timeless, fantastic, and/or monstrous qualities. Getting beyond myth, I want to draw attention to a recognizable "poetry of extinction" that has, in a somewhat ad hoc and intermittent fashion, confronted the disappearance of individual species and the ecological implications of such a declension.

Moreover, I contend that it is possible to discern a zoopoetics that underlies this form of writing. The rest of this chapter outlines, first, the theoretical and historical background that enjoins animal disappearance; it is then followed by two very different responses, one from the American poet W. S. Merwin and the second from English musician and poet Richard Skelton. Their work provides instantiations of a zoopoetics of extinction, taking into account both human and nonhuman involvements with the natural world, and the consequences that supervene therefrom.

INTO THE VOID: DISAPPEARANCE AND MYTH

As the history of natural science shows, the notion of species extinction only acquired scientific credibility at the end of the eighteenth century. In 1798, the same year that Coleridge's "The Rime of the Ancient Mariner" appeared, the French naturalist and zoologist Georges Cuvier presented a controversial paper to the Société d'Histoire Naturelle de Paris. Using a set of detailed drawings, Cuvier showed how the lower jaw of an Indian elephant differed significantly from that of a mammoth; the latter, therefore, could not be regarded as a different kind of elephant, but as a separate species—one that was now extinct. Furthermore, underlying this and other species' extinctions was a "deluge" or cataclysmic event that took place just prior to the advent of human civilizations. If current geological systems cannot accommodate such a fact, said Cuvier, then those systems ought to be modified (see Rudwick 1997, 33–34).

Several decades after Cuvier, Charles Darwin presented his own theory of species extinction. Indeed, in *On the Origin of Species* (1859), he made it central to his key concept. "Natural Selection," he wrote, "almost inevitably causes much Extinction of the less improved forms of life" (Darwin 1985, 68). But Darwin was not simply endorsing Cuvier's model. He was also modifying it, removing the "cataclysmic" forces that actuated extinction and replacing it with a more graduated process of "background" extinctions. This positing of small-scale forces and changes accords with Darwin's belief that the natural order was defined by "balance" and "uniformity." The "economy of nature," as he called it, is a homeostatic system that encompasses "distribution, rarity, abundance, extinction, and variation" (116). Thus, Darwinian extinction is counterpoised by *replenishment*. Some species are obliterated so that others can thrive; such is the process of natural selection, which can also function as a kind of "space-clearing" operation (see Beer 2009, 322). What is especially significant, in terms of present-day concerns, is that Darwin's conception of evolutionary change does not entertain the possibility of a void or vacuum.

In the twenty-first century it is possible to talk of disparate yet clearly delineated "cultures of extinction." In contrast to Darwin's vision of perdition and rejuvenation, these cultures are fixated on *loss*—absolute loss, without remainder or renewal. The sixth great extinction event, the starting point of the so-called "Anthropocene epoch," is what gives an edge, and a sense of urgency, to this pessimistic vision of terminal depletion. When we reflect on the precariousness of our relationship to the biosphere, writes Claire Colebrook, "we start to think about climate as a general condition that binds humans to an irreversible and destructive time" (Colebrook 2013, 52). The alarming prospect of anthropic eradication has, thus, quickened concerns about biocide, and about the consequential disappearance of animal species.

The very real possibility of species extinction also brings to the fore some intractable philosophical problems. The void that Darwinian evolution abnegates is known as *horror vacui*, or the fear of empty spaces. This fear is referred to by the diagnostic term *kenophobia*, a psychic malady that associates emptiness with solitude and abandonment; both *horror vacui* and *kenophobia* underpin the well-known saying, "nature abhors a vacuum." More than just a piece of generic folk wisdom, this adage comes out of Aristotelian philosophy. In the *Physics*, Aristotle argues that the notion of the "void" does not make sense, neither as a condition of movement nor as a space for a hypothetical body. It is contrary to reason because the void's imagined homogeneity defies the principles of both *differentiation* and *directionality*, with its absence of spatial markers: because the relationship between a solid body and a medium (through which the body moves) collapses, and because the contraction and condensation of physical objects would also no longer be possible. From all of these perspectives, the void simply cannot exist (Aristotle 1999, 93–102). However, the anthropocentric myth is not just about human ascendancy and preeminence, it is also about propagation and dominion, as if generational continuance implies a kind of immortality. From this angle, *horror vacui* is objectionable not because of "fear of the void," but because it projects a human-shaped hole into the fabric of existence. *Homo sapiens* is, therefore, revealed to be *Homo fragilis*—a precarious species whose longevity can no longer be taken for granted.

If the albatross is the "millstone" animal, the one that invokes guilt and frustration, primarily, and the notion of endangerment only secondarily, then the dodo is the "extinction" animal *par excellence*. This flightless bird has an even more dubious honor than the albatross, as it was the first known species to be hunted into extinction by human predators (see Stearns and Stearns 1999, 16–17).[2] First described in 1598 by Dutch sailors who landed in Mauritius, and last sighted there in 1680, the dodo has achieved its iconic status posthumously. And, as with the albatross, a celebrated literary work has helped in vouchsafing that status. It was immortalized by Lewis Carroll in *Alice's Adventures in Wonderland* (1865) and taken to be a sly self-portrait. The dodo also fortifies the pointed connection between *extinction* and *myth*. Its disappearance as a species means that representational artifacts—paintings, illustrations, written accounts—have given the bird the aura and piquancy of a creature of myth, which even the subfossil records of its material existence cannot entirely dispel.

But species extinction can also be understood in more mundane terms. As John Berger asserted in "Why Look at Animals?," for the past two hundred years animals have been steadily "disappearing," in the sense of becoming increasingly marginal to Western life. It is more than just the commercial exploitation of animals, a practice that has caused them to "disappear" in a physical (and statistical) sense. Berger acknowledges that animal imagery and animal representations are all around us, in the form of toys, cartoons, decorations, superstitious sayings, and fables—and even animals themselves, as the ubiquitous household pet (the "new animal puppet," sterilized and isolated, in the name of domestication) (Berger 1991, 26). But therein lies the problem. As objects of knowledge, and of vision or spectacle, animals recede into the human imaginary. The zoo, says Berger, is the "living monument to [animal] disappearance" (ibid.), the place where every exotic creature is on display. But because only very precise conditions can countenance such a display—confinement, theatrical décor, imposed passivity—these creatures' every look and gesture only serves to confirm their indubitable marginality.

In a discussion about the "science of grammatology," Jacques Derrida argues that the discourses surrounding scientific research cannot avoid the taint of metaphysical presuppositions (Derrida 1981, 35–36). In similar fashion, Judith Roof suggests that a "poetics" has come to be associated with the discourses about DNA, in the form of "analogies, figurations and unacknowledged narratives" imported by scientists (Roof 2007, 3). Stephanie S. Turner applies this notion of the "literary" to extinction, noting that it can be "re-imagined" according to the predicates of genomic science. The disappearing animal is eclipsed by the *reappearing* animal, made manifest when loss is offset by recovery. She writes: "[T]he development of molecular biology means that species like woolly mammoths and Neanderthals are not lost after all, but continue to exist as the genetic codes residing in their remains, codes we are getting better and better at reading and interpreting" (Turner 2007, 58–59).

Extinction, then, is becoming "open-ended," because DNA is endlessly reproducible. As a consequence of this open-endedness, the temporal manifold is reduced to a homogeneous unity—a "perpetual present," best understood in mythic, rather than chronometric terms. As Turner puts it: "Fabulous and primal, [genome time] characterizes the DNA molecule as the *ne plus ultra* unit of life, establishing a worldview that naturalizes immortality as an inherent, coded quality" (2007, 59). Thus, the legibility, indeed, the hermeneutical capacity of DNA indices allows biological information to introduce a new, counterapocalyptic narrative into the field. Instead of irrevocable disappearance, the "readable" genetic code convokes persistence across time—dormancy and recuperation, then, rather than loss without return.

This change is integral to the asseveration that a "mythic turn" has taken place in extinction studies—from which it can be surmised that the literary-poetic elements of animal disappearance must be recognized and acknowledged. But, rather than as a recent development, driven by scientific ingenuity, it might better be seen as a necessary, yet contestatory, precondition of the field itself. When a writer such as W. S. Merwin approaches the complex situation of *disappearance* and *reappearance*, he confronts a delicate and potentially tortuous state of affairs. Ranging across the different forms of animal disappearance—from occlusion or absence to death and extinction—the poetry that he was writing half a century ago is plaintive and admonitory, even as it seeks to embrace the void.

In the Black Garden: W. S. Merwin's Evacuated World

Environmental depredation has been a pressing concern for W. S. Merwin since 1952, when his first book of poems appeared. By the mid-1960s, that mounting disquiet brought on a personal crisis, which both stymied and reshaped his poetry. "I got to the point where I thought the future was so bleak that there was no point in writing anything at all," he said, twenty years later. "And so the poems kind of pushed their way upon me when I wasn't thinking of writing" (Elliott and Merwin 1988, 6). The "poems" in question became *The Lice* (1967), the collection now generally regarded as Merwin's signal poetic achievement.[3] Notable for its lack of punctuation [a strategy designed to mimic, says Merwin, the "movement and lightness of the spoken word" (Hirsch and Merwin 1987)], *The Lice* reimagines the natural and animal worlds as all but eradicated, viewed from the vantage point of some (unspecified) future time.

Merwin's crisis was not just a response to the impending disappearance of certain species, but also to his increasing awareness that poetry, too, was becoming extinct (Merwin 1966, 269). Many of the poems in *The Lice* bear this out formally, through language that is pared-down and stark, yet also forcible and concentrated. As these poems unfold, the lack of punctuation seems to suggest that one of the bases of language—its grammatical infrastructure—is disappearing, in advance of a more widespread linguistic-poetic extinction. Animal extinction is closely aligned with this diminishing role of poetry in the postwar world, as if animals and poetic expression were covertly bound to each other. Merwin exploits the mysterious nature of that bind, decades ahead of the current wave of animal scholarship, as if recognizing the zoopoetic relationship that conjoins the two.

At the same time, the (mostly) short pieces in *The Lice* are tonally tied to another enduring poetic tradition. Hank Lazer describes the collection as a "planetary elegy," an "extended myth of uncreation, the story of the disappearance of the animal world" (Lazer 1982, 262). To posit an "elegy of uncreation" is, unavoidably, to court paradox. If we take the elegiac mode to be a form of writing that "enables fantasies about worlds we cannot yet reach, even as it facilitates investments in a world that will outlast us" (Cavitch 2007, 1), then Merwin's lamentation could be seen as a challenge, even as a retort. The world that he imagines is not so much "unreachable" as not worth reaching, hence not one in which human beings can have any kind of "investment." As his speaker declares, in "The River of Bees":

> On the door it says what to do to survive
> But we were not born to survive
> Only to live (Merwin 1967, 33)

In this context, "to survive" means to conceive of a future for one-self (or, more broadly, one's species) and to recognize that survival is inseparable from sustainability. On the other hand, "to live" suggests a narrowing of possibilities, of being indentured to the moment and its immediate needs. Another poem, "Whenever I Go There" concludes with the apothegm: "Today belongs to few and tomorrow to no one" (Merwin 1967, 24). A future that is uninhabitable by either human beings or animals is one that stretches the resources of the elegy to its limits, by shutting down the "future investment" that is so intrinsic to the form.

As already suggested, within Merwin's broader ecopoetic project in *The Lice*, there is a more focused inquest into animal extinction. Having said that, the poem at the start of the collection, "The Animals," is curiously tentative and exploratory. Set in a barren, timeless landscape, the animals of the title are notably absent:

> And myself tracking over empty ground
> Animals I never saw (3)

The speaker is, in Ed Folsom's words, a "ruined American Adam," his would-be Eden, "alien and unnameable" (Folsom 1987, 235). This disconsolate figure—indeed, a speaker who cannot speak ("I with no voice")—discharges his duty of identifying the unseen animals by "Remembering names to invent for them." In a poem about distance, absence, and human-animal estrangement, this indicates an attempt to bridge the gap, by negotiating between taxonomic "remembering" and poetic "invent[ing]." His final plea devolves into a single encounter and affirmation:

> Will any come back will one
> Saying yes
> Saying look carefully yes
> We will meet again (Merwin 1967, 3)

The fractured language and faltering syntax challenge the note of apparent certainty on which the poem ends. And the penultimate line is as much an address to the reader ("look carefully") as it is a promise of what is to come—the unseen animals that will reappear, albeit without entirely shedding the aura of absence that this poem so hauntingly establishes.

As well as describing general, nonspecific animals, *The Lice* contains poems about individual animals, in the process of dying (a pigeon, a small bird, a whale)[4]; and, in two instances, poems about large masses of animals. "The Herds" describes a solitary individual who climbs "northward" to "celebrate our distance from men." (56) As he lays down at dusk and sees some hoof tracks, the sound of the herds reaches him from afar. But no sooner has the sound—real or imagined—resonated than the wider world of nature reasserts itself, in the form of the "ancient sun," the "glass mountain," and the "flocks of light grazing." The last of these is a phenomenological verity: a herd of sheep, perhaps, momentarily transformed into pure creatures of light by the early morning sun. The scene then abruptly shifts, as the reality of the situation is revealed:

> And the water preparing its descent
> To the first dead (56)

If we take the "dead" to be one or more of the herd, this sudden disclosure locates animal mortality within a larger cycle of continuance. The herd species, in other words, will persist in leaving tracks and sounds in its wake, despite the fact of physical expiration.

Another *Lice* poem, "In a Clearing," presents the same scenario: a speaker watching the flow of herds, in darkness and in silence. But, rather than conveying a perceptual anomaly, the act of observation yields thoughts of a more metaphysical nature (which also bring into play, via analogy, the poem's title):

> Passing through senses
> As through bright clearings surrounded with pain
> Some of the animals
> See souls moving in their word death
> With its many tongues that no god could speak (70)

Animal mortality, thus, means more than just surrendering to the natural cycle of events. Indeed, to sense that one's existence is finite—a sense that, says Merwin, animals also possess—is to have a kind of "soul awareness," and, rather than being just one thing, this imputed animal awareness is more variegated than ours ("its many tongues"), if just as mysterious. Even more than in "The Herds," death is equated with light:

The word
Surrounds the souls
The hide they wear
Like a light in the light
And when it goes out they vanish (70)

Death awareness is at once a form of protection ("The hide they wear")
and an inextricable part of existence ("a light in the light"). In Merwin's
"herd-world" light belongs to darkness, and both are codependent on
the existential integrity of life.

It would be difficult to see either "The Herds" or "In a Clearing"—
or "The Animals," for that matter—as "protest" poems. Animal disappearance is explored in these instances as an extra-anthropic matter, as
the provenance of nature or metaphysics. "For a Coming Extinction," by
contrast, is an impassioned animal rights polemic. In the new century, it
seems more prescient than ever:

Gray whale
Now that we are sending you to The End
That great god
Tell him
That we who follow you invented forgiveness
And forgive nothing (68)

The ontological divide between human and animal is first of all wid-
ened—it is *we*, with our assumed cognitive superiority, who are sending the gray whale to *The End*—and then it is annulled, "we who follow
you," indicating that our own demise is also imminent. Merwin's gray
whale is, thus, the harbinger of a wider, more imposing extinction,
"Leaving behind it the future / Dead." As for the animal itself:

When you will not see again
The whale calves trying the light
Consider what you will find in the black garden
And its court (68)

The barren Eden of "The Animals," a terrain void of life, is recon-
ceived here as an otherworldly anti-Eden, the traditional biblical
topos transformed into a "black garden" of extinct animals. What the
gray whale will find in this tenebrous afterdeath is a record of animal

annihilation: "The sea cows the Great Auks the gorillas / [...] Our sacrifices." As with "forgiveness," the notion of "sacrifice" is shorn of its traditional humanistic associations and shown to be complicit in practices of cruelty.

Ursula Heise notes that the poem is less a portrayal of whales than of human beings; less an attempt to come to terms with the endangered species itself, and more an appeal to the perpetrators, the animal killers. As a consequence, she writes, "The whale's death turns out not to mean anything other than humans' grim and deadly self-affirmation," a specular maneuver that "cuts off any possibility of response" (Heise 2016, 47). Merwin's poetry does occasionally adopt this pose, yet it is never so clear-cut or high-handed as Heise suggests. "After the Dragonflies," for example, a post-*Lice* poem that continues its elegiac mood and temporal involutions, has the speaker reminiscing about a time when "Dragonflies were as common as sunlight." He likens them to "memory," in their movements, back, forth, and sideways. Now, however, there are people who never saw one, much less noticed that "the veins in a dragonfly's wings / were made of light." This loss is then complicated by an interspecies reversal:

> when we appeared in their eyes
> we were strangers
> they took their light with them when they went
> there will be no one to remember us (Merwin 2016, 19)

Light, a Merwinian trope in *The Lice* (as we have seen), is equated here with memory, and with human / insect recognition. And as in "For a Coming Extinction," one disappearance (the dragonflies') foreshadows or anticipates another (ours). Which of these is the speaker mourning? It is "their light" that illuminates the poem and that obliges us to remember them; the poem itself, then, is an act of remembrance. Our coming extinction, conversely, means that we will be forgotten—a fact presented almost as an afterthought, albeit a dolorous one.

Discussing zoopoetics and mass extinction in Merwin's work, Aaron Moe focuses mainly on the post-*Lice* poems. However, he makes the useful point that reading Merwin through the "growth of the self," as Jarold Ramsey does, serves (deliberately or not) to temper or weaken the poet's ecological and ecocritical concern with extinction (Moe 2014, 96). Merwin is, finally, more concerned with self-erasure or self-extinction than (as Heise claims) with "self-affirmation." Cary Nelson alludes to this when he suggests that the poetry in *The Lice* "presses towards a silence achieved through self-depletion" (Nelson 1977, 576). This is borne out in the cryptic poem "It is March," in which Merwin's speaker contemplates his future absence:

It is March and black dust falls out of the book
Soon I will be gone (Merwin 1967, 17)

The past has vanished, the future is paralyzing, and the speaker is antic-ipating nonexistence. He concludes on a note of enigmatic deferment: "Whatever I have to do has not yet begun." (17) (Dying, perhaps? Or preparing for oblivion?) In one of the most celebrated of the *Lice* poems, Merwin even "commemorates" the anniversary of his death—in advance of actually dying—by unknowingly passing the day "When the last fires will wave to me" (58). The poem in question, "For the Anniversary of My Death," is a quintessential elegy of uncreation. The speaker admits to being "Surprised at the earth," for reasons of gratitude ("the love of one woman") and regret ("the shamelessness of men"), and finds himself reluctant to leave it. The death that he acknowledges may not yet have happened, but that undetermined *yet* is simply a matter of perspective.

The "extinction" poems in *The Lice*, thus, contemplate the end in a threefold way: as extinction of species, as extinction of poetry and poetic language, and as extinction of self. The three are tightly inter-woven. If it is, as Nelson suggests, a "poetry that becomes empty in the very act of opening itself to the world" (Nelson 1977, 576), that is because the world is in the process of emptying itself out. This condi-tion is mirrored in the numerous allusions made throughout *The Lice* to the cosmic blackness of the night sky. The book itself, however, is defined by a (non)textual *whiteness*. Many of the poems comprise a dozen lines or fewer, suspended precariously in a homogeneous white field. The effect is nothing if not disconcerting: a *horror vacui* of the page, inviting—or, perhaps, rather compelling—the reader to negoti-ate the absence of words, the treacherous gaps between poems, and the potential extirpation of meaning that ensues. "It is not a creative void that Merwin faces," notes Edwin Folsom, but "a destructive void which opens its dark abyss, ready to swallow the poet and all of life with him" (Folsom 1978, 66).

In this regard, it is significant that, although the poems in *The Lice* are generally seen as "post-apocalyptic," their mode of presentation is neither straightforwardly predictive nor anticipatory. For Merwin's sense of the depleted present, in his poetics of extinction, is haunted by the future. The time is out of joint, in other words—something that Derrida, drawing on *Hamlet*, refers to as a "hauntology" (Derrida 2006, 201–202). In this spectral experience of time, that which is *no longer* is conjoined with that which is *not yet* (see Hägglund 2008, 82). Merwin constructs his poetry so that the voice calling back from the absent future makes the present fully culpable for the catastrophic losses to come. Thus, the postapocalyptic temper of *The Lice* cannot be dismissed on the grounds that "it may not happen"; for Merwin it has already happened, even if the temporal order has yet fully to reveal it.

Like Merwin, Margaret Ronda notes that the resources of the elegy are put under pressure when the subject of species extinction—or, more broadly, the end of nature—arises. She suggests that the "emergent literature" associated with this way of thinking is necessarily elegiac, as it "demands an emphasis on what is *not*, on the negative workings of creative imagination in light of a concept's withering-away" (Ronda 2013, n.p.). The mourning that accompanies this "negative imagination" is also shaken because its object, the hitherto constant and self-renewing natural world, has become "impossible and unthinkable" (ibid). What this means for the elegy is that it, too, becomes "impossible"—an impossibility that is conveyed, not through mourning the absent object, but (as Freud famously argued) the *other* affective response to absence and loss, which is melancholia. For Ronda, then, the elegiac effect of confronting extinction, of mourning for the future and all its lost entailments, is a "melancholia without end." This, in turn, means being forced to confront "obligation, culpability and guilt," and to recognize that human action is a "determinative force" (ibid).

Merwin conveys his sense of human culpability and determination via the notion of an *immanent* apocalyptic upheaval. It is pithily conveyed in a poem from an earlier collection, "This Day of This Month of This Year of This." The speaker presents a litany of personal and observational attributes, the most striking of which is:

> With my teeth graveyard for the nameless
> With extinction my ancestor (Merwin 1963, 74)

Future and past, destiny and history, are made congruent, haunto-logically folded into one another. Alternately, they could be seen as akin to a genetic inheritance: "extinction" lies dormant, until the propitious moment arrives to transform what has hitherto been a recessive trait into a dominant one.

The notion that "extinction" can be "my ancestor," aside from its epigrammatical acuity, also bears some relation to myth. In particular, it is a reminder that myths use "imaginative patterns" to shape our men-tal habits, that they are "ongoing dramas inside which we live our lives" (Midgley 2004, 5). Such patterns, such ongoing dramas can, of course, take a wide and diverse variety of shapes. One that has gained a lot of traction since Merwin's mid-1960s zenith (and still has purchase today) is predicated on "endism"—the notion that, as Frank Kermode (1967, 28) famously put it, the "paradigms of apocalypse continue to underlie our ways of making sense of the world." But Kermode also warns against the dangers of "mythical thinking," because it favors the status quo. He writes: "Myth operates within the diagrams of ritual, which presupposes total and adequate explanations of things as they are and were; it is a sequence of radically unchangeable gestures" (39). The meaning and sta-bility that myth provides is, thus, difficult to challenge or contest.

Seen in this light, Merwin's "extinction-as-ancestor" supposition exudes a *countermythic* force: it dislodges the myth of extinction that invariably slips into the pattern or drama of survival. The Darwinian dialectic of *loss and renewal*, for example, insists that extinction must be seen as a kind of hiatus, rather than as a terminal and irreversible condition. Merwinian extinction, by contrast, disallows any consola-tory gestures. As William Rueckert (1987, 48) notes, "Merwin will not mythologize the future, for the words die on the way to that realm." If "the words die", that is because language is being squeezed out of existence, haunted by impending absence and loss. Cary Nelson takes it a step further, setting Merwin's mid-1960s poetry against the paradig-matic instance of modernist myth. There are, he says, "disruptions and discontinuities" akin to those in *The Waste Land*, but they are there "without any recourse to mythic synthesis" (Nelson 1977, 583).[5] As an explanatory system, myth works to integrate diverse and even paradoxical elements—something that Eliot perfected in his high-modernist years. Merwin's view of the coming extinction, however, is as a kind of solvent, a breakdown of correspondence and a rescission of meanings.

Merwin may have claimed that the crisis poems of *The Lice* "kind of pushed their way upon me," but the collection is neither attenuated nor impoverished. Because the impending crisis is a threefold extinction (species, poetry, and self), its parts are inextricably linked to one another; animal disappearance is more than just an ecopoetic matter. Moreover, although the void that Merwin confronts is "destructive" rather than "creative," the vividness and resourcefulness of his poetic temper—and the metaphorical superabundance of the work—belies any hint of lassitude or acquiescence. Even as the logic of evacuation guides and informs much of *The Lice*, Merwin's linguistic perspicuity manages to overcome the *via negative* of death, disappearance, and loss. His zoopoetic imagination bears out this tension, casting suspicion on the role of myth in extinction studies, while proposing nonappropriative ways of apprehending human-animal relations.

TRACE DECAY: RICHARD SKELTON'S PHANTOM BESTIARY

Merwin's "elegies of uncreation," as we have just seen, attempt to find more elemental and pared-down ways of addressing the destruction of ecosystems and the disappearance of species. Yet, the precariousness that this reveals is partly offset by Merwin's ecopolitical awareness, lending some of the more cryptic aspects of his mid-1960s poetry a polemical edge. If it were possible to remove that (political) awareness, and that edge, how would nature's precarious condition manifest itself? Would it shine through in other ways? One approach to these questions can be made through what Gary Snyder, Merwin's fellow poet and contemporary, calls the "dark side of nature": the side where parasitism, predation, and appetite rule. Life outside the human, diurnal world, says Snyder, is not simply a harmonious union of species and ecosystem: "It is also nocturnal, anaerobic, cannibalistic, microscopic, digestive, fermentative [...] there is a world of nature on the decay side, a world of beings who do rot and decay in the shade" (Snyder 2008, 170). A zoopoetics of extinction, thus, needs to take account of this "decay side," where human agency is eclipsed by nature's own entropic tendencies.

One of the most recent poetic explorers of the dark(er) side of nature is Richard Skelton, the English musician and poet. Skelton's writings possess an aura of enchantment, even as they address the plight of animal disappearance—an effect achieved through the finely honed sense of local particularity that permeates his work. "Landscape, language and loss are the three great subjects of [Skelton's] work" (Macfarlane 2015,

181), writes Robert Macfarlane—in particular, the landscapes and animal species of Cumbria, a county in England's northwest. Mountainous,
wet, and sparsely populated, Cumbria has been a prime locale for English
verse since the Lake Poets immortalized it in the early nineteenth century. Skelton's haunted and evocative poetic writings, ethereal yet oddly
material, both continue and dissolve this tradition—a poetry of animal
and mineral traces or residues that stir the topographical imagination.
It is possible to see this work as elegiac, but in a different vein from
Merwin's, and considerably sparser and more fine-spun. Skelton's is a
poetry of objects, as well as of vanished animals, with bones and feathers
becoming especially charged artifacts for his poetic vision. As metonymi-
cal reminders of nonhuman species, they exist on the borderline between
animal and mineral, simultaneously present and absent.

A good, if enigmatic, example of Skelton's "object-oriented"
approach is the six-line "Thing-Poems," which simply lists a number of
indicative objects:

Coil of barbed wire and string

Fragment of moss-fastened vertebrae

Thistle seed head and stalk

Bone of small animal

Mottled feather

Curved section of roof tile (Skelton 2016, 27)

The line-breaks signify disparity, suggesting that each object or set be read
as a poem unto itself. Three of the "things" listed are of animal origin:
"moss-fastened vertebrae," small-animal bone, and "mottled feather."
As descriptions, they are neither specific nor nonspecific (with the partial exception of "mottled feather"), and they steer clear of abstractions.
Juxtaposed with insentient matter—barbed wire, string, thistle seed, roof
tile—the effect is eerily unsettling. These animal remains are reminders, first and foremost, that there were creatures (whatever they may have
been) that once housed or exhibited them. In addition, the lack of context
fosters an almost palpable spectrality, as if their ghostly semibeings were
struggling to reassert their claims to existence.

Writing about Merwin's poem "The Animals" and its meditation on
absence, Aaron Moe suggests that "it is very difficult for the body of an
animal to reappear in a poem if that animal does not exist" (Moe 2014, 97).

He suggests that Merwin overcomes, or at least rethinks, this difficulty in a more oblique fashion, in the "shift from naming animals to naming the absence of animals" (ibid). Skelton, however, approaches animal absence through contrast, sometimes naming them, sometimes not. Perhaps the most explicit example of this is a short prose poem simply entitled "Gone." Its subject is birds, some more specific than others:

> The grey bird is gone. Its cry no longer frames the captive landscape. The curlews, gone. Their birthing halls deserted. The watcher, *aderyn corff*, is absent. Blended into nothing. Swifts, vanished.(Skelton 2016, 28)

In short order Skelton conjures up a "grey bird," some "curlews," a watching "*aderyn corff*" (a *corpse* or *death bird*) and "Swifts." But they are only evoked in order to be removed: They are "gone," "no longer" present, "absent," as "nothing," and "vanished." The lexicon of absence is being worked through here, in all its artfulness, and it proves to be surprisingly nuanced. After a long, parenthetical remark about negotiating a "violent gale," "Gone" concludes with a characteristic discovery:

> And here by the path on Hoar Stones Brow, I find a large, black feather *Crow rudder*. The only testimony—on this blank morning—that the air bore something on its back. Lifted high on its shoulders. Singing.(Skelton 2016, 28)

The vivid immediacy of this "only testimony" pushes back against the welter of absences. In other words, the black feather of the crow is a pointed vestige that Skelton effectively uses as an act of restoration. And similarly to Merwin, it is metaphorical ingenuity that enables this restorative act: the "back" and "shoulders" of the air are given creatural form, and likened to an ethereal beast that sings. But where Merwin recollects the absence(s) of herds, whales, and dragonflies, Skelton brings them back to the world through implication, his writings "freezing" or "preserving" animal traces—a kind of zoopoetic equivalent to genomic analysis of DNA.

Another case in point is "Notes on the Landscape," a prose poem about recovery that demonstrates another aspect of Skelton's method. It begins:

> West Pennine Moors: the early sources have not been exhaustively excerpted. A

glacial effect on phonology: O.E. ā becomes
ō south of the Ribble. Some names now lost
with ground-nesting birds. (Skelton 2016, 119)

This stanza exemplifies Skelton's "three great subjects": landscape (the
moors); language (phonological changes below the Ribble, a major river
about eighty kilometers south of the Pennines); and loss (ground-nesting
birds and their names). It reads like the jottings of a historian, clipped
and matter-of-fact, with no emotional attestation from the speaker. The
loss of both *names* and *species* is neither elegiac nor melancholic, but simply a matter of adducing the "early sources."
     The second stanza, however, modifies the nature of this loss. It com-
prises two striking claims:

The wing of a curlew paid testimony to
the early forms. Its call mimicking that of
riven wood, adopted chiefly to illustrate
dialect sound-changes. (Skelton 2016, 119)

Skelton's somewhat phlegmatic historian has traded places with his orni-
thological enthusiast, alert to the semiotics of species diversity, and to the
nuances of sound and form, birdcall, and regional dialect. The speculative note being struck here is folded into a broader observational remark
about morphology.
     Elsewhere in Skelton's work, the curlew figures as the "bird of
absence," the hauntological creature forever on the verge of disappearing
(as well as "Gone", discussed previously, there is also "Hordern Stoops,"
which begins: "The curlews are long gone" [2015, 68]). In "Notes,"
however, the bird's absence is not so clear-cut. Stanza three stays with
the curlew, drawing landscape and language ever closer together while
recalibrating loss:

The curve of its bill and the byht of a
river, throwing light on the early history
of the county. The pre-industrial landscape
preserved in egg colours: greenish-dun to
olive-green (blotched with dark brown and
dark shades of green, thought to intimate
early forms of writing). (Skelton 2016, 119)

The collocation of animal part (the curlew's curved bill) and body of water (the river's bend, or "byht" in Anglo-Saxon) bespeaks a secret relationship that hinges on the notion of the palimpsest. Skelton is demonstrating a key principle of ecocritical thinking, as it confronts a landscape's legibility or "readability." To read a landscape as a text means to recognize its impermanent and fluctuating quality, its temporal constraints and proneness to agencies within (species inhabitation, climate differentials) and without (human incursion). A landscape can contain or project a story, as a result of this impermanence (see Wells 2014); Skelton, however, is suggesting that a landscape can also be a poem, by reading those changes as hidden continuities, or the transference of attributes across time. The poet's eye, in this regard, is able to discern more than the cultural geographer's, wedded as the latter is to the belief that "traditional landscape analysis inevitably offers only a limited scope of enquiry" (Holdsworth 1997, 44). The work of recovery is, therefore bidirectional. Even as landscapes retain traces of animal life (bones and feathers), living animals can display signs of historical sedimentation, if only they are read incisively enough.

In a characteristically Derridean move, the term *hauntology* contains an echo or trace of the word *ontology* (Derrida 2006, 10). This is not merely a homophonic or linguistic conceit. As Derrida makes clear, he is proposing a conceptual displacement: that the sureties of ontology (present/absent, living/dead, being/nonbeing) be supplanted by the logic of the specter (the trace, the apparition). Skelton demonstrates a similar logic in his aesthetics of hauntology. In doing so, his work awakens the same precarious quality that inflects the present-day culture(s) of extinction—only *Homo fragilis* barely figures in it, and it is the natural world of insentient matter and sentient species that is poised between the actual and the evanescent. For Skelton "reads" the Cumbrian moors and lakes and birds as a kind of ghost world, where time is out of joint and the present haunts the past. This amounts to a mirroring of the Merwinian future anterior, which looks back on the present from some unspecified time yet to come.

But Skelton is also a poet of space, as we saw in "Gone." This side of his writing comes through clearly in "Lines of Flight," one of Skelton's more buoyant pieces:

> I watch a solitary crow follow the
> Yarrow upstream. Tracing its own

river in the sky. Higher, much higher,
gulls wheel and meander, bicker and
squabble.

Could I know the landscape without
ever seeing it? Limn its ghost,
mirrored in these intangible paths—
these lines of flight? (Skelton 2015, 40)

The crow's flight path over the Yarrow River becomes a self-defined, overhead trail, a line that is continuous with the community of gulls flying higher still. As well as paralleling the river's currents, the crow's (and the gulls') lines of flight reflect the landscape—ghostly, fugitive, intangible, and transient. It is a fitting image of what could be described as the materiality of the ghost, and it gives some perspective to Skelton's concern with "remainders," his conviction that nature is haunted by its decay side. In this way of seeing, nature does not follow the path of *loss and renewal* so much as *loss and vestigial signification*. Loss is, therefore, not absolute, even if recovery is only imputable through (nonhuman) memory and material remainder rather than through some kind of ecological redistribution. For both Merwin and Skelton, acts of remembrance and restoration can sidestep the snares of appropriation that abide in poetry's metaphorical capability. More than this, each writer brings a hauntological element to zoopoetics, suggesting that animals are no more themselves than when their nonexistence is contemplated and made subject to the deceptions and sureties of language.

Notes

1. Although the *OED* gives priority to both species and figuration, when it comes to actual usage of the word "albatross," the latter vastly outweighs the former.
2. Thom van Dooren questions if this is the case, but concedes that the dodo was "among the first" species to be written about in this way (2014, 3).
3. By the same token, *The Lice*, "one of the most important books of poetry to appear in the sixties" (Watkins 1975, 192), is also considered to be Merwin's "bleakest, most apocalyptic and agonized book" (Hirsch and Merwin 1987), and "as deep an expression of fatalism and despair as one is likely to find in contemporary literature" (Watkins 1975, 193).

4. The poems in question are "Fly" (Merwin 1967: 73), "The Room" (48) and "For a Coming Extinction" (68–69).
5. For a counterargument to Rueckert's and Nelson's assertions, see Christhilf (1986).

WORKS CITED

Adorno, Theodor W. 1983. *Prisms*, trans. Samuel and Shierry Weber. Cambridge, MA: MIT Press.
Aristotle. 1999. *Physics*, trans. Robin Waterfield. Oxford: Oxford University Press.
Beer, Gillian. 2009. Darwin and the Uses of Extinction. *Victorian Studies* 51 (2): 321–331.
Berger, John. 1991. *About Looking*. New York: Vintage.
Cavitch, Max. 2007. *American Elegy: The Poetry of Mourning from the Puritans to Whitman*. Minneapolis: University of Minnesota Press.
Centre for Humans and Nature. 2014. 'Questions for a Resilient Future: How Far Should We Go to Bring Back Lost Species?' http://www.humansandnature.org/how-far-should-we-go-to-bring-back-lost-species–question-13.php. Accessed 29 April 2017.
Christhilf, Mark. 1986. *W. S. Merwin the Mythmaker*. Columbia, MO: University of Missouri Press.
Colebrook, Claire. 2013. Framing the End of the Species: Images without Bodies. *symplokē* 21 (1–2): 51–63.
Coleridge, Samuel Taylor. 1969 [1798]. The Rime of the Ancient Mariner. In *Poetical Works*, ed. Ernest Hartley Coleridge, 186–209. Oxford: Oxford University Press.
Darwin, Charles. 1985 [1859]. *The Origin of Species by Means of Natural Selection; or the Preservation of Favoured Races in the Struggle for Life*, ed. J.W. Burrow. London: Penguin.
Derrida, Jacques. 1981. *Positions*, trans. Alan Bass. Chicago: University of Chicago Press.
———. 2006. *Specters of Marx: The State of the Debt, the Work of Mourning and the New International*, trans. Peggy Kamuf. New York: Routledge.
Elliott, David L., and W.S. Merwin. 1988 [1984]. An Interview with W. S. Merwin. *Contemporary Literature* 29 (1): 1–25.
Folsom, L. Edwin. 1978. Approaches and Removals: W. S. Merwin's Encounter with Whitman's America. *Shenandoah* 29: 57–73.
Folsom, Ed. 1987. 'I Have Been a Long Time in a Strange Country': W. S. Merwin and America. In *W. S. Merwin: Essays on the Poetry*, ed. Cary Nelson and Ed Folsom, 224–249. Urbana: University of Illinois Press.

Hägglund, Martin. 2008. *Radical Atheism: Derrida and the Time of Life*. Stanford: Stanford University Press.

Heise, Ursula K. 2016. *Imagining Extinction: The Cultural Meanings of Endangered Species*. Chicago: The University of Chicago Press.

Hirsch, Edward, and W.S. Merwin. 1987. W. S. Merwin: The Art of Poetry, No. 38. *The Paris Review* 102. http://www.theparisreview.org/interviews/2692/the-art-of-poetry-no-38-w-s-merwin. Accessed 29 April 2017.

Holdsworth, Deryck W. 1997. Landscape and Archives as Texts. In *Understanding Ordinary Landscapes*, ed. Paul Groth and Todd W. Bressi, 44–55. New Haven: Yale University Press.

Kermode, Frank. 1967. *The Sense of an Ending: Studies in the Theory of Fiction*. Oxford: Oxford University Press.

Lazer, Hank. 1982. For a Coming Extinction: A Reading of W. S. Merwin's *The Lice*. *ELH* 49 (1): 262–285.

Macfarlane, Robert. 2015. *Landmarks*. London: Hamish Hamilton.

Merwin, W.S. 1963. *The Moving Target*. New York: Atheneum.

———. 1966. Notes for a Preface. In *The Distinctive Voice: Twentieth-Century American Poetry*, ed. William J. Martz, 268–272. Glenview: Scott, Foresman.

———. 1967. *The Lice: Poems*. New York: Atheneum.

———. 2016. *Garden Time*. Hexham: Bloodaxe.

Midgley, Mary. 2004. *The Myths We Live By*. London: Routledge.

Moe, Aaron M. 2014. *Zoopoetics: Animals and the Making of Poetry*. Lanham, MD: Lexington Books.

Nelson, Cary. 1977. The Resources of Failure: W.S. Merwin's Deconstructive Career. *Boundary 2* 5, vol. 2: 573–598.

Ronda, Margaret. 2013. Mourning and Melancholia in the Anthropocene. *Post45*. http://post45.research.yale.edu/2013/06/mourning-and-melancholia-in-the-anthropocene/. Accessed 29 April 2017.

Roof, Judith. 2007. *The Poetics of DNA*. Minneapolis: University of Minnesota Press.

Rudwick, Martin J.S. 1997. *Georges Cuvier, Fossil Bones, and Geological Catastrophes: New Translations and Interpretations of the Primary Texts*. Chicago: University of Chicago Press.

Rueckert, William H. 1987. Rereading *The Lice*: A Journal. In *W. S. Merwin: Essays on the Poetry*, ed.Cary Nelson and Ed Folsom, 45–64. Urbana: University of Illinois Press.

Safina, Carl. 2002. *Eye of the Albatross: Visions of Hope and Survival*. New York: Holt.

Skelton, Richard. 2015. *Landings*. Cumbria: Corbel Stone Press.

———. 2016. *The Pale Ladder: Selected Poems & Texts 2009–2014*. Cumbria: Corbel Stone Press.

Stearns, Beverley Peterson, and Stephen C. Stearns. 1999. *Watching, from the Edge of Extinction*. New Haven: Yale University Press.
Snyder, Gary. 2008. *A Place in Space: Ethics, Aesthetics, and Watersheds*. Berkeley: Counterpoint.
Turner, Stephanie S. 2007. Open-Ended Stories: Extinction Narratives in Genome Time. *Literature and Medicine* 26 (1): 55–82.
van Dooren, Thom. 2014. *Flight Ways: Life and Loss at the Edge of Extinction*. New York: Columbia University Press.
———. 2015. Editorial Profile: Thom van Dooren. *Environmental Humanities*. http://environmentalhumanities.org/about/ep-vandooren/. Accessed 29 April 2017.
Watkins, Evan. 1975. W. S. Merwin: A Critical Accompaniment. *Boundary 2* 4 (1): 186–199.
Wells, Christopher W. 2014. Reading Signs: The Landscape as Text. *Resilience: A Journal of the Environmental Humanities* 1 (3): 107–111.

PART III

Entanglement

Spinning Theory: Three Figures of Arachnopoetics

Matthias Preuss

Presages also are drawn from the spider; for when a river is about to swell, it will suspend its web higher than usual.
(Pliny 1855, XI.28)
'To read what was never written.' Such reading is the most ancient: reading prior to all languages, from entrails, the stars, or dances.
(Benjamin 1999, 722)

Literary animal studies is concerned with the marginal, with critters that populate the fringes. In pursuit of arachnids in literature and its theory, this contribution examines three different zoopoetological figures in Ovid's *Metamorphoses*—the *spinning spider*, the *weaving spider*, and the *secreting spider*. Each of these figures conveys a different way in which animals contribute to poetry and, thus, supports Aaron Moe's affirmation that animals are indeed "makers" (Moe 2013, 2): They can provide the *content*, the *form*, and the *medium* of literature. What is more, each figure also implicates a different way to think about literature—as *expression*, as *text*, and as *secretion*. These ways are paraphrased at the end of each section in terms of the theoretical writings of Roland Barthes.

M. Preuss
Ruhr-Universität Bochum, Bochum, Germany

© The Author(s) 2018   193
K. Driscoll and E. Hoffmann (eds.), *What Is Zoopoetics?*,
Palgrave Studies in Animals and Literature,
https://Doi.org/10.1007/978-3-319-64416-5_11

Departing from the understanding of figures as "material–semiotic nodes or knots" (Haraway 2008, 4), in what follows, I will unfold the material and semiotic aspects of each figure. To contextualize and historicize the tropes, I will relate them to the ancient knowledge about spiders as set out in the writings of Aristotle and Pliny the Elder. In my analysis, I distinguish between three interrelated levels of animal materiality: *subject matter, textuality*, and *corporeality*. Drawing on Nicole Shukin's (2009) rubric of *rendering*, as well as the works of Bruce Holsinger (2009) and Sarah Kay (2011) on parchment, I flesh out the notion of *corporeality*, which I propose as an antidote to a reductive semiotic approach to animals in texts. Textual webs are to be taken seriously as traces that do not necessarily indicate a former animal presence but that consist of actual animal matter. This conception of literature as *secretion* resists the tendency to consume animals in theory. Spiders are more than mere metaphors, and they seldom come alone. When we begin to pull at the threads of arachnopoetic imagery, marine snails emerge and flayed goats come to the fore. The following analysis not only serves as a reminder of the fundamental entanglement of different life-forms (both nonhuman and human), but also points out the poetic machinations that are involved in pursuing literary animal studies and the becoming (zoo) poetic of literary theory.

TAKING UP THE THREAD (DISGUST)

In quotidian encounters, arachnids, and more specifically spiders, tend to provoke disgust. When these diminutive arthropods crawl, fall, jump, fly, or simply lurk they can trigger a rejection response in human animals that involves nausea, avoidance, and an intense sensitivity to contamination (Davey 1994, 17, 20). The overwhelming feeling of disgust that can seize the body of a person who comes across a spider is, however, culturally constructed rather than biologically induced and is not founded in the evolutionary history of *Homo sapiens* (23). Furthermore, it seems to be a European, urban, and relatively 'modern' rather than a universal phenomenon (Davey et al. 1998). The seemingly 'natural' negative reaction to spiders (cf. Menninghaus 2003, 184) has a cultural history; it has its place and its time. Arachnophobia was *made* and, consequently, it can be *unmade*.

In critical encounters, one sometimes notices a similar rejection of spiders, another contemporary form of "tarantism" (Russell 1979), or at least an 'uneasiness' about handling arachnids (and the like). This equally "unnatural" and, at times, deliberately strategic theoretical and method-ological bias in literary animal studies includes the preference for some 'objects' of research (e.g., "charismatic megafauna") and the neglect of others, usually small or tiny ones, such as spiders. However, the prob-lem at hand is not the difficulty of how to touch upon *certain classes* of rather revolting animals, but how to account for animal bodies in texts *in general*. Although literary animal studies is attentive to animals in texts, there is a risk of reducing them to *textual animals* and neglecting *corporeal* aspects of their lives and deaths.

In the "thought image" (*Denkbild*) "Gloves" from *One-Way Street*, Walter Benjamin muses on a paradox that emerges from the corpo-real contact zone between humans and critters, providing an allegory for the theoretical approach toward animals. Here, disgust is a model that describes the handling of any animal, not only explicitly repulsive ones. The fear of skin-on-skin contact, Benjamin writes, results from an "obscure" sense for an unsettling affinity between human and non-human animals. By shying at and shrinking from all-too-human beasts, humans perform an alterity that is not simply given. They autoposit themselves as sovereigns in the animal kingdom. In the wake of rationali-zation as a distancing move, however, they lapse into the other extreme: "All disgust is originally disgust at touching. Even when the feeling is mastered, it is only by a drastic gesture that overleaps its mark: the nau-seous is violently engulfed, eaten, while the zone of finest epidermal con-tact remains taboo" (Benjamin 1996, 448).

Although Benjamin's account has the undeniable tendency to inflate and universalize a rather 'European' scene (that might have occurred in a Berlin broom closet), it does, nevertheless, provide a witty sophism against anthropocentrism: "He [man] may not deny his bestial relation-ship with animals, the invocation of which revolts him: he must make himself its master" (ibid.). It is not physical mastery over animals but rather intellectual mastery over a violently enforced ontological hierar-chy that must be aimed for. The affirmation of a mimetic correspond-ence across species boundaries turns the tables and initiates a 'revolution' of human-animal interactions. Benjamin sets the objective (*Aufgabe*) to 'own' the difference and reach out. However attainable it may be, this objective can provide a methodological orientation in the field of con-temporary literary animal studies. Benjamin figuratively hints at the adequate approach to animals: scholars should take off their gloves and prepare to get a full feel of animal skin.

In what follows, I will prepare the terminological and theoretical ground for a 'reading without gloves' that dares to get in touch with *zōa* through and in *poetry* in the broadest sense without consuming them (i.e., without incorporating them into an anthropocentric semiotics).

TRANSITION (FROM ZOOPOETICS TO ZOOPOETOLOGICAL FIGURES)

To conceptualize the relationship between text and animals in a 'non-consuming' manner, Aaron Moe introduced *zoopoetics* as a "theory" that recognizes that nonhuman animals "are makers" who cocreate poems through their specific "gestures and vocalizations" (Moe 2013, 2; cf. 2014). Acknowledging multispecies agency, poems cannot be attributed to humans alone; they are the product of a "joint venture" (ibid.), and this "universal" making is "based upon material gestures" and has a "bodily" dimension (4). For Kári Driscoll, zoopoetics is concerned with the *reciprocal* constitution of animals and language. This includes "zoopoiesis," "the creation *of* the animal as much as the creation *by means of* the animal" (Driscoll 2015, 223). When handling animals in texts, however, it is precisely the 'glove of language' that is hard to slip off. How can we treat and read animals in texts otherwise—not only as semiotic animals (that *mean* something but are *only textual* after all)?

One of Donna Haraway's instruments for reaching beyond semiotics is the term 'figure,' which merges matter and meaning: "Figures help me grapple inside the flesh of mortal world-making entanglements that I call contact zones. Figures are not representations or didactic illustrations, but rather material-semiotic nodes or knots in which diverse bodies and meanings coshape one another" (Haraway 2008, 4). Haraway's allusion to "knots" or "nodes" (cf. Haraway 2016, 10–16) in networks of things (including human and nonhuman animals) already bespeaks the degree to which the makings of web-building spiders have invaded critical terminology, and underlines the material substrate of metaphors in and for theory. The following analysis of spider metaphors in Ovid's *Metamorphoses* relies heavily on this notion of 'figure' to address not only the semiotic but also the material aspects of the tropes and to distinguish different levels of materiality.

Literary texts are "self-reflexive construct[s]" (Culler 1997, 33) (i.e., they reflect upon their making; they have an *implicit* theory of *poiesis*, an *implicit* poetics). The self-reflexive dimension of literary texts can be called their *poetology*—a notion that allows us to differentiate between 'internal' and 'external' theories of making (as the latter can take the shape of a heteronomous and prescriptive set of rules at times). A zoopo-etological reading, as I conceive of it, looks for zoopoetics *in* poetry and accounts for the involvement of nonhuman animals in implicit theories of making. More specifically, it traces the material gestures and bodies of nonhuman animals in the text and treats literary life-forms as reflexive figures that speak to the interimplication of life (matter, nature) and lit-erature (text, culture).

After these preliminary, conjunctive, and explorative remarks circling around *what* a zoopoetological reading of a text could be, the following pages seek to demonstrate *how* a zoopoetological reading of a text could be performed by taking a closer look at the first 145 verses from book VI of Ovid's *Metamorphoses*. The hand-to-hand fight between Arachne and Minerva playing out in this passage can be regarded as the *locus classicus* of the spider as a zoopoetological figure.

THE SPINNING SPIDER (ARACHNE'S ABDOMEN)

The beginning of book VI of Ovid's *Metamorphoses* narrates the strug-gle (*agōn*) between Arachne, the mortal daughter of a Lydian dyer from Colophon by the name of Idmon, and Minerva, the goddess of wisdom and patroness of the arts and crafts, who sprung fully armed from Jupiter's head. The odd couple compete in the art of weaving after Arachne boldly claimed her skill surpassed the dexterity of the deity. As Minerva is not inclined to waste an opportunity to penalize un-godly activities and insubordination, a showdown inevitably follows. The antagonists place themselves in front of two identically constructed looms and begin to fabricate textiles. Both tapestries depict scenes of transformation and, thus, provide a two-part *mise en abyme* of the *Metamorphoses* as a whole: "Threads too of golden wire were woven in, / And on the loom an ancient tale was traced" (Ovid 1986, VI.69–70).

Already in the invocation at the very beginning of the *Metamorphoses*, the text is announced as *carmen perpetuum*, a "continuous song" (I.5) that spans the time from the creation of the world out of chaos until Ovid's present (and beyond). The 'ancient tale' is another name for the song that features Arachne. The description of the textiles in the text is also a description of the text as textile. The text addresses how it is made and how other texts are made; it implies a theory of making poetry.

The poetological dimension of the text resides precisely in the representation of the production process of pieces of art (about the long 'history' of transformations) that potentially include the text of the *Metamorphoses* itself. The implicit theory of poetry operates with a certain similarity of tapestry and book. This metaphorical traffic shapes the concept of the text in such a way that it attains textile qualities.

When the weaving is done, Minerva finds Arachne's work of art flawless and true to life. Not amused, the goddess tears it to shreds and strikes the proud woman in the face with the shuttle. Thereupon, Arachne erratically tries to hang herself, but Minerva stops her in midair and turns her into a spider:

> And as she turned to go, she sprinkled her
> With drugs of Hecate, and in a trice,
> Touched by the bitter lotion, all her hair
> Falls off and with it go her nose and ears.
> Her head shrinks tiny; her whole body's small;
> Instead of legs slim fingers line her sides.
> The rest is belly; yet from that she sends
> A fine-spun thread and, as a spider, still
> Weaving her web, pursues her former skill.
> (VI.139–145)

In the lines quoted above, the poetological or metatextual metaphor of 'weaving' is related to the web making of a spider. To grasp the poetological potential of this figure, it is helpful to consult the historical proto-zoological knowledge about spiders that circulated in Ovid's time. What was known about spiders serves as the backdrop against which the figure operates.

In Aristotle's *History of Animals*, composed centuries before Ovid's *Metamorphoses* but still authoritative at the time (and beyond), Aristotle praises spiders with reserve but grants that some of them are "industrious" and "resourceful" (Aristotle 1984, IX.38.622b). Pliny the Elder, in the 11th book of his *Natural History*, composed and published some decades after Ovid's *Metamorphoses*, shows less restraint and marvels at the "wondrous art" practiced by spiders and deems it "worthy of our especial admiration," making the poetological metaphor more plausible. It is above all the autarky or self-sufficiency of arachnoid textile production that fascinates the naturalist. Pliny lauds a wolf spider (*Lycosidae*) for the "remarkable [...] skill which it displays in its operations": "These spin a large web, and the abdomen suffices to supply the material for so extensive a work" (Pliny 1855, XI.28). This corresponds to the long-held conviction that spiders spin webs "from their interior as an excretion" which Aristotle attributes to the pre-Socratic Democritus (Aristotle 1984, IX.39.623a). Pliny markedly emphasizes the abdominal cavity. His description seems to echo Ovid's verses in the accentuation of the bloated belly. The animal body part serves as a container for the resources that are processed. The organ is regarded as the origin of the work—that is why the "abdomen suffices." *Pars pro toto*: the belly embodies the beast.

The *spinning spider*, characterized by its abdomen, is the first figure of animal *poiesis* in the *Metamorphoses*. It implies a conception of literature as the excretion or *expression* of something that was contained within the author. The single thread that is formed into a work of art originates from a self-sufficient spider subject: All the resources needed for spinning it finds within itself.

As a sign, the swollen venter embodies Arachne's inflated claim to superiority and sovereignty. Her hubris is modulated into a hybridization and ends in a full transformation into a "lesser" life-form. As an artist, she dares to violate a metaphysical "law of genre" (Derrida 1980) that lays down the incommensurability of divine, human, and animal *poiesis*. She challenges the authority of the goddess and the primacy of divine authorship. The symmetry of the loom symbolizes the parallels in the antagonists' power politics. Ultimately, Minerva and Arachne contribute to the same fabric that bespeaks the apotheosis of the artist or the author. Two equally dominant subjects attempt to gain mastery. Arachne's heretical anthropocentrism appears as an authoritarian gesture in line with the divine will to power. She transgresses the order, but she is not able to take the place of the goddess. Her aspiring movement is reversed; she is humbled, and tumbles down the *scala naturae*.

Regarding the material side, the figure helps to foreground the *subject matter* of the narrative poem. The resources (once contained within the author) are released and spun into the work—they become *content*. During this form-giving process the raw intestinal material is refined. As a zoopoetological figure, the spinning spider implicates a hermeneutic approach to literature that centers on the author who is "thought to *nourish* the book, which is to say that he exists before it, thinks, suffers, lives for it, is in the same relation of antecedence to his work as a father to his child" and who tries to "*express*" an "inner 'thing'" (Barthes 1977, 145–146). "The *explanation* of a work is always sought in the man or

woman"—or animal, as a whole or in part—"who produced it, as if it
were always in the end, through the more or less transparent allegory
of the fiction, the voice of a single person, the *author* 'confiding' in us"
(143). The single thread can be read accordingly as "a line of words
releasing a single theological' meaning (the 'message' of the Author-
God)" (146).

On the one hand, the figure of the spinning spider naturalizes the
notions of authorship and expression by turning anthropomorphic
descriptions of spiders around and taking them literally; on the other
hand, it blurs the distinction between human and nonhuman makings
by depicting spinning as a common mimetic practice that crosses species
boundaries.

THE WEAVING SPIDER (PURPLE STAINS)

The spinning spider may be the most conspicuous, but it is not the
only arachnopoetological figure lurking in the *Metamorphoses*. From
a safe distance, what the beginning of book VI spells out is a literal
(*'littera'* = letter) metamorphosis of the proper name "Arachne" into
the Latin designation for a zoological genus, "Aranea." Although the
Greek "Arachne" [Ἀράχνη] and the Latin "Aranea" both mean "spider," the former refers theriophorically to a mortal human being who
is saved from death by being turned into an animal specified by the latter. According to Frederick Ahl (1985, 228), this anagrammatic shift,
and the translation it implies, structure the text. Departing from his
analysis, I argue that the defiance that provokes the conflict and seals
Arachne's fate is also already inscribed in her name. "Arachne" can
be read as the anagrammatic negation (*an-*) of an ordering principle
(*arché*), as a declaration of war against divine and mundane hegemony
(*an-archía*). Her telling name evokes the resistance against princes and
principles; and her negating force is encapsulated in the *alpha privati-
vum* at the heart of "Ar*an*ea." "*Arché*" also means "origin"; the play
of the letter compromises the originality of the author. As Ahl points
out, some critics tend to discount anagrams as "accident[s] of language" and "random occurence[s]" (1988, 24) precisely because of
the difficulty to credit them to an author. He holds that ancient writers
"treat[ed] the alphabet as the element of language which could be rearranged," which makes "letters [...] the building blocks of much ancient

linguistic reality" (27). He concludes that they produce a "complex fabric" ("w[oven] together") and that "elements of wordplay are not [...] occasional"; "they *are* [their] art" (43). My point, however, is not that Ovid willfully encrypted Arachne's anarchic drive. Rather, I would like to stress that anagrams produce meaning beyond intention—on the level of the letter. The signifier "Arachne" and the elements it is composed of point to a poetic quality of written language itself.

In the opening verses, Arachne's lineage is addressed in a paradoxical manner that demonstrates how the question of (artistic) filiation is infused with another meaning. The relationship between parent and daughter (*filia*) is sidestepped and the focus is shifted toward the plural of different threads (*fila*) that a text is made of:

> The girl
> Had no distinction in her place of birth
> Or pedigree, only that special skill.
> Her father was Idmon of Colophon,
> Whose trade it was to dye the thirsty wool
> With purple [*tingebat murice lanas*] of Phocaea.
> (Ovid 1986, VI.7–9)

Instead of Arachne's origin—which is declared insignificant—the genealogy of the *Metamorphoses* is treated in these seemingly redundant remarks. One major source is spelled out explicitly: a lost catalog of transformation stories compiled by Nicander of Colophon in the second century BCE. The text names one of the purple threads that is worked into the fabric. The signifier "purple" acts as a contrasting agent that lends salience to the heterogenic threads the book is made of. It surfaces three times; the text is shot through with purple. In this regard, it resembles the fabrics that are produced by Arachne and Minerva on the diegetic level. The second occurrence underlines that it is not Arachne as an author who is rendered visible by coloration. Her erubescence is not lasting; she pales (VI.46–48). The third occurrence of "purple" conclusively settles on the multiplicity and heterogeneity of threads. Reading is complicated by the difficulty to distinguish. It takes a reader attuned to the subtlety of the allusions to appreciate the craftsmanship of the weaver:

Here purple [*purpura*] threads that Tyrian vats have dyed
Are woven in, and subtle delicate tints
That change insensibly from shade to shade [*discriminis umbrae*].
(VI.61–62)

Purple speaks volumes. The Latin-Greek collision of *color* and *phoné* (voice) in the name Colophonius becomes the aptonym that marks and condenses the poetological trait of the text.

In contrast to the spinning spider—an animal that inhabits the diegetic world—the weaving spider emerges as a figure from the manipulation of letters and preceding texts. Yet, there are traces of other animals: the purple stains implicate the entangled natural and cultural history of an almost inconceivable mass of marine snails. "Purple" translates to the Latin *murex* or *purpura*. These are the ancient names of two species of muricids, *Bolinus brandaris* and *Hexaplex trunculus* native to the Mediterranean (as well as the North Atlantic *Nucella lapillus*) which became synonyms for the dye harvested from their mantle cavity (*totum pro parte*) and for the garments tinged using Tyrian purple (Schneider 2006). The works of Aristotle and Pliny offer meticulous descriptions of the elaborate harvest of this precious product. Interestingly enough, Aristotle covers the treatment of the snails under the heading "generation in the case of testaceans" (Aristotle 1984, V.15.546b). It is the reproduction of the snails that facilitates the production of the dye, because to procreate, the animals "cluster together like a bunch of grapes" (V.15.547a). After they are collected in creels, the smaller ones are crushed alive, bigger ones are ripped apart. A "sufficient number" of snails must be collected and kept alive until they are processed (V.15.547a). Unlike the thread of the spinning spider, the dye is a "sort of excretion" that presupposes the obliteration of the individual body. One singular abdomen is not sufficient this time. There is no belly, just a pulp. The origin is crushed.

Pliny's account echoes Aristotle's, but it is considerably more detailed and dwells on the culture of purple. Like Ovid, he distinguishes a panoply of different hues and describes how they serve symbolically as a means of social distinction (Pliny 1855, IX.60–64). Pliny seems surprised by the sublimation necessary to assign value to these colors. Although he is inclined to "excuse this frantic passion for purple," he notes that "the smell of it is offensive, and the colour itself is harsh" (IX.60). The best Tyrian purple has "exactly the colour of clotted blood" (IX.62).

Pliny refers to the *toga praetexta* (IX.63) that distinguishes magistrates, priests, and young men from the commoners who wear white. Ovid's text takes this designation seriously. In the *Metamorphoses*, the purple threads (*praetextus*) mark the earlier text (*prae-textus*)— Colophon's catalog—that is woven into the later one. Consequently, the *Metamorphoses* can no longer be regarded as original.

Taking these considerations into account, the spinning spider gives way to the second zoopoetological figure: the weaving spider which interweaves antecedent heterogeneous threads. It implies a conception of literature that emphasizes the *form* of a text and its intertextuality. The anagrammatic play of the letter that allows the weaving spider to appear on the page ("Aranea") illustrates on a smaller scale how texts are assembled from diverse elements. The spinning author is replaced by a weaving writer who is initially a reader of other texts. These texts are broken down into fragments that constitute the material base of new texts. Writing, as it is figured by the weaving spider, is essentially quoting.

Semiotically, purple has a conventional meaning: It is regarded as the Roman color of power. Tyrian purple is among the most important status symbols in the classical world (cf. Reinhold 1970). During the reign of Augustus, the dye was reserved exclusively for the emperor, and wearing purple in public was a punishable offense. The symbol of the sovereign authority of man over man also bears the material traces of an arrogated and metaphysically secured power of disposal over animals. The purple stains (*maculae*) are reminders of the excessive killing of animals involved in the production of the dye. Looking like "clotted blood," they turn the text into a literary monument for the human and nonhuman victims of sovereign power and highlight its tyrannical trait. The contrast between the no-name dye of Phocaea, which Arachne's humble background is associated with, and the imperial Tyrian purple shows the magnitude of Arachne's ambition and assumption and her artistic excellence at the same time (cf. Harries 1990, 65). The color is a means to problematize the assertion of authority and sovereign control over texts as well as human and nonhuman animals. In addition, the shades of purple can be read as nuances in poetic tone that are decisive in the competition between Arachne and Minerva: "The subtle graduations of colour produced by the weaving process [...] prefigure those subtle shades of meaning which will make all the difference between [...] the two pictorial narratives" (73).

Whereas the figure of the spinning spider emphasizes the *subject matter*, the material side of the figure of the weaving spider foregrounds *textuality* and the composition from heterogeneous elements. The color renders the text opaque, so that the meaning that was supposed to shine through becomes secondary. The purple threads are a visual metaphor for this visibility of language as the raw material of literature. Linguistically speaking, the figure marks the signifier and detaches it from the signified.

The literary theory implicit in the figure of the weaving spider resembles a postmodern approach to literature that centers on *(inter)textuality* and holds that "writing is the destruction of every voice, of every point of origin," that writing is the "negative" where the "identity" of the "body writing" is lost (Barthes 1977, 142). Literature as *text* has "no other origin than language itself" and is the "multi-dimensional space in which a variety of writings [...] blend and clash": nothing but a "tissue of quotations." The writer that replaces the author "can only imitate a gesture that is always anterior, never original"; she can only "mix writings" (146). Therefore, texts have "to be *disentangled*," not "*deciphered*" (147).

THE SECRETING SPIDER (CRYPTIC CORPSES)

The weaving spider is hard to spot. However, there is an even more cryptic and elusive specimen in the *Metamorphoses*: the secreting spider. The tapestries that Arachne and Minerva produce—exemplary texts within the text—are unreadable. Both Arachne and Minerva are unable to receive the message of the other because they are weaving simultaneously. Accordingly, both fail to convey their meaning. On the one hand, Minerva depicts herself as victorious warrioress in the center. She surrounds this allegory with scenes of divine punishment by transformation. These scenes are offered as hermeneutic aids—"examples to instruct / her rival" (Ovid 1986, VI.84)—for slow-witted mortals like Arachne. On the other hand, Arachne concocts a catalog of celestial crimes and shows godly perpetrators in their true colors: "To all of them Arachne gave their own / Features and proper features of the scene" (VI.121–122). But it is crucial that both textiles can only be read—as a warning or, respectively, as an accusation—after the fact, when the damage is done, and it is already too late.

Ekphrasis, the literary description of images, constitutes such a belated reading. The two-dimensional arrangement of pictorial 'still frames' in space is converted into a linear sequence of words that allows the characters to file past the reader. By way of this medial translation from image to text, Arachne is granted the final word in the argument; the representation of her textile follows that of Minerva's. The description of her piece also takes up more space, is more complex, and brims with rhetorical *enargeia*. However, the unreadability that necessitates the translation must not be forgotten. To make the decision of who won the weaving contest the basis for a reading of the Arachne episode not only means 'taking sides,' but also taking part in a competition for primacy and principate. It amounts to an enthronement and overemphasis of the reader whose judgment is decisive.

Arachne repeatedly and fatally fails to read the warning signs (Harries 1990, 71–76). She underestimates Minerva's vengefulness and her readiness to put up a fight. These traits are epitomized in the *aegis*, the armor or cloak protecting her torso: "Herself she gives a shield, she gives a spear / Sharp-tipped, she gives a helmet for her head; / The aegis guards her breast" (Ovid 1986, 123; VI.78–79). Etymologically, the word '*aegis*' is derived from the old Greek expression for 'goatskin' (Parker 2006). This is a mythological reference to Amalthea, foster mother to Zeus who is represented either as a she-goat suckling the infant god or as a nymph feeding him goat's milk. But why is it the goat*skin*, of all things, that is featured in a prominent place like Minerva's breast? Since the third century BCE, parchment, or *membrana*, the cleaned, depilated, and tanned leather of goats (as well as donkeys, calves, and sheep) was used as a writing material alongside papyrus. Indeed, from that time forward, literary works were transcribed from papyrus rolls to parchment codices due to their superior durability (Hurschmann 2006b). Accordingly, "Ovid's works were transmitted by a continuous series of manuscript copies, first in the form of papyrus rolls, and then, from the fourth century AD on, in the form of the codex book with which modern readers are familiar" (Possanza 2009, 315). Thus, it is very likely that the poet owes part of his enduring reputation to the considerable number of goats that were killed to make his writings last. It is the "familiar neatness and authority of the printed page" that "mask the complexities of the historical process" (312) of transmission and the animal matter involved.

Bruce Holsinger's work on medieval parchment culture prompts us to consider the animal as the "material substance of the literary object" (Holsinger 2009, 619) and reminds us of the "mass deaths of countless sheep, lambs, calves, and goats for the means of literary transmission" (ibid.). He points out the "habits of criticism" that "by necessity erase the category of the animal in their pursuit of allegory" (620). In a similar vein, Sarah Kay points out that "[h]owever refined the parchment, it still bears traces of the living animal from which it derives" (Kay 2011, 13–14) and urges readers and literary scholars to "explore an ethics of medieval reading located on the surface as opposed to in the so-called depths of a text" (20).

Returning to the figure of the spider, the historical writings about arachnids offer an analogous reflection upon the product of the art of spinning or weaving *qua* animal substance. Aristotle insists that a spider's web is an organ, a part of the spider's body. The web is made *by* the spider, but it is also made *of* the spider. Nevertheless, it seems to be a body part that does not fully belong to the body but stands *apart* at the same time:

> Spiders can spin webs from the time of their birth, not from their interior as an excretion, as Democritus avers, but off their body as a kind of tree-bark, like the creatures that shoot out with their hair, as for instance the porcupine. (Aristotle 1984, IX.39.623a)

Pliny, by contrast, is fascinated not only by the way the weaving spider conceals itself—"How carefully, too, it retires into a corner [...] so carefully shut up from view, that it is impossible to perceive whether there is anything within or not!" (Pliny 1855, XI.28)—but also by the way it makes its web disappear: "With what wondrous art does it conceal the snares that lie in wait for its prey in its checkered nettings!" (ibid.). In the case of the spider, the animal substance escapes the view. Also the marine snails mentioned before are hidden from the view—"they keep themselves in concealment" (IX.60)—but only until the harvest. Their precious bodily fluids are labeled a "secretion" (ibid.), something that has been separated or severed from the body to which it belonged. Similarly, the spider's web is a secretion, an extension of the animal body.

The secreting spider that is encrypted within the *medium* is the third zoopoetological figure offered by the *Metamorphoses*. It implies a materialist conception of literature as *secretion*, one that considers how animals are fed into texts as literary objects and focuses the *corporeality* of literature. The secreting spider is a memento that every piece of writing (*scriptum*) can be read as a crypt (*cripta*) for the animals that are implicated in it—often at the expense of their lives and physical integrity.

By way of its concealment, the secreting spider betrays what Arachne (unlike Calliope) lacks—the expertise in artistic dissimulation, necessitated by the insight that "the favour of the gods (and god-emperors) could be won by skillful blending of praise of flattery with bolder and even more risky material" (Harries 1990, 77). In this (dis)respect Arachne resembles the young Ovid, who was banished by Augustus for his irreverence in the *Ars amatoria*. She defies the long rhetorical "tradition of 'figuring' language in the interests of both tact and safety" (Ahl 1984, 174) to avoid sanctions by the hands of the authorities. This tradition is incorporated in Pygmalion's vivid statue: "Such art his art concealed [*ars adeo latet arte sua*]. In admiration / His heart desired the body he had formed" (Ovid 1986, X.252). But to read a spider—even an absent one—in this anthropocentric manner also means contributing to the "disappearing animal trick" that critics have employed to render animals "a non-issue" by turning them into "metaphors," into "figures of and for the human" (McHugh 2009, 24). This usually "ends with the human alone on the stage" (ibid.). In Ovid's text, however, a spider is left hanging halfway between life and death. This leaves us to consider the animal remains as well as the animal that remains (secretly lurking) in the text.

As for the material aspect, the figure of the secreting spider helps us to address visibility and materiality with respect to literature, two issues that, according to Giovanni Aloi, are "elephants in the room" regarding the relationship of animal studies and art:

> Whether they representationally appear on the canvas or not, animal products are in the mix of the materials used for the making of the objects we discuss—they have been rendered invisible but they are undeniably present. (Aloi 2015, 10)

The secreting spider 'gives a face' to the simultaneous omnipresence *and* invisibility of animals as media (cf. Holsinger 2009, 616–617); it is a catachrestic figure. Whether we write *with* a quill, write *on* skin, or wrap books *in* skin, animals are comakers of literature in many corporeal ways. Under the conditions of the capitalist mode of (re)production, *rendering* has reached its apex, as Nicole Shukin points out: "Rendering signifies both the mimetic act of making a copy, that is, reproducing or interpreting an object [...] and the industrial boiling down and recycling of animal remains" (Shukin 2009, 20). The rubric of rendering is a powerful analytical tool not only for the industrial era, since the cultural technique of rendering also has a pre-industrial history. It is useful to point out the "discomfiting complicity of symbolic and carnal technologies of reproduction" (21) in different historical constellations. What is more, it encourages us to consider both the semiotic and the material aspect of animals. Thus, it also constitutes a "critical practice" (24) that is neither "reductively materialist" nor "reductively culturalist." In other words, it is a model for a 'reading without gloves' that treats animals in literature neither exclusively as signs nor exclusively as bodies, but tries to establish the entanglement of both aspects in animal figures.

Animals bodies have been and still are the very medium and the material substrate of *poiesis*. As such, they tend to be overlooked because they merge with the product. In literary theory, the phantasm of a dissolving spider becomes the figure of Roland Barthes's critical revision of the theory of intertextuality with respect to the body:

> *Text* means *Tissue;* but whereas hitherto we have always taken this tissue as a product, a ready-made veil, behind which lies, more or less hidden, meaning (truth), we are now emphasizing, in the tissue, the generative idea that the text is made, is worked out in a perpetual interweaving; lost in this tissue—this texture—the subject unmakes himself, like a spider dissolving in the constructive secretions of its web. Were we fond of neologisms, we might define the theory of the text as an *hyphology* (*hyphos* is the tissue and the spider's web). (Barthes 1975, 64)

In this fragment, Barthes paraphrases the "death of the author" as a shift in the use of metaphors *in* and *for* theory from the tissue to the web. This retrospective is more than a mere repetition "in other words." Rather, it discloses a critical agenda: A program that has allegedly already been implemented is transposed into the subjunctive mood. The web appears animated—it almost weaves itself—and it conceals "secrets" within the "secretions." The weaving spider that replaced the spinning spider makes way for the secreting spider. The "death of the author" was the "birth of the reader" (148) and also her apotheosis as a "super-reader." But the theorist (as a reader) can claim as little authority as the author, if she attempts to get a hold of the truth of a text by accounting for other texts within a text. The subject of theory seems to be abandoned here in favor of a sensorium for secretive traces of life-forms. The secretions of the spiders' spinnerets act as lubricants for the discourse (cf. Barthes 1975, 64–65). Barthes metaphorically opens the concept of the text toward a multiplicity of bodies, although his anthropocentric fasci-nation with "our erotic body" (17) prevails.

Gérard Genette's master trope for the hypertext, the "*palimpsest*," relies heavily on disfigured mammalian hides. Nevertheless, the *corporeal* conditions guaranteeing that this concept works, remain unspoken:

> [The] duplicity of the object, in the sphere of textual relations, can be rep-resented by the old analogy of the palimpsest: on the same parchment, one text can become superimposed upon another, which it does not quite con-ceal but allows to show through. (Genette 1997, 398–399)

The goatskin mentioned in the *Metamorphoses* is the material substrate and prerequisite for the emergence of palimpsests. As long as papyrus was in common use, writing media were rarely reused because it was cheaper and more expandable than parchment (Hurschmann 2006a). The resistance of the material allowed it to be scraped with pumice stone or wiped free of written text with a sponge, and, thus, the repeated reuse of the page—while conserving traces of the previous text—was possi-ble. Animal bodies have not only provided a medium among others that allowed for literature to take shape; they have also made possible a way to think about literature. The physical properties of animal matter cata-lyzed the material culture of the palimpsest and, thus, brought forth the leading metaphor for intertextuality. Contemporary literary theory is inconceivable without an understanding of the animals that have been flayed since ancient times; it feeds on an entangled cultural and natural history with nonhuman leading parts.

CONCLUSION

The preceding attempt at a 'reading without gloves' examined three different figures of arachnopoetics in Ovid's *Metamorphoses*: the spin-ning spider, the weaving spider, and the secreting spider. Each of these figures implicates a different way of thinking about literature—as *expres-sion*, as *text*, or as *secretion*. There is one major difference between the spinning spider and the weaving spider versus the secreting spider: no animals were harmed in the creation of the first two metatextual tropes, whereas the third incorporates the remains of animal bodies. It is this *corporeal* dimension of animal participation in literature that this contri-bution sought to emphasize.

Spiders have served as metaphors for poets since the earliest literary texts that were delivered to posterity. Yet, spiders are more than tropes. Spiders are also more than just spiders. The explication of the figures unearthed a web of semiotic and material relations between multiple species, and between multiple substrates of animality. Animals contribute to literature in various ways; some even give up their hides for literature. Therefore, literature surely cannot be attributed to humans alone. On the one hand, this is suggestive of the mimetic similarity between human and nonhuman animals (even spiders) that fascinated Benjamin and challenges the mastery of the human—not only with regard to literature. On the other hand, it leaves us to consider the animal remains that are transformed into literary objects—a metamorphosis that easily escapes our attention. This is the morbid facet of animal *poiesis* that must be taken into account when we speak of animals as "makers" (Moe 2013, 2) and of "creation *by means of* the animal" (Driscoll 2015, 223). Forms of life and forms of death are entangled in intricate ways—and literature is one knot in this web.

Works Cited

Ahl, Frederick. 1984. The Art of Safe Criticism in Greece and Rome. *The American Journal of Philology* 105 (2): 174–208.

———. 1985. *Metaformations: Soundplay and Wordplay in Ovid and Other Classical Poets.* Ithaca, NY: Cornell University Press.

———. 1988. *Ars Est Caelare Artem (Art in Puns and Anagrams Engraved).* In *On Puns: The Foundation of Letters*, ed. Jonathan Culler, 17–43. London: Blackwell.

Aloi, Giovanni. 2015. Animal Studies and Art: Elephants in the Room. *Antennae: The Journal of Nature in Visual Culture* (Special Editorial): 1–30.

Aristotle. 1984. History of Animals, trans. d'A.W. Thompson. In *The Complete Works of Aristotle: The Revised Oxford Translation*, ed. Jonathan Barnes, 1:774–993. Princeton: Princeton University Press.

Barthes, Roland. 1975. *The Pleasure of the Text*, trans. Richard Miller. New York: Farrar, Straus, and Giroux.

———. 1977. The Death of the Author. In *Image—Music—Text*, ed. and trans. Stephen Heath, 142–148. London: Fontana.

Benjamin, Walter. 1996. One-Way Street, trans. Edmund Jephcott. In *Selected Writings: Volume 1, 1913–1926*, ed. Marcus Bullock and Michael W. Jennings, 444–488. Cambridge, MA: Belknap Press of Harvard University Press.

———. 1999. On the Mimetic Faculty, trans. Edmund Jephcott. In *Selected Writings: Volume 2, Part 2, 1931–1934*, ed. Howard Eiland, Michael W. Jennings, and Gary Smith, 720–722. Cambridge, MA: Belknap Press of Harvard University Press.

Culler, Jonathan. 1997. *Literary Theory: A Very Short Introduction*. Oxford: Oxford University Press.

Davey, Graham. 1994. The 'Disgusting' Spider: The Role of Disease and Illness in the Perpetuation of Fear of Spiders. *Society and Animals* 2 (1): 17–25.

Davey, Graham, Angus McDonald, and Uma Hirisave. 1998. A Cross-Cultural Study of Animal Fears. *Behavior Research and Therapy* 36: 735–750.

Derrida, Jacques. 1980. The Law of Genre, trans. Avital Ronell. *Critical Inquiry* 7 (1): 55–81.

Driscoll, Kári. 2015. The Sticky Temptation of Poetry. *Journal of Literary Theory* 9 (2): 212–229.

Genette, Gérard. 1997. *Palimpsests: Literature in the Second Degree*, trans. Channa Newman and Claude Doubinsky. Foreword by Gerald Prince. Lincoln: University of Nebraska Press.

Haraway, Donna. 2008. *When Species Meet*. Minneapolis: University of Minnesota Press.

———. 2016. *Staying with the Trouble: Making Kin in the Chthulucene*. Durham, NC: Duke University Press.

Harries, Byron. 1990. The Spinner and the Poet: Arachne in Ovid's Metamorphoses. *Proceedings of the Cambridge Philological Society* 36: 64–82.

Holsinger, Bruce. 2009. Of Pigs and Parchment: Medieval Studies and the Coming of the Animal. *PMLA* 124 (2): 616–623.

Hurschmann, Rolf. 2006a. Palimpsest. In Cancik and Schneider, *Brill's New Pauly*. http://dx.doi.org/10.1163/1574-9347_bnp_e904490.

———. 2006b. Parchment. In Cancik and Schneider, *Brill's New Pauly*. http://dx.doi.org/10.1163/1574-9347_bnp_e913430.

Kay, Sarah. 2011. Legible Skins: Animals and the Ethics of Medieval Reading. *Postmedieval* 2 (1): 13–32.

McHugh, Susan. 2009. *Animal Farm*'s Lessons for Literary (and) Animal Studies. *Humanimalia* 1 (1): 24–39.

Menninghaus, Winfried. 2003. *Disgust: Theory and History of a Strong Sensation*. Albany, NY: State University of New York Press.

Moe, Aaron M. 2013. Toward Zoopoetics: Rethinking Whitman's 'Original Energy'. *Walt Whitman Quarterly Review* 31 (1): 1–17.

———. 2014. *Zoopoetics: Animals and the Making of Poetry*. Lanham, MD: Lexington Books.

Ovid. 1986. *Metamorphoses*, trans. A.D. Melville. Oxford: Oxford University Press.

Parker, Robert. 2006. Aegis. In Cancik and Schneider, *Brill's New Pauly*. http://dx.doi.org/10.1163/1574-9347_bnp_e109870.

Pliny. 1855. *The Natural History*, trans. Henry T. Riley. The Perseus Digital Library. London: H.G. Bohn.

Possanza, Mark. 2009. Editing Ovid: Immortal Works and Material Texts. In *A Companion to Ovid*, ed. Peter E. Knox, 311–326. Chichester: Wiley-Blackwell.

Reinhold, Meyer. 1970. *History of Purple as a Status Symbol in Antiquity*. Brussels: Latomus.

Russell, Jean F. 1979. Tarantism. *Medical History* 23 (4): 404–425.

Schneider, Helmuth. 2006. Purple. In Cancik and Schneider, *Brill's New Pauly*. http://dx.doi.org/10.1163/1574-9347_bnp_e1014860.

Shukin, Nicole. 2009. *Animal Capital: Rendering Life in Biopolitical Times*. Minneapolis: University of Minnesota Press.

Impersonal Love: *Nightwood*'s Poetics of Mournful Entanglement

Peter J. Meedom

> *beat life like a dinner bell, yet there is one hour*
> *that won't ring—the hour of disentanglement.*
> (Barnes 2001 [1936], 125–126)

Living beings in Djuna Barnes's *Nightwood* (2001 [1936]) prove difficult to read by virtue of their poetics of entanglement; they exist precisely in so far as they are cowritten by the history of impersonal life. The loquacious heart of Barnes's interwar novel, the gender-bending quack Matthew O'Connor, ceaselessly professes death and dying as part of life and love as a kind of loss equaling death. For O'Connor, to love a person means to become entangled in his or her impersonality, in the heterochrony and heteronomy reaching beyond personal life. What kind of practice does loving the impersonality of the personal require? In this chapter, I will argue that the zoopoetics of *Nightwood* takes the shape of entanglement tying together personal and impersonal life that shifts how we think about the role and function of animality in "perhaps the

P. J. Meedom
University of Oslo, Oslo, Norway

© The Author(s) 2018
K. Driscoll and E. Hoffmann (eds.), *What Is Zoopoetics?*,
Palgrave Studies in Animals and Literature,
https://doi.org/10.1007/978-3-319-64416-5_12

213

most complex and atypical portrait of animality in modernist literature" (Rohman 2008, 26). Moreover, O'Connor's discourse of impersonal love necessitates significant engagement with the way posthumanist thinkers, such as Donna Haraway, Elizabeth Grosz, Rosi Braidotti, and Cary Wolfe, think about relationality and temporality. As we come to learn, O'Connor proposes a mournful practice to affirm the failure of knowing the precise nature of entanglement, exactly how one is delivered to forces beyond one's power. O'Connor enjoys a privileged position in the novel—the other main characters (Felix, Nora, and Jenny) seek his counsel "to learn of degradation and the night" (145); he's an expert in the troubles of the heart. Although baffling and defying standard logic, the character and purpose of O'Connor's proposed mournful practice can be reconstructed through his many informal sessions with Felix Volkbein and Nora Flood, who both love and fundamentally fail to understand the vagrant, enigmatic Robin Vote. *Nightwood* invites reflection on what it means paradoxically to extend beyond oneself to others and, thus, suffer the embeddedness of loss and death within life: "Love is death, come upon with passion; I know, that is why love is wisdom. I love her as much as she is condemned to it [...]. We love each other like death" (124–125). Here, Nora is referring to the center of desire in the novel, Robin, who in her elusiveness and attraction comes to embody the difficulties of living with entanglement. Although Robin does not die in the novel, love is consistently depicted as a kind of death, as dying and decay, as a process of loss or dispossession. One of the major difficulties arising out of this discourse concerns how love relates to this continuous process of loss vis-à-vis death as a final (or possibly transitionary) event for personal life.

Let me begin by briefly recounting the narrative of *Nightwood*: Robin marries a false Baron, Felix Volkbein, who is fixated on forging an aristocratic lineage to escape his precarious Jewish identity. Against her will, she bears him a male heir. She abandons her family and moves in with Nora, an American expat living in Paris, but eventually leaves her too—departing on her nighttime wanderings, drinking, and taking up with a widow, Jenny Petherbridge. Nora consults O'Connor for advice and insight about her own feelings of distress, ownership, and abandonment. O'Connor, though, is not without his own troubles. We learn quite early that O'Connor himself is "a soul in physical stress" (26)—having fought for France in the war and losing a kidney, he suffers above all from the ramifications of gender fluidity to which the social world proves inhospitable.

In order to enter the netherworld of *Nightwood* and begin to grasp the stakes and scope of O'Connor's largely overlooked discourse, I propose to imagine him as an analogue to Freud's psychoanalytic practice which directs itself not toward "those energies which, owing to repression, are inaccessibly confined in [the] unconscious, as well as those which [the] ego is obliged to squander in the fruitless task of maintaining these repressions" (Freud 1959, 256), but, instead, toward affirming and learning to live with what Barnes names "the beast on the other side, with the stench of excrement, blood and flowers" (80).

In a way similar to Freud, O'Connor describes personal life as wildly and unpredictably various in its desires, irresolvably conflicted, and, again like Freud, he concerns himself with what cannot be assimilated into the narrative of the analyzed. However, whereas Freud conceived of the individual as a single unit, whose division was essentially a defensive measure, O'Connor insists that there is no possibility for love to occur without becoming entangled in the impersonality of the person you love and suffering the loss inherent in this process. He provides, in essence, a talking cure, but one that is directed at the impersonality of the personal rather than the attention to the personal accorded by psychoanalysis. In other words, O'Connor envisions a posthumanist practice to encompass the impersonal beyond the personal framework suggested by Freud. I seek to further existing criticism on *Nightwood*'s textual politics in the direction of posthumanism, specifically the attempts to get away from the individualizing of persons, to celebrate a world of relations rather than subjects.

A doctor of existence or anatomist of life, rather than a medical man, O'Connor never overtly flaunts his curative abilities: "I am no herbalist, I am no Rutebeuf, I have no panacea, I am not a mountebank" (17). It cannot be expected that O'Connor will cure anyone or anything. As an unlicensed doctor, he spends most of his time discoursing on topics of extramedical suffering—the "universal malady" (29), dispensing impenetrable wisdom. While incongruity best describes O'Connor's soliloquies, we do find consistency in how he repeatedly attempts to describe personal lives that have painfully broken with self-identity. O'Connor spouts death and loss within life, which critics have largely ignored or else taken at face value in order to affirm the novel's triumphant deconstruction of the human-animal boundary. Rather than framing it is a simple or indeed clichéd metaphor of love, O'Connor's discourse of life proposes death as part of life. As we shall see, this subverts the position Carrie Rohman takes, for example, when she affirms that the boundary-troubling agency of "the animal" revises the human. Instead, *Nightwood* proposes a much more complex poetics of entanglement, in which there can be no talk of overcoming or transcendence (either upward or downward), but only of getting deeper into "the mess"—similar to what Donna Haraway (2016) calls "staying with the trouble," or as Rosi Braidotti (2013, 141) puts it, "'We' are all in *this* mess together." In trying to find a ground between the strong impersonality of vitalists like Braidotti and the focus on personal finitude in Derrida and Cary Wolfe, this chapter argues that entanglement necessitates the integration of both levels.

My discussion of "entanglement" owes much to the work of Karen Barad, where agents not only interact in phenomena, but are constituted in and through them. On these grounds, Barad proposes the term "intra-action":

> Distinct agencies do not precede, but rather emerge through, their intra-action. It is important to note that the "distinct" agencies are only distinct in a relational, not an absolute, sense, that is, agencies are only distinct in relation to their mutual entanglement; they don't exist as individual elements. (Barad 2007, 32)

Barad's agential realism seeks to reconcile epistemology and ontology on a general philosophical level—with *Nightwood* I propose to think about what entanglement means in a sense of both heteronomous entanglement with others and heterochronous temporality. What proves so difficult to comprehend in O'Connor's incessant ramblings is that to apprehend these two aspects of entanglement, he suggests, comes to rest on mourning the loss that enables it.

Heteronomy and heterochrony disturb the domestication of death and nature by questioning the notion that only human beings in their humanity make up lovable persons. In proposing the term "impersonal love," I am drawing on Dominic Pettman's (2017) recent notion of "creaturely love," which sees all love as inherently both more and less than human. Pettman's key intervention consists in shifting how we think about what we love in who we love to be more a matter of creatureliness than a question of humanity. My reason for choosing the "impersonal" is not only to try to avoid the most insidious aspects of the reified categories of "human" and "inhuman"/"animal" that continue to haunt the discourse of animal studies and posthumanism; it is also a matter of finding a term that allows us to think beyond the personal, especially when the personal is always cocreated by and develops with something larger than itself. With the impersonal rather than Pettman's "inhuman," I regard *Nightwood*'s poetics of mournful entanglement to direct us beyond the singular being and toward impersonal life. With impersonal life I, thus, imply what Brian Massumi (2014. 96) calls "[l]ife [that] in all its dimensions pertains to the transindividual, never to the individual considered separately." My use of the term "the personal" is deliberately underdetermined; it simply implies a discrete being to whom something matters and not an ontological statement bent on fixing *who* can be a person and *what* cannot. It is precisely this conceptual obsession that cuts off possible affective registers in favor of the problematic notion that science or ontology can finally tell us who we are, and following from this, whose lives shall count as lives. Instead, I propose to consider the personal as temporary and negotiable—ultimately the personal only appears through an act of recognition.

Roaring with the Earth

How does recognizing entanglement—one's own shadow—come to be a mournful activity? How does recognizing entanglement fortify an alternative view of the earth, how does it reinvent love? Thinking about entanglement is a considerably difficult task, which is why I enlist a range of thinkers to unfold some of the political and philosophical ramifications of this term. In significant ways, with O'Connor, Barnes brings into play Freud's notion of "mourning" as well as Darwin's vision of the living world as an "entangled bank." O'Connor's discourse speaks to the long and difficult work of inheriting two nineteenth-century thinkers that both forged a new temporality without the redemptive future of Christianity: Darwin and Freud loom large in the novel, and I will spend parts of this chapter clarifying how the novel enters into dialogue with these figures concerning mournful entanglement.

In what is perhaps the central passage in O'Connor's many soliloquies, mourning and impersonal life entangle themselves as desired practice and ultimate reality:

> We are but skin about a wind, with muscles clenched against mortality. We sleep in a long reproachful dust against ourselves. We are full to the gorge with our own names for misery. Life, the pastures in which the night feeds

and prunes the cud that nourishes us to despair. Life, the permission to
know death. We were created that the earth might be made sensible of her
inhuman taste; and love that the body might be so dear that even the earth
should roar with it. Yes, we who are full to the gorge with misery, should
look well around, doubting everything seen, done, spoken, precisely
because we have a word for it, and not its alchemy. (Barnes 2001, 75)

In this characteristically convoluted discourse, O'Connor touches on
several aspects this chapter will seek to unfold. First, the images could
be characterized collectively as "entanglement" in that they, on several
levels, show the living being's entwinement with the earth, with death,
with others—condensed in the baffling sentence: "We were created that
the earth might be made sensible of her inhuman taste; and love that the
body might be so dear that even the earth should roar with it." In other
words, O'Connor tries to imagine personal life from the point of view
of impersonal life in the full knowledge that it doesn't have a point of
view—this becomes the grounds for reinventing love as beyond the personal (heteronomy) as well as for extending back into earth time (heterochrony or "the past in the present" to use Henri Bergson). Second,
the emphasis on "misery," "reproach," "despair," and "doubt" suggests
a painful experience of living with entanglement that serves to establish the generally mournful tone of the novel. And, although life would
seem to permit knowledge about "death," knowledge is repeatedly cast
into doubt when the "alchemy"—the way it works—eludes words and
expressed knowledge. Mourning, then, also works to affirm the inability
to know this.[1]

O'Connor's discourse on earthly entanglement foregrounds heteronomy: Being alive means being "mixed up with" or entangled with
"others," as O'Connor explains, "The body has a politic too, and a life
of its own that you like to think is yours" (137). In Donna Haraway's
parlance, we would express this as "partners do not precede the relating" (Haraway 2008, 4). But, whereas, Haraway consistently and eloquently studies relationality, "the permission to know death" through life
seems to call for another framework attentive to the impersonal beyond
interpersonal becoming. First, however, let us ask what it is about
O'Connor's mournful entanglement that departs from Freud's notion of
mourning.

In August 1913, Sigmund Freud made a day hike through the
Dolomites with two friends, one of them a poet, possibly Rilke.[2]

In his essay "Transience" (1915), Freud recounts their discussion of how nature and flowers are prone to destruction and decay and, in this sense, possess an ill-fated beauty. For the poet, the knowledge of extinction disturbed the appreciation of beauty that was already lost. In contrast to the poet's pessimistic view, Freud saw value, even a heightened beauty, in transience, arguing that scarcity and finitude instill a worth of a different kind:

> What spoilt their enjoyment of beauty must have been a revolt in their minds against mourning. The idea that all this beauty was transient was giving these two sensitive minds a foretaste of mourning over its decease; and, since the mind instinctively recoils from anything that is painful, they felt their enjoyment of beauty interfered with by thoughts of its transience. (Freud 1957b, 306)

Continuing this line of thought a few years later in "Mourning and Melancholia" (1957a [1917]), Freud argues that normal mourning is a form of psychic work in which the self detaches from the world and retreats into itself so that it can, slowly and painfully, disengage the energy it has invested in a love object that no longer exists in order to be able to reclaim that lost energy for itself. In melancholia, the psyche refuses to accept the reality of the loss and takes the lost object into the psyche instead. Freud argues that "[m]elancholia is in some way related to an object-loss which is withdrawn form consciousness, in contradistinction to mourning, where there is nothing about the loss that is unconscious" (1957a, 244). The process of mourning, then, marks a separation from the world in contrast to melancholia. Rather than a retreat into the self, the kind of mourning expressed by O'Connor in *Nightwood* denotes an expansion that attempts to recognize entanglement beyond oneself, and further entails a practice in which the mourner tries to affirm impersonality.

In this respect my reading benefits greatly from Branka Arsić's understanding of grief as an unending practice premised upon an affective vitality by which it "changes the mode of being—the ontology—of what is not into what is, but it can do so only as long as it perpetuates itself, imbuing what is lost with its own force" (Arsić 2015, 32). Eschewing individualist personal identity in favor of an impersonal view of all matter, Arsić argues, leads to the possibility of collective, communal grief. Similarly, O'Connor professes a nonteleological understanding of matter as that which circulates, and in the following I shall explore how O'Connor's notion of entanglement can be productively related to the kind of heterochrony envisioned by Darwin.

Darwin's image of the entangled bank helps us think about how entanglement proposes a temporality of deep time as heterochronic presence. Let me quote the famous penultimate paragraph of *On the Origin of Species*:

> It is interesting to contemplate an entangled bank, clothed with many plants of many kinds, with birds singing on the bushes, with various insects flitting about, and with worms crawling through the damp earth, and to reflect that these elaborately constructed forms, so different from each other, and dependent upon each other in so complex a manner, have all been produced by laws acting around us. (2008 [1859], 360)

Leading us from a beautiful prospect to the hidden powers at work, Darwin leaves us with a sense of wonder at the formal prowess of impersonal life but also with an indelible mark of loss. All present living beings carry the deep history of life with them—this is heterochrony. For the attentive reader, their bodies tell stories of an immense impersonal history composed collectively by uncounted personal lives and deaths. The argument here is that Darwin and Freud redescribed nature in such a way that we ought to reconceive the old regrets about transience and accept an entangled existence, suffering and all, as a source of joy. *Nightwood* points to the earth as the place to be. ("Bow Down" is, after all, the recurring imperative of the novel.) Freud and Darwin—together with O'Connor—try to make life more bearable by redescribing its conditions, finding the sublime in the impermanent, and condemning as an enemy of life the very idea of immortality.

Entanglement describes how personal and impersonal life become embedded in each other, or, as Brian Massumi notes, how the "transindividual folds into the infraindividual, which folds back out into the transindividual" (Massumi 2014, 94). Entanglement's multidirectionality unseats the organizing logic of before/after, of following against, or with, against the succession that makes adaptation and advancement the hallmarks of a superior species.

Juxtaposing Darwin with Barnes demands comment, when it was precisely the politicization of natural selection and the typological thinking of fixed biological matter that made it easy to exploit and frame "natural" differences within culture, and in turn, to persecute and kill "the unwanted," "lives unworthy of life," etc., as we encounter them in *Nightwood*'s interwar culture of life and death. Elizabeth Grosz has persuasively argued how Darwin's thought could hardly have been further removed from a belief in living matter as bounded fixity. Drawing on Bergson, Grosz writes that "life, even the simplest organic cell, carries its past with its present as no material object does" (Grosz 2008, 6). The reference to an "original past, a past which has never been present" resonates strongly with Bergson's concept of the "past in general" from *Matter and Memory* (1896). For Grosz, we should think of species "in terms of trajectories emergent from individual transformations" (2004, 8). In other words, Grosz argues on the basis of Darwin that species are not fixed ontological categories but work indeterminately.

Because nature largely was (and is) conceived as the realm of necessity itself, biology has proved susceptible to virtually any political orientation and use. The political use of Darwin, then, has more to do with a penchant for arguments of necessity than with any inherent political valence of biological or evolutionary theories. If we, instead of emphasizing the struggle for life of Social Darwinism, foreground Darwin's complex work on change and entanglement, we begin to notice how O'Connor's convoluted discourse on entanglement is not only a melancholy lament of personal loss, but more properly an attempt to describe an imperative to love the impersonal, however troubling and possibly painful it will turn out to be.

Nightwood's repurposing of depravity not only refers to the outcasts and eugenically rendered unproductive, typically implied by degeneration, decadence, and depravity, but also proposes an affective register attuned to impersonal life's heterochrony and the heteronomy of personal life known as entanglement:

> In the acceptance of depravity the sense of the past is most fully captured. What is a ruin but Time easing itself of endurance? Corruption is the Age of Time. It is the body and the blood of ecstasy, religion and love. "Ah, yes," the doctor added, "we do not 'climb' to heights, we are eaten away to them." (Barnes 2001, 106)

To recollect such sensation is to turn into another sensation; feeling what is being lost is no longer confined to the past, but is maintained through the act of mournful entanglement. Stated differently, the depravity or decadence mentioned here is not one of dandy excess—it is rather the depravity of earthbound creatures devoured by affection for others through an act of impersonal love.

When we take entanglement into consideration, *Nightwood*'s "bowing down" refers not only to possible social submission, but also to a possible countermovement against the erect posture of the human *ekstasis* from nature. The "lowest" and most "degraded" elements are not overcome; they remain essential to life. While I agree with Dana Seitler's argument that *Nightwood* attempts to make "social problems identifiable and resolvable in the body that extends beyond the limits of generic convention" (Seitler 2008, 115), I am less convinced that the "characters who populate this unstructured landscape are figured as sexual subjects in a state of bestial devolution" (121), which, for Seitler, means performing the kind of strategy that renders decay and degeneration positive by a normative inversion. Rather than ostracizing the unproductive as being "against life," mourning recognizes the remnants, failures, and losses inherent in impersonal life. For O'Connor, recognizing entanglement means affirming this kind of heterochronic presence: "The reason I'm so remarkable," O'Connor tells a priest, "is that I remember everyone even when they are not about" (Barnes 2001, 147).

In a sense, humans are living fossils or infraindividual remnants of former life—"the rudiment of a life that has developed, as in a man's body are found evidences of lost needs" (47). Holding close to the breast or having the "fossil" of someone embedded turns the lapse of time into time's recovery—as witnessed here in Barnes's description of love: "In Nora's heart lay the fossil of Robin, intaglio of her identity, and about it for its maintenance ran Nora's blood" (51). The love of Robin and Nora is traversed by the transformation from an isolated individual to a presence or force that permeates the earth. What is mourned, then, becomes simultaneously the deep time of fossils as well as the recognition of so-called depraved, unworthy lives. Earthly entanglement is a painful expansion of personal life, yet it does not belong to any one individual and cannot be satisfied in any object. Mourning as an act of life, then, directs itself simultaneously to the past in the present—the deep heterochronic time of fossils—and outward toward the "depraved," "unworthy" lives "while flesh is on them" (76).

LOVE'S STRANGE KINSHIP

Entanglement is not a way out, but a painful way deeper into the earthly mess. The role and function of impersonal love in *Nightwood* as deliberated by O'Connor by and large hinges on the relationship of Nora and Robin that has typically served as the key point of contention in critical readings of animality. In the following, I shall argue that *Nightwood*'s poetics of mournful entanglement fundamentally collides with the notion of animality as nonidentity proposed by Carrie Rohman. The kind of entanglement I am depicting here necessitates integrating the personal with impersonal. While I am informed by thinkers such as Braidotti, Haraway, Deleuze and Guattari, and Wolfe, the purpose here is to show how this desired integration makes obvious certain limitations in their different lines of thought.

The first encounter with Robin occurs when the doctor is called by a hotel clerk to check on a guest, only to arrive (accompanied by Felix) to find a woman asleep, described in an extended tableau—a veritable collection of natural metaphors: Robin smells of fungi, "earth-flesh"; she "is the infected carrier of the past," "her flesh was the texture of plant life [...] as if sleep were a decay fishing her beneath the visible surface [...] the property of an unseen *dompteur*" (31). Similar to Merleau-Ponty's notion of flesh (*chair*) denoting the intertwinement of bodies, Barnes, too, stresses the "strange kinship" with animals (Merleau-Ponty 2003, 168).[3] Moreover, the heterochrony depicted here—Robin's curious embodiment of "decay," the "past," and the "earth-flesh"—makes her eminently desirable. Felix's attraction seems vested in Robin's natural antiquity: "not so much the work of man as the work of wind and rain and the herd of the seasons" (Barnes 2001, 37). With Robin, Felix can seemingly experience a "great past" without the burden of history—she carries "the 'way back' as animals do" (36). When the unnamed narrator depicts Robin, it is with "the iris of wild beasts who have not tamed the focus down to meet the human eye [...] a woman who is beast turning human [...] as the unicorn is neither man nor beast deprived, but human hunger pressing its breast to its prey" (33–34). Throughout the novel, Barnes plays with the figure of taming used in humanist discourse, that of becoming human by exercising the faculty of reason. In these descriptions, however, Robin seems to belong to the linear conception of evolution, having "somewhere about her [...] the tension of the accident that made the beast the human endeavour" (61). Yet we are also fundamentally witnessing the other characters' penchant for representation—for providing ways and means for making desires known, for making Robin legible in and through them. Robin is associated with silence and the absence of language (although she does, in fact, speak and act, something critics tend to elide). Her being different contributes to her illegibility but cannot, I argue, be exhaustively explained by a "return" to the animal.

At the end of the novel, Robin is found in an abandoned, decaying chapel by Nora and her dog, and she performs an inexplicable, wordless gesture of falling down, crawling, and crying in front of a scared dog. This gesture keeps repeating in Barnes's fiction, often in a form that underlines it as a gesture, a literary motif, rather than the psychologically justifiable action of a humanlike character. While their first encounter was determined by the exchange of regards and sympathies between Nora, Robin, and an unhappy lioness in the circus, this time it is the voice of a dog calling them together in a chapel close to Nora's house. Nora enters the chapel and witnesses the much-discussed interaction of Robin and Nora's dog:

> Then she began to bark also, crawling after him—barking in a fit of laughter, obscene and touching. The dog began to cry, running with her, head-on with her head, as if to circumvent her; soft and slow his feet went. He ran this way and that, low down in his throat crying, and she grinning and crying with him; crying in shorter and shorter spaces, moving head to head, until she gave up, lying out, her hands beside her, her face turned and weeping; and the dog too gave up then, and lay down, his eyes bloodshot, his head flat along her knees. (153)

Is this an act of violence marking an "entrance into the cultural order," as Diane Warren has suggested, reading it as "the final collapse of the subversive potential of boundary crossing" (Warren 2008, 139)? Or is it an "ambiguous translation into pure beastliness" aiming at "a kind of 'transcendence downward'" as Kenneth Burke (1966, 13) argues? According to Dana Seitler's (2008, 27) more recent reading, the ending marks the point where "sexual perversity as a form of atavism is literally enacted as a character's return to the form of an animal." But these readings raise the question: From which perch or promontory does this downward movement descend? Is the animal a previous state to which the human can "return"? Contrary to these readings, I argue that *Nightwood* does not present us with a recognizable description of the human as residing above the animal.

In her otherwise instructive reading on identity, language, and animality in *Stalking the Subject* that helpfully foregrounds how *Nightwood* "refuses the disavowal of animality onto marginalized others" (Rohman 2008, 133), Rohman, nonetheless, equates the "undecidable," "nonlinguistic," a "wholly unconscious" quality of Robin together with the ending as a kind of animality capable of revising "the category human"—for Rohman this heralds the novel as a "posthumanist triumph" (157). Rohman's argument is somewhat hard to follow: Is the posthuman equal to animality as nonidentity, which therefore revises the human? When arguing, for instance, that "Robin represents nonidentity as a privileged form of being" (148), it seems to me that Rohman goes too far when reinforcing a notion of animal life as pure being or, equally problematic, as a form that transcends all concepts—the "allomorphic" animal to employ Greg Garrard's (2011, 167) typology. Although Rohman is keen to point out that Robin's "character undercuts the traditional notion that human and animal are separate realms" (Rohman 2008, 143), Rohman's emphasis largely falls on inversing the value of the nonlinguistic from negative to positive—the "redeeming nature of Robin's subjectivity" (157)—which does not allow for the mutual inclusion of human-animal lives that I want to stress here. It is precisely the notion of unconscious or innocent animal life that *Nightwood* plays out as a discursive fantasy. In the following characteristically dense passage, O'Connor contrasts such innocent ignorance with the recognition of the impersonality of personal life:

> And everything we do is decent when the mind begins to forget—the design of life; and good when we are forgotten—the design of death. I began to mourn for my spirit, and the spirits of all people who cast a shadow a long way beyond what they are; and for the beasts that walk out of the darkness alone, I began to wail for all the little beasts in their mothers, who would have to step down and begin going decent in the one fur that would last them their time. (Barnes 2001, 94)

Here, O'Connor ventures that *human* innocence is precisely the forgetting of death as part of life, thus, failing to recognize how the personal extends beyond itself—"a long way beyond what they are." *Nightwood* qualifies death as part of life, that life is life only when including death and, thus, not life opposed to death: "A man is whole only when he takes into account his shadow as well as himself—and what is a man's shadow but his upright astonishment" (107). For O'Connor, mourning is the only practice he knows that can affirm the inability to know the impersonality of the personal.

Because humanism is based on an exclusion of animality, becoming-animal is a subversive strategy, or so the argument goes. However, in his third thesis "on the Animal *to Be Avoided*" in *What Animals Teach Us About Politics*, Brian Massumi notes that to prophesy "the end of the human and the dawn of a posthuman age," in fact, assumes "the ability to categorically separate the human from the animal" (Massumi 2014, 91). Of course, becoming in the sense originally proposed by Deleuze and Guattari resists the implication that you could attain a state at which this becoming would be at an end. For Deleuze, becoming is not necessarily a "good thing," even though this is how it is routinely presented. Becoming is hard and painful and entails loss; in other words, at times, it can also result in "fascist becoming." In this sense, Rohman's triumph occludes the dangers and loss incurred by becoming entangled. *Nightwood*'s ending is simply difficult to claim for any conclusion. Performing together, as Robin, Nora, and the dog do, affective potential that far from suspends life in the kind of drunk, melancholic stupor O'Connor seems to court toward the end, it animates the novel with a final bout of restless, indeterminate energy. The ending is an abrupt gesture of bowing down; itself a risky, momentary entanglement of humans and dog. Notably, it is an act of mourning together—they are both "crying," Robin "weeping" too, the dog "with bloodshot" eyes—bringing them closer without ultimately effacing differences. Robin and the dog do not become one another; they hold in play a sense of difference. Entanglement does not return us to the separate personal but to relations, yet we should not downplay the risks when committing to a boundless desire of tracking, as the enigmatic final chapter underscores. Mourning does not necessarily involve a progressive ethical stance toward others, yet it seeks to make more life possible without guarantees. Life is continuous change and, therefore, continuous loss—we cannot successfully hold on to what we hold dear. Refusal to mourn is a refusal to live.

With the poetics of entanglement, *Nightwood* straddles the personal and impersonal in ways challenging posthumanist thinkers like Braidotti, who want us to consider death from the point of view of impersonal life interpreted through the negative vitalism of Gilles Deleuze; he views life and death within the same vital continuum and as another stage in the organism's transformation and, therefore, not as the property of a singular being, but as a relentless and diversifying principle that flows both within, and beyond, the bounds of the organism as pure excess and potentiality. As Deleuze insists in *Pure Immanence*, life does not end "when individual life confronts universal death" but is rather "everywhere, in all the moments that a given living subject goes through" (Deleuze 2001, 29). He suggests that this embeddedness of the organism in the world occurs on a register beyond the conceptions of time and duration that would normally adhere to the personal. Coconstituted from within and without, the personal relation to death in Deleuze's vitalist philosophy demonstrates its enclosure within the vital continuum contra the perspective of finitude foregrounding individual exposure. Embedded in a negative structure of loss, mourning, difference, and vulnerability, the personal—when seen within the framework of finitude—appears limited, with death as the final terminus. For Braidotti and Deleuze, then, political and ethical thought only bent on personal finitude maintains a sharp and problematic division of the living from the dead when it interprets death as the definitive end of being.

Emphasizing precisely this kind of personal finitude, Jacques Derrida's *The Animal That Therefore I Am* and Cary Wolfe's critique of "double finitude" both foreground the shared corporeal vulnerability and mortality of humans and other animals, and in particular the human's own subjection to the "materiality and technicity of language that is always on the scene before we are, as a radically human precondition for our subjectivity" (Wolfe 2009, 571). Rather than aligning itself perfectly with the strong impersonal strand of Braidotti and Deleuze or the personal perspective of finitude proposed by Wolfe and Derrida, *Nightwood*, as I argue, enfolds these two levels through entanglement by bowing down to heteronomy as well as heterochrony. O'Connor's lamenting discourse on impersonal love points toward a different engagement with the impersonality of the personal, hence the difficult imagery of cardiac fossils, entangled moths in their extinctions, and other logical incongruities I hope to clarify in this chapter.

Affirming entanglement as a formal principle means not seeking to recover losses for individual restoration, but rather opting for a community in which losses are transferred and shared. In this way, the ending

of Barnes's novel seems to me to be similar to Haraway's concern for
an active engagement, a response, or playful mode of being that seeks
to get beyond anthropocentric epistemologies that tend to divide affect
from knowledge. Haraway writes that "greeting rituals are flexible and
dynamic, rearranging pace and elements within the repertoire that the
partners already share or can cobble together" (Haraway 2008, 26).
The "shorter and shorter spaces" between Robin and the dog could be
read as differences of degree, not of kind, between creatures that are
no longer in a binary world but in a world of multiple differences and
mutual loss. Haraway's objective in developing a theory of companion
species is to create assemblages of human and animal that upset the perspective of the human as a singular, discrete, independent, and undivided
being. As such, she helps us to see how companion species are not dogs
or cats but composite beings, a species that comes into being through a
way of becoming-with other kinds. I want to suggest, however, somewhat in tension with Haraway's perspective, that there is in *Nightwood*
a portrayal of a particular form of relation that is a being together
between different kinds, but one that loses meaning if we see it as a state
the attainment of which would necessitate some kind of transformation or transcendence into hybridity. In place of the notion of hybridity,
Nightwood not only presents entanglement but also preserves a sense of
difference, of personal life extending into the impersonal. Pure impersonality is not something we can claim for ourselves: "A strong sense of
identity gives man an idea he can do no wrong; too little accomplishes
the same," as O'Connor reminds us (Barnes 2001, 126).

Mournful Entanglement

In many ways, *Nightwood* is a novel about legibility, about reading entanglement even when it strains our habits to treat bodies as conceptual surfaces, consolidated and ordered into "readable" forms. O'Connor—the
"consultant" for all other characters—at one point seeks the council of a
priest to unburden himself, for once, of all his troubles. The advice given
contains a crucial point about legibility and living beings for the novel as
a whole:

> And once Father Lucas said to me, "Be simple, Matthew, life is a simple
> book, and an open book, read and be simple as the beasts in the field; just
> being miserable isn't enough—you have got to know how." So I got to

thinking and I said to myself, "This is a terrible thing Father Lucas has put on me—be simple like the beasts and yet think and harm nobody." (118)

Preoccupied with the disjuncture between the supposed order and harmony of nature with the bloody reality of life (and thought), O'Connor recognizes that his insight into entanglement bars him from any such simplicity. The priest, of course, speaks within a point of view of creation in which beasts are simple because life—authored by God—is eminently and immediately legible. The book of nature, let us remember, has been the paradigm of the legible text in the Western tradition. In the attempts to attain perfect knowledge of the natural world, men have often compared the natural world to a book or a text, because whatever can be read can in principle be understood (cf. Blumenberg 1981, 47–57). The book here works metaphorically as an elemental unity, a closure against recalcitrance and the unfamiliar. As such, the book of nature fuses nature and culture in such a manner as to fully humanize nature and render it legible in a total gesture of comprehensibility. Entanglement works precisely to obscure such a vision of nature's simplistic legibility, emphasizing the lack of authority beyond earthly life: "God is what we make him, and life doesn't seem to be getting any better" (89). The creature "man" is divested from the creator, and, thus, "damned and innocent from the start" (108). How should we live if we take unredeemable transience seriously? If we are not fallen creatures, but simply creatures outside "salvation history," we cannot be redeemed (Garrard 2011, 146).

What emerges in the proliferating images of O'Connor's speech is, in fact, a discourse of the epistemological and personal consequences of entanglement—as he later says: "Don't learn anything, because it's always learned of another person's body" (Barnes 2001, 132). Freud discovered how modern people endanger themselves by the ways in which they protect themselves—one of the ways being their tendency to disallow vulnerability and loss, pinpointed, too, by O'Connor as the inescapable reality of entanglement. *Nightwood* challenges us to face our exposure to the world, rather than immunize ourselves: "they [persons] are only of value when they have laid themselves open to 'nuisance'—their own, and the world's" (135). Moreover, we should note that O'Connor is himself entangled and does not occupy a privileged position outside the mess. Entanglement has personal consequences for those who desire knowledge, often voiced by O'Connor himself: "Can't the morning come now, so I can see what my face is mixed up with?" (20).

If the "morning" came in this sense, it would mean the end of night, and, thus, the end of life, a judgment day that would preclude the very mortality and vulnerability and the others one is so painfully and thrillingly "mixed up with." Thus, the doctor's maddening monologues can be ascribed to a failed "know thyself"—the doctor himself has been denied self-knowledge, "I've never been one thing that I am, to find out what I am!" (146). Circling back to the passage quoted earlier on roaring with the earth, we can now say that we cannot know the alchemy of life because we have been written by it, and, thus, to know ourselves would be to know the inhumanity or rather impersonality that we strangely both are and are not. Hence, the failure of the Delphic imperative is preprogrammed, on the side of death and impersonality.

O'Connor is both the vehicle for others and his own desire to know what acts upon him, what he consists of, only to learn that the more he knows, the more dispossessed he appears. In his discourse on impersonal life, O'Connor is obsessed— not with representation, but with how actually to learn from impersonal life without falling back on the self-identical: "I have a narrative, but you will be put to it to find it" (87). To learn "of another person's body" achieves what O'Connor wants knowledge of entanglement to perform, namely to lead to mourning as an expansive, potentially miserable yet affirmative practice. The (dis)reputable doctor becomes something akin to a visionary artist; a therapist whose objective it is to acquaint his interlocutors with the causes of their suffering and to show the way to insight through reinvention. Like Freud, O'Connor displaces his culture's favored modes of description and explanation for love and compassion. The disturbing discovery heralded by O'Connor is the entanglement of personal and impersonal life (the design of life and death) that calls for the making of sentences, the forging and forcing of analogies. And like Freud, too, the work is not merely dutiful, but essentially imaginative and visionary; a "bowing down" to meet others in the condition of entanglement. O'Connor, then, is not a doctor of the self like Freud, but of the "inhuman" or impersonal character of the personal.

In O'Connor's philosophy of mournful entanglement, the formation of personal history is traumatically opened toward the earth, yet entanglement is negated or destroyed when it is hosted by a fixed object or subject. The inarticulate roaring with the earth mourns the loss and can turn one's life into an endless lament—"now *nothing, but wrath and weeping*!" (149, original emphasis). For Barnes, mourning is not a period of afflicted time or an obstacle that the person needs to overcome in order to live once again free from loss; it is "closer to an ontological operation of restoration of the loss than the modern psychological commitment to protecting the interest of the mourner" (Arsić 2015, 20). In a convoluted description of Nora, we learn that she is "a part of the function to the persons she stumbled against; as a moth by his very entanglement with the heat that shall be his extinction is associated with flame as a component part of its function" (Barnes 2001, 54). Openly flouting the principle of noncontradiction, Nora is both herself and not herself with others. The sentence highlights relation—"part," "entanglement," "associated," and "component"—thus, creating a dense, even obscure, image of an enfolded being whose vitality contains death. Instead of the second life of the soul, entanglement promotes the life of the world that continues after one's own death. The mind-boggling simile propels *Nightwood* away from idealizing the body as an unwritten truth opposed to the mediation of language and toward a sensible life of entanglement with others—this is a crucial aspect of the zoopoetics of entanglement. In this manner, recognizing entanglement entails trying to come to terms with loss and death as part of impersonal life.

In conclusion, what characterizes the poetics of entanglement in *Nightwood* is the way in which living beings are chronically entangled in both a vertical and a lateral sense. Firstly, the vertical *scala naturae* (humans above animals), which the advent of historical sciences supplanted with a temporal hierarchy from regressive and degenerate to highly developed and civilized, is here formally rearranged into heterochrony. This is directed, too, against the genealogy of breeding and pedigree: "Never say higher or lower," Darwin wrote in the margins of a book (qtd. in Shanahan 2004, 288). Secondly, mourning redirects the gaze laterally toward fellow creatures in a multispecies world, a counterpolitics to the biopolitical production of war and biological typologization that renders certain lives expendable and many others degeneratively unproductive. Mourning offers an affective paradigm of impersonal love insofar as it reckons with entanglement in the guise of heteronomy and heterochrony. In mourning, we care far beyond the limits of life; we love beyond death. The mourner maintains a fidelity to her loss and takes finitude—the limit that inscribes life—as the basis for relationality. Recognizing deep time of life's history makes the personal level sensible to the immanence of death in life, which O'Connor incessantly emphasizes. In O'Connor's philosophy of mournful entanglement, the formation of personal history is traumatically opened toward the earth. The earth itself has become a living memorial. The care for the dead is perpetually renewed through the activity of mourning.

NOTES

1. In a similar vein, Paul Sheehan argues for a "zoopoetic restoration" in his chapter in this volume.
2. According to Herbert Lehmann (1966, cf. Schur 1972, 302), the characters referred to are respectively Lou Andreas-Salomé and Rainer Maria Rilke. This has not been confirmed, although Rilke did visit Freud one month after the preparation of the text, in December 1915 (cf. Freud and Ferenczi 1996, 98).
3. Merleau-Ponty's attempt in *Phenomenology of Perception* to avoid the philosophical dichotomies of activity-passivity and subject-object with his concept of the "prepersonal" as an original past—constituting a forgotten or unconscious dimension of embodiment—shares certain ground with what I am trying to do in this chapter. The prepersonal is an "anonymous life which subtends my personal one" (Merleau-Ponty 1962, 165); it is "[b]odily existence which runs through me, yet does so independently of me" (ibid.).

WORKS CITED

Arsić, Branka. 2015. *Bird Relics: Grief and Vitalism in Thoreau*. Cambridge, MA: Harvard University Press.

Barad, Karen. 2007. *Meeting the Universe Halfway: Quantum Physics and the Entanglement of Matter and Meaning*. Durham, NC: Duke University Press.

Barnes, Djuna. 2001 [1936]. *Nightwood*. London: Faber and Faber.

Blumenberg, Hans. 1981. *Die Lesbarkeit der Welt*. Frankfurt am Main: Suhrkamp.

Braidotti, Rosi. 2013. *The Posthuman*. Cambridge: Polity.

Burke, Kenneth. 1966. Version, Con-, Per- and In-: Thoughts on Djuna Barnes's Novel, Nightwood. *The Southern Review* 2: 329–346.

Darwin, Charles. 2008. *On the Origin of Species*, ed. Gillian Beer. Oxford: Oxford University Press.

Deleuze, Gilles. 2001. *Pure Immanence: Essays on a Life*, trans. Anne Boyman. New York: Urzone.

Freud, Sigmund. 1957a. Mourning and Melancholia. Translated under the general editorship of James Strachey, in collaboration with Anna Freud, assisted by Alix Strachey and Alan Tyson. In *The Standard Edition of the Complete Psychological Works of Sigmund Freud*, 14: 243–258. London: The Hogarth Press.

———. 1957b. On Transience. Translated under the general editorship of James Strachey, in collaboration with Anna Freud, assisted by Alix Strachey and Alan Tyson. In *The Standard Edition of the Complete Psychological Works of Sigmund Freud*, 14: 305–307. London: The Hogarth Press.

———. 1959. The Question of Lay Analysis (1926). Translated under the general editorship of James Strachey, in collaboration with Anna Freud, assisted by Alix Strachey and Alan Tyson, In *The Standard Edition of the Complete Psychological Works of Sigmund Freud*, 20: 179–258. London: Hogarth Press.

Freud, Sigmund, and Sándor Ferenczi. 1996. *The Correspondence. Volume Two: 1914–1919*, trans. Peter T. Hoffer, ed. Ernst Falzeder and Eva Brabant, with the collaboration of Patrizia Giampieri-Deutsch, under the supervision of André Haynal. Cambridge, MA: Belknap Press of Harvard University Press.

Garrard, Greg. 2011. *Ecocriticism*. London: Routledge.

Grosz, Elizabeth. 2004. *The Nick of Time: Politics, Evolution, and the Untimely*. Durham, NC: Duke University Press.

———. 2008. *Chaos, Territory, Art: Deleuze and the Framing of the Earth*. New York: Columbia University Press.

Haraway, Donna. 2008. *When Species Meet*. Minneapolis: University of Minnesota Press.

———. 2016. *Staying with the Trouble: Making Kin in the Chthulucene*. Durham, NC: Duke University Press.

Lehmann, H[erbert]. 1966. A Conversation between Freud and Rilke. *The Psychoanalytic Quarterly* 35 (3): 423–427.

Massumi, Brian. 2014. *What Animals Teach Us About Politics*. Durham: Duke University Press.

Merleau-Ponty, Maurice. 1962. *Phenomenology of Perception*, trans. Colin Smith. London: Routledge.

———. 2003. *Nature: Course Notes from the Collège de France*, trans. Robert Vallier. Evanston, IL: Northwestern University Press.

Pettman, Dominic. 2017. *Creaturely Love: How Desire Makes Us More and Less Than Human*. Minneapolis: University of Minnesota Press.

Rohman, Carrie. 2008. *Stalking the Subject: Modernism and the Animal*. New York: Columbia University Press.

Schur, Max. 1972. *Freud: Living and Dying*. New York: International Universities Press.

Seitler, Dana. 2008. *Atavistic Tendencies: The Culture of Science in American Modernity*. Minnesota: University of Minnesota Press.

Shanahan, Timothy. 2004. *The Evolution of Darwinism: Selection, Adaptation and Progress in Evolutionary Biology*. Cambridge: Cambridge University Press.

Warren, Diane. 2008. *Djuna Barnes's Consuming Fictions*. Aldershot: Ashgate.

Wolfe, Cary. 2009. Human, All too Human: 'Animal Studies' and the Humanities. *PMLA* 124 (2): 546–575.

Between Encounter and Release: Animal Presences in Two Contemporary American Poems

Ann Marie Thornburg

I

When I was a child, I spent part of one summer visiting a small empty house where no human lived. A family member lived between its walls for a while and moved out, followed by others who did the same. We spent long days there: she smoothing rough edges, I approaching perimeters, both indoors and out. I liked to be alone in the upstairs bedroom, alternately occupying myself with my things and my plaster-walled environment. I can no longer remember if the floorboards were warped, or if they only seemed warped when I looked at them through an adult's prescription glasses. I liked using the glasses to distort or enhance the world I could see, and would wear them (perhaps foolishly) until my head throbbed as if a small tin band had stopped between my eyes. I do not have words to re-envision and record both what and how I saw. I only remember this: the floor bulged up, and I could never walk across its sloping surface, only through.

A. M. Thornburg
University of Notre Dame, Notre Dame, IN, USA

© The Author(s) 2018   235
K. Driscoll and E. Hoffmann (eds.), *What Is Zoopoetics?*,
Palgrave Studies in Animals and Literature,
https://doi.org/10.1007/978-3-319-64416-5_13

Downstairs there was a door through which, I was told, a pet dog, left alone for the day, had chewed. The door had been repainted a numinous white. The possibility of a dog's self-made opening (the chewed-open hole, plastered over) remained visible, like a moon floating beneath cloud cover.

Outdoors I did accidental violence, which was violent all the same, to tiny frogs, and listened for the tan boxer who moved around the patchy grass in a neighbor's yard, a kind of double about whose own life I can barely speculate. One afternoon I let myself into the house next door. The porch door was unlocked, so I pulled it open and entered a space where someone else lived. They were not home. I sat down on the hard, yellow-striped couch, picked candies from a bowl, and ate them. Here I was. But why? What did I expect of this space, this world, and the many worlds within? I sat a while longer, uneasy in a stillness so still it practically vibrated. I got up and left.

II

Poems featuring animal presences often narrate encounters between a first-person speaker (often one, but sometimes more) and an animal, presenting the scene of encounter as something to encounter in a poem. These encounters involve multiple parties: both the poem's speaker and the animal (who often names or is presented as the occasion for the poem), and also the poem's reader, who watches the poem's speaker encounter an animal. Poems featuring animals can work with notions of sameness and difference by examining their human and animal subjects' nearness to or distance from one another, as I will show in a poem by Diane Seuss and another by Carl Phillips. What are the terms of these encounters, and who sets them? What are their trajectories? I select these two poems because they both present unsettled scenes of encounter with domesticates. Cows and dogs may strike some readers as excessively present the world over. However, following Kári Driscoll and Eva Hoffmann in their introduction to this volume, I am reminded that a productive zoopoetic reading of the following poems acknowledges that within them a dog is not only a metaphor, and a cow is not only a cow. I also approach these poems as a poet who is working in anthropology. It may be that scenes of encounter, a focus of anthropological work, are especially apparent to me. I am not a literary scholar and therefore find myself productively unmoored by the task of attempting something like literary scholarship here.

Poets do many things in poems featuring animals: angle toward mysteries; use animals to understand themselves; reject anthropomorphisms in favor of animals' perspectives, which are investigated with intensities tempered by acknowledged limits on the expressive capacities of human language and perceptual apparatuses; embrace anthropomorphisms and sometimes "speak for" animals; register inspiration and awe. They also explore what it means, variously, to be: animal, human, wild, domestic, liminal, tiny, huge, inside, outside, solitary, communal, everywhere, nowhere, disappearing, multiplying, predator, prey, alive, dead, and more. In this chapter, I present yet other modes of encountering animals in poems, modes that foreground the social and imagined natures of encounter. Both Diane Seuss's and Carl Phillips's poems emphasize a speaker's intimacy or identification with another animal, something I will discuss through the language of positioning. The speakers stand either in proximity to, or at a distance from, the animals they engage. These encounters are ended or suspended through gestures of release from positions negotiated through (sometimes with and sometimes against) ontological category differences that can be used to separate humans and animals. However, far from signaling the speaker's giving up on relating or giving into vague celebrations of difference, these gestures are supported by processes of self-scrutiny that acknowledge the precarity of relating. Here, though, precarity is not only a quality of the relating, but a quality of those in relation, because, as Donna Haraway (2003, 17) notes, parties in relation "do not precede" that relation. While relating may be a stabilizing activity, it does not always have this effect. The forms of release practiced in these poems position animals as separate but entangled subjects. Human speakers, meanwhile, narrate their positions and appear to initiate these self-conscious acts. This, however, highlights not only the ambiguity of relations between humans and animals but also their co-constitution and multidirectionality, and the fleeting gestures of autonomy that punctuate or even characterize these relations.

My analyses enter the domain of zoopoetics, if we understand zoopoetics as modeling rapprochement between humans and other animals. In a formulation of "zoopoetics" that takes up American poetry, literary critic Aaron Moe (2013) describes the intersubjective activities of poets who attend to animal bodies by acknowledging animals as fellow "makers" (of structures such as birdsongs and spider webs), and continuing or emulating their work in the production of poems. For Moe, a "multispecies event" occurs when "a poet undergoes the making process of *poiesis* in harmony with the gestures and vocalizations of nonhuman animals" (2). Language is wrought into "forms"—by which Moe designates sonic and semantic effects—that mimic animal activity. Such poems' meter and diction would evoke what the human poet imagines to be extralinguistic, often communicative, gestures through motor and sensory capacities assumed markedly different than humans': wing-beats, chest-pulses, catching the scents hovering in air (2). Zoopoetics can render seemingly autonomous, sometimes inconspicuous, and often "wild" animal lives, appealing to an investment in preserving "nature" as a distinct zone of life and world-making that runs parallel to human culture and may have something to teach it. Poems such as Seuss's, however, bring us into encounter with familiar domesticates to whom humans may be in closer proximity. Readers' ability to recognize these proximities may also provoke reconsideration of the proximities associated with categories such as "wild": what is the wild, and where? And where, furthermore, are humans in relation to it? How do ripples of human activity touch spaces that may seem distant from one vantage point? Which distinctions do we attempt to preserve within attachment and entanglement, and which do we wish to efface?

The desire to note moments of harmony between the human and animal worlds (which may be viewed as discrete before they harmonize) is understandable, particularly in response to acknowledgments of the Anthropocene, its multiple scales, and the destructive relations occurring within it. But zoopoetics might also productively account for moments in which human watching and animal doing fail to harmonize into an "event" worth recording as a poem that acknowledges another's body or appropriates its embodiment. Moe's work is generative for thinking through the social (encounter) in relation to the textual (poems). This, however, invites the question of how zoopoetics can account for the overwhelming presence of human notions of relationship in describing the lives of animals and engaging in multidirectional communication with animals. Anthropologist John Hartigan (2014, 2) encourages us to "think the social," which Moe does through his engagement with the poetic process "without privileging the exceptional case of humans." But, Hartigan wonders, how might we "do this without totemizing 'natural' objects in order to reify social categories?" (ibid.). If the available categories are subject (human) and object (animal), the kinds of productive engagements, relations, and affects poems about animals might register are limited, and not simply because humans and animals are predictably placed in such categories, but because such categories might not be the most useful for considering human-animal communications and entanglements. Nevertheless, zoopoetics' acknowledgment of communicative possibilities between humans and animals helps us grasp, usefully but imperfectly, the multidirectional movement of human and animal recognitions, relations, becomings, and unravelings. Defining zoopoetics also means acknowledging and troubling the idea of the singular category "poems about animals." Zoopoetics seems to demand a more specific engagement between humans and animals, one that crests above the level of content (if this, indeed, is what "about" signals). Nonetheless, poems that appear to be "about" animals may also involve or imply a kind of watchful engagement or deliberate distancing between those creating and populating their scenes.

The poems I consider focus on entanglements with domestic animals—the animals with whom many people often share space and who support and are supported by human living in a variety of ways. As entanglements, these relations involve assumptions, are multidirectional, and depict precarious moments of contact. I find anthropologist Kathleen Stewart's (2012) conception of precarity useful for thinking about alternative or additional positions along trajectories of encounter. Stewart takes precarity "to be one register of the singularity of emergent phenomena—their plurality, movement, imperfection, immanence, incommensurateness, the way they accrete, accrue, and wear out" (518). For Stewart acknowledging precarity "means stepping outside the cold comfort zone of recognizing only self-identical objects" (518) and being attentive to, among other things, the positions of figures relative to one another, and the power dynamics and affective stakes of those positions.

In the two poems that follow, the speakers find themselves caught up in animal presences. They admit to or catch themselves engaging in the affective capture and attempted possession of the poems' animal subjects, and they move through processes of self-scrutiny that involve repositioning, ultimately resulting in temporally uncertain gestures of release. "Love" features prominently in both.

III

The first poem is by Diane Seuss, whose poems feature speakers who encounter the incongruities of social worlds and remain ambivalent about their livability. These speakers often start off along precarious trajectories that deposit them at dimly connected waypoints. In this poem, the world of the calf, and the imagined worlds that grow up around it, are such points.

> *It was the idea of the calf I loved*
> and not the calf though it licked me with its tongue
> covered in taste buds like barnacles. I'd sleep with my head
> on its warm side. Pretend to sleep. Pretend to like to be alone.
> (Seuss 2010, 5)

This poem narrates the suspension of an expected affectionate response. The speaker immediately asserts a relation to the calf that is retrospectively self-aware. The speaker did not "love" the calf, but the "idea of the calf." The poem's title delivers the assertion about the object of the speaker's love (an idea about a feeling about the calf instead of, simply, a feeling about the calf itself). It may be important for the speaker to clarify their relation to this precarious emotional zone. "Love" is charged with pathos and filled with a vague potential that is tempting to enact. Disavowing their presumed love of the calf places the speaker in the category of non-animal lover, and further, in the subcategory of non-animal lover who also does not love young, vulnerable, abandoned animals. After this bald assertion, the speaker goes to work illustrating why they loved the idea of the calf by pointing, evocatively, to parts of the calf's body and elaborating their imagined relationship with the calf: the "tongue / covered in taste buds like barnacles"; the warmth of its side, its unoffered companionship, and its story, which elicits an arm's-length identification:

> Though I wished I was in the fieldstone house
> with the narrow winding staircase and a spigot in the wall that gushed
> lemonade, playing caroms with the old folks. The calf came
> with a story. It had been rejected by its mother. (5)

The speaker describes an imagined experience (or experience of imagining) that does not initially seem committed to relating. Here the "idea of the calf" allows the speaker to feel like the kind of subject they may be invested in becoming:

> I liked the idea of feeling sorry for it and tying orange ribbons
> around its ears. Its black watery eye, a planet
> of black water and no continents. If you sailed
> that sea you'd have to sail forever. [...] (ibid.)

By positioning themselves in sympathetic relation to the calf, the speaker can feel themselves to be more empathic and possibly less lonely. However, the speaker's self-conscious awareness of this positioning inflects its effects. Ultimately, feelings toward the calf are recognized as "ideas about the calf," which move in relation to the speaker's self-positioning.

Liking an idea embodied in a living animal might be a mode of relating. Relating is predicated on the speaker's enjoyment of the idea of having a feeling toward the calf ("I liked the idea of feeling sorry for it"). In identifying points along a trajectory that leads to expressed—but not felt—feelings, the speaker suggests that their response to the imagined calf did not begin with feeling or even a stable subject position. Feminist theorist Sara Ahmed notes that sympathy "might describe a pedagogy: learning how to respond well to another person's situation as an attunement to how they feel" and "acquiring the ability to say or do the right things" (Ahmed 2015, n.p.). The speaker does not detail the history of this pedagogy, but this poem suggests that they have learned what to say and do, and further, "like" the idea of the imagined effects of this saying and doing. When the "idea of the calf" as embodied by the "calf itself" sends out a feeling, it is received as part of the speaker's forming "idea of" the calf. The speaker registers, in Ahmed's terms, "a demand that [they, the speaker] return feeling with like feeling" (2015, n.p.). The speaker seems to comment on this demand by admitting that they attempted to respond with an appropriate feeling, and perhaps use this response to develop their subject position. The poem itself, which takes a wider view, remains neutral about the ethics of this self-making. "The idea of the calf" inspires pretend activities for the speaker that open other pretend worlds: "pretend[ing] to sleep" and "pretend[ing] to be alone" precede "wish[ing]" to inhabit the folksy fantasy space of the "fieldstone house." This pretending does not erase the possibility that the also-unknowable speaker may have been abandoned, like the calf. The calf and its staged world might be inventions designed to test feelings toward past events and future trajectories: the speaker has the ability to imagine their own suffering while calling it the calf's. The world that is described and, perhaps, created is compact and textual, and yet is filled with the expansive promise of imaginative representation. Thus, the speaker's control shifts in relation to the scope of the worlds evoked, both real and imagined.

After spending time in the imagined "fieldstone house," we learn that the calf "came with" the sad story of its abandonment. The speaker does not "come with" a story, but we may read the calf's story as projection because the speaker seems to be a self-reflective figure. The poem details their strange, slightly sad production of a story that is entangled in the narrative of the calf, if not appropriated from it, or imagined through it. If anything could be said to "inspire" this poem, it might be the mother cow's failed making as evidenced by her failed caring, and the construction of a self vis-à-vis the suffering calf. After all, the mother cow "rejected" the calf, a response different than abandonment: rejection does not imply the distance enacted through the activity of leaving, and leaving behind. A rejected calf, by contrast, might still see, be seen by, and be generally involved in a dynamic of noticing and ignoring together with its mother. This dynamic also plays out in the poem as the speaker self-consciously rejects the calf.

The sentence "I invented sadness" could be less productively read as a narcissistic assertion, or, more productively, as a nod to the ways in which, according to literary critic Gillian White (2014, 115), lyric-reading norms focus on an "I" who is presumed to be the unique source of a poem's expressions. In this poem, Seuss does not question the existence and coherence of her poems' already-defined "voice" and that voice's conflation with her biography and presumed personality. Instead, Seuss's poem and speaker wonder about how poems and their speakers come to select and interact with objects of care:

> [...] When it got the bloat and died
> I invented sadness, reached down into my emptiness
> like a wishing well and drew up a small wooden bucket
> of tears. They knocked down the lean-to with the green tractor.
> The calf was never mine, though I said it was. (Seuss 2010, 5)

Here "the presence of their speaker" is foregrounded "as if to exaggerate, explore, and sometimes explode the tacit premises of the lyric-reading models" that assert that "poems were produced to be analyzed into legible moral content, as speech, by academic critics [or other readers]" (White 2014, 108).

The speaker's claim to have "invented" sadness also routes back to their ambiguous representational practice: the speaker's reasons for inventing and representing are not easily determined, while the fact of the poem's staging by the speaker is reasserted. Thus the speaker is identified as someone who can invent both figures and feelings that readers have likely encountered before. What readers potentially encounter anew in this poem is a speaker who recognizes the ways in which those figures and feelings can be reproduced and claimed as original, toward personal and public ends that are uncomfortably truncated.

Although the poem's speaker, whose presence is repeatedly referenced throughout the poem, drives the poem's unfolding, the calf's "black watery eye" stands in the center of the poem's wistfully strange and vaguely maudlin world. It is a sheeny sense organ that remains inscrutable while sliding into the position of metaphor for the calf's distance from the speaker. Like a planet, the calf's imagined world magnetizes the speaker, pulling them toward "a dream of possible lives" that become "ordinary affects so real they become paths [the speaker] can actually travel on" (Stewart 2007, 116). And travel the speaker does, until they finally reject the abject calf, asserting that it does not belong to them. Here, precarity does not resolve itself so much as move into another trajectory of self-making enabled by a disavowal of ownership: the calf is not the speaker's. What we know of the speaker, in the end, is that they did not love the calf, but the idea of it. This, however, is what we knew about the speaker at the beginning of the poem. It could seem, then, that the calf—and by extension animals in poems generally— recedes from view even as its qualities are elaborated. Poems that seem to be "about" animals might detail the kinds of feelings a speaker thinks they do or should have toward them, which surface as assertions about how animals are in the world. This poem does not aim to display who animals are (and are differently), nor to reveal what they "really" think, feel, or do, but this does not mean that it denies them the possibility of "really" thinking, feeling, or doing. Through its grounding in the speaker's self-reflective fixity, however, the poem suggests that humans, too, can recede from view both in and through their relations with animals. What the speaker and the calf become together is, of course, recorded as a poem about the speaker and their story about the calf. While the speaker and calf may have been implicated in a "multispecies event," this event is not clearly the result of intersubjective harmonizing. In fact, it is difficult to locate a singular "event" wherein the speaker has finally worked through their relations with the calf. I can point to the poem's small entirety, but this seems an unsatisfying and possibly inaccurate gesture. Engagements unfold within the poem, and these engagements involve temporalities and modes of knowing. The speaker's performance of attempted self-understanding through the calf, and the calf's own knowing or not, are finally rendered mysterious, inaccessible, or perhaps even irrelevant to the speaker and the calf. Modes of knowing are also tied to questions about forms of certainty: what has happened and who, exactly, is involved? In the end, if there is an "event" in this poem it is not a point of arrival, but instead an open question about what constitutes a "multispecies event" to begin with.

IV

Snow is weather's movement made visible. We enter and exit, moving out of weather (indoors) and into weather (outdoors). This movement between out and in reminds me of the shifting relations—between owner and dog, literal and figurative, holding on and release—that unfold in Carl Phillips's 2008 poem "White Dog." Here, as in Seuss's poem, humans' and animals' positions in relation to one another first seem to create empathically charged situations that then shift through relations that reflect, and reflect on, the stability of these positions, and their formations. Phillips's poems, like Seuss's, often position their speakers at a distance from the worlds they could join and the scenes in which they might participate.

White Dog
First snow—I release her into it—
I know, released, she won't come back.
This is different from letting what,
already, we count as lost go. [...] (Phillips 2008, 28)

What kind of release is set off by dashes in the first line? Unfastening a leash or unlatching a gate, with the foreknowledge that the dog will not return? A gesture of abstract letting go? Or something that does not seem, on its surface, so serious: a game in which the dog does not come back? If the dashes are a formal innovation, this innovation is not only apparent on the poem's surface. Instead, the dashes are a part of the speaker's work with and against contingencies. The dashes emerge from an event in which "harmony" means shifting the mode of relating from acknowledging commensurateness by holding another to disavowing commensurateness and letting that other go. The type of release (mental or metaphorical) remains ambiguous, and its achievement will ultimately prove difficult to establish. If the speaker releases the dog in their mind only, is this "release" to be embodied in everyday relations? Can it be? If, conversely, the speaker physically releases the dog, does the speaker do so with the knowledge that the dog will encounter new or different contingencies and be engaged in the new or different tensions of intersubjective relating? What, also, if the dog returns? Would this be a relief or disappointment, an anticlimactic or an unanticipated climax? The poem continues:

> [...] It is nothing
> like that. Also, it is not like wanting to learn what
> losing a thing we love feels like. Oh yes:
> I love her. (2008, 28).

"White Dog" enacts the owner-speaker's relation to the released dog. It accumulates assessments as it moves toward a conclusion that is negotiated through the buffering simile ("It's as if I release her / because I know") the speaker uses to reposition themselves. Within the bounds of the speaker's control, the dog, too, positions herself in relation to the speaker. While the dog may not have a say about her release, she does depart when the speaker releases her. In the poem's first two stanzas, the owner discards two possible motives for releasing the dog: she is not already "count[ed] as lost" as a failed object of care (as is the calf in Seuss's poem), nor is the release a staged inquiry into loss in general. This suggests that, for the speaker, the dog is a particular object who is recognized as a distinct subject. The speaker indulges the temptation to compare by denying it outright. Negative similes appear twice: "It is nothing like" and "it is not like." Drawing negative comparisons in order to clarify singular feelings can reveal differences but can also obscure similarities. This human speaker may, indeed, be identifiable as human because they categorize their relation to the dog across species lines. The speaker's verbal gestures of disavowal ("it is nothing / like that") do categorical work. Yet this assertion renders the speaker's prior assertion of distinction ambiguous. Thus, the speaker's observation registers the tensions that drive categorizations, unsettling categories in the process: "it" may be distinct from "that," or, alternatively, "that" could be nothing.

A bare assertion of love stands at the beginning of the third stanza, routing back to the released dog, but also pushing toward the owner. Loving another (the dog) necessarily involves the construction of a self (the owner) who professes love:

> I love her.
> Released, she seems for a moment as if
> some part of me that, almost,
> I wouldn't mind
> understanding better, is that
> not love? She seems a part of me, (2008, 28)

The dog "seems as if some part of" the owner who might be "better" understood, but then is recognized as not the owner, and, a few lines later, not human. Perhaps the speaker moves into negative comparison to signal they are talking about a dog in a register typically reserved for human beloveds: a register that allows for, and even celebrates, slippage between subjects. The speaker once again begins to move along a trajectory prepared to accommodate an appeal to sameness, but is forced to recognize apparent difference. The stakes of this difference are not stated outright, but there is a power differential between human owners and dog pets, something that no amount of repositioning can entirely erase. In her work on companion species relations, Donna Haraway (2003, 33) denies that the fantasy of a companion animal's "unconditional love" is a universal good. The assumption of domestic animals' (particularly pets') unconditional love obscures the fact that they have needs, the meeting of which are often contingent on human responsiveness. Love is subject to external conditions, and it can be harmful to presume that a concept or feeling as contingent and potentially vague as love is unconditional (39). The dog next appears "suddenly" distinct, and "seems entirely like what she is: a white dog." In asserting the dog's distinctness, the owner still inflects the literal with the figurative. The gulf between speaker and dog simultaneously widens and closes as relations are clarified through the dynamic of approaching an other through a self. The dog is both "a part of" the owner and "entirely like what she is." By acknowledging that there are mysterious parts of themselves that they would "almost" like to understand better, the owner also suggests that there can be no claim to total understanding of what it is like for the dog to be herself. Here, also, the dog is no longer abstracted by the snow, but visible "against" it:

and then she seems entirely like what she is:
a white dog,
less white suddenly, against the snow,
who won't come back. I know that; and, knowing it,
I release her. It's as if I release her
because I know. (Phillips 2008, 28)

This poem does not attempt to represent the dog's world, nor does it ignore the fact of the dog's own subjectivity. The owner-speaker instead remains alert to the limitations of their position. This supports the clarity of the poem's stopping point. Here, recognizing apparent difference leads to an ambiguous release that may be physical (allowing the dog to choose where her body goes) or mental (letting go of an attachment to the dog). This gesture may be tinged with a roving, self-correcting sadness, but may equally be born out of a seeming indifference to proper caring—being a good owner who does not let a pet loose—that might constitute an ethics. Anthropologists Bhrigupati Singh and Naisargi Dave (2015, 233) invoke ethics as "a mode of relatedness, even if the relation is as ephemeral as a mood that may escape measure or description, lying somewhere between mourning and indifference." Indifference, then, does not signal a failure of imagination or response, but a kind of rigor that resists, as evidenced by Phillips's halting lines, the pulls of identification and empathy which typically foreground the responses of the describing party.

Poet Camille Dungy (2009) writes the following about the poem in her introduction to *Black Nature: Four Centuries of African American Nature Writing*:

For a people who have been classified as entirely separate, as a subspecies or as a possession, the demands of empathy and the repercussions of a lack of empathy are all the more apparent. The limits of pathetic fallacy and dominion are tested in poems that address the folly of drawing analogies between our relationships with other creatures and the workings of the human heart [...]. The dog is no extension of the speaker, and what love and connection the speaker holds for and with her must be held with the knowledge that she is her own completely separate entity, free to remove herself from the speaker entirely, and not subject to human emotions. (2009, xxii–xxiii)

For Dungy, the poem, with its questions and corrections, dramatizes the assumptions the speaker is pulled to make about the dog. Through this process, the speaker is reminded that the dog is not merely an extension of them. (However, while power and dominion are tested, I am not sure the dog is represented as "free to remove herself entirely," as the speaker first decides to "release her into [the snow].") At the beginning of the poem the dog's whiteness may be revitalized along with the snow's whiteness. However, at the moment of release, the dog is "less white, suddenly," perhaps because the snow appears whiter. (The dog is also marked as female in the poem.) And yet the speaker notes that through the gesture of release she also "suddenly" becomes "entirely like what she is." Not just white, but more specifically and differently white, and also a dog. She is marked as multiply distinct. Here, too, the dog's metaphorical or physical movement makes her more visible. Questions of visibility and invisibility, race, gender, and more, are also an important part of the zoopoetic purview. For, as Dungy reminds us, implications of species difference reference recollections and present-day realities of bodies in historically specific, racialized relation. Poems such as Phillips's create spaces in which questions of race and gender may appear unsettled. However, it is also critical to ask questions such as: Who, exactly, is the poem's speaker? And what does it mean for a gesture of release and distinction to involve whiteness?

Literary scholar Alexandra Isfahani-Hammond (2013) prefaces her discussion of the "embarrassing matter[s] of feeling" connecting her relationship with her dog Akbar to her scholarly "turn to species inquiry," and further reminds us that "white privilege [has] reli[ed] on discourses of speciation." This "reminder" is a powerful observation and critique. Isfahani-Hammond works through these felt intellectual tensions (between social-historical awareness of human suffering and subjugation, on the one hand, and the feelings she has for her dog and, in turn, animal suffering, on the other) in the following way, generously reminding those of us working "across" species lines to attend to how and why these lines are drawn in the first place:

Respect for sentient *bios*—across not only racial, ethnic, gender, class but also species lines—is only cautiously revealed in a world wherein humanity is the sole, ever-shifting gauge for protection against abjection. In the course of my research on what J. M. Coetzee terms the transspecies "sympathetic imagination," I have been energized by announcements like *e-misférica*'s of the "turn to animals [sic] studies," and the abundance of journals, conferences, symposia and academic programs centered on the nonhuman. On the other hand, I have also encountered within this "turn" a great deal of scholarship wherein compassion is rigorously withheld; far from subjects for moral consideration, non-humans are objects of figurative curiosity. This disavowal of suffering constitutes a sinister new form of thingification at the avant-garde of literary debate. (2013, n.p.)

This is a poem about relating that privileges its speaker's position while also acknowledging that the speaker relates to the dog in ways that are not always self-evidently understandable or commensurate. Still, the speaker attempts to understand something about relating to another self without either mystifying the other through claiming their ultimate unknowability or asserting a clear and, therefore, limited understanding. The dog leaves when her owner presents this opportunity. She seems to choose. That this opportunity could be granted, and that she could take it, act as formal constraints that allow the poem to achieve its rigorous aim: to constellate the responses, ranging from affectionate self-identification to self-conscious alienation of one self (human) to another (animal), and to finally trace trajectories toward release. While release itself could become a "multispecies event," singular moments of event, charged though they may be, may be charged differently, or unknowably, for those involved or caught in them. Furthermore, releasing may not be a liberatory gesture, but instead a mere suspension. This is not to say that relations do not also involve durations of apparent sameness or moments of symmetry. However, Stewart's notion of precarity reminds us that shifting and unsettled relations may, surprisingly, settle or harmonize, but that they also may not.

V

Almost daily I drive by a horse stable, and almost always the horses are outside, standing and moving in relation to one another. Although they are kept by humans, and are in a variety of shifting and contingent relations with them, I almost never see the humans. Once I did see a few people standing in a small cluster near a horse. Perhaps one of them was learning to ride. Usually, though, I only see the horses and a scatter of farm implements. Usually the horses seem not to move. They are not bolted to the ground, but instead hover in place, tails brushing the air. Yet I know they shift, even if those shifts look to me like nothing or like the way things were before. When it gets cold some of the horses are covered by blankets. They drift toward the barn. Fresh bales of hay appear and the horses circle them.

One day, though, as I drove past, I saw one horse run toward or away from another. I was just passing the scene, so I do not know what happened before or after. I acknowledge the ongoingness of this relational unfolding, while not really knowing how many horses, humans, places, objects, and more shape it. Was this a moment of encounter, of release, or of something in-between? This question assumes that encounters mark beginnings and releases mark ends, but that is not usually so. The horses are still out there near the barn, not timeless but present, not fixed but moving, positioned and positioning themselves in relation to one another, just as I have positioned myself in relation to them.

WORKS CITED

Ahmed, Sara. 2015. Becoming Unsympathetic. *Feminist Killjoys: Killing Joy as a World Making Project*. 16 April. Goldsmiths, University of London. Accessed 15 March 2017. https://feministkilljoys.com/2015/04/16/becoming-unsympathetic/.

Dungy, Camille T. 2009. Introduction: The Nature of African American Poetry. In *Black Nature: Four Centuries of African American Nature Poetry*, ed. Camille T. Dungy, xix–xxxv. Athens, GA: University of Georgia Press.

Haraway, Donna. 2003. *The Companion Species Manifesto: Dogs, People, and Significant Otherness*. Chicago: Prickly Paradigm Press.

Hartigan, John, Jr. 2014. *Aesop's Anthropology: A Multispecies Approach*. Minneapolis: University of Minnesota Press.

Isfahani-Hammond, Alexandra. 2013. Akbar Stole My Heart: Coming Out as an Animalist. *emisférica* 10 (1). Accessed 15 March, 2017. http://hemisphericinstitute.org/hemi/en/e-misferica-101/hammond.

Moe, Aaron M. 2013. Toward Zoopoetics: Rethinking Walt Whitman's "Original Energy." *Walt Whitman Quarterly Review* 31 (1): 1–17.

Phillips, Carl. 2008. *The Rest of Love*. New York: Farrar, Strauss, and Giroux.

Seuss, Diane. 2010. *Wolf Lake, White Gown Blown Open*. Amherst: University of Massachusetts Press.

Singh, Bhrigupati, and Dave Naisargi. 2015. On the Killing and Killability of Animals: Nonmoral Thoughts for an Anthropology of Ethics. *Comparative Studies of South Asia, Africa, and the Middle East* 35 (2): 232–245.

Stewart, Kathleen. 2007. *Ordinary Affects*. Durham, NC: Duke University Press.

———. 2012. Precarity's Forms. *Cultural Anthropology* 27 (3): 518–525.

White, Gillian. 2014. *Lyric Shame: The "Lyric" Subject of Contemporary American Poetry*. Cambridge, MA: Harvard University Press.

Heading South into Town: ipipipipipipip, ah yeah, um, we're gonna, yeah, ip

Catherine Clover

Elizabeth Street Coburg   low cloud   still   mild   low light
dry   *tsu dya*   voice at the bus stop male indistinct *nn m nn nn nn eep*
eep eep-eep eep eep eep eep eep eep eep   Lorikeets fly over in groups west
east   *ahh ahh ahh ahh eep eep eeep eeep eeep ee-up ee-up ee-up ee-up*
    flying overhead   walking   south   *eeup eeup eeup eeup eeup*
        uh mm ooh umm m m umm mm mahmah oo uh-uh   indistinct voice
on radio in passing car siren   *uh-uh uhhhh   uh-uh   uhhhh uh-uh*
uhhhh   uh-uh uhhhh   uh-uh uhhhh   *uh-uh   uhhhh   uh-uh uhhhh*
    single dove   *ohhhhhhhhhh*   *ohhhhhhhhhh*
    ohhhhhhhhhh   Magpie low pitch dropping whistle   *ak*
ock ka-chok   Wattlebird   middle distance   *ee-up eeup*
            Lorikeet   *whoo oo oo-oo-oo*   *whoo oo oo-*
oo-oo   *eehooo-oooahoooo*   *ee-ee*   Grey Butcherbird middle
distance   *ah-wee-ah-oh-ahh   ah-wee-ah-ah-oh-ah*   Magpie
A dog barks from a passing car   stereo thump *dun-dun-dun-dun*
    sere monlo si ner lo no chan moy he's bet dye de ke-eltszy sie den uh stoeke ha ha
        nau   *yate yeh oh yeh* voices at the bus stop
            treet treet treet treet   Common Myna

C. Clover
RMIT University Melbourne, Melbourne, Australia

© The Author(s) 2018   253
K. Driscoll and E. Hoffmann (Eds.), *What Is Zoopoetics?*,
Palgrave Studies in Animals and Literature,
https://doi.org/10.1007/978-3-319-64416-5_14

INTRODUCTION

This chapter addresses the possibility of a shared language with common wild urban birds through attentive listening and sonic strategies
that address animal voice, language, and interspecies communication.
The chapter combines creative practice with exegesis: embedded in the
text is a creative work that uses the medium of written language. Like a
textual field recording, this work follows the motion of a journey from
Melbourne's suburban north to the center of the city and details a contingent interaction between people and birds through hearing, listening,
voicing, speaking, reading, and languaging. The creative work is closely
considered through a self-reflexive process, and this includes how artistic thinking can work with and through the current ecological crisis,
specifically our relationship with and treatment of other animals (in this
case common wild urban birds), as well as what the flexibility of art—as
a means to morph and shape-shift across disciplinary boundaries—offers.

The artwork embedded in this text, titled *Heading South into Town*,
emerges from a listening practice. It is constructed from listening in the
field, which occurs in two ways: either incidentally, as when an overheard
voice or exchange, bird or human, captures my attention; or intentionally, as when I plan a visit to a specific site or allot a particular period of
time to listening. Both forms of fieldwork contribute to this text. With
Heading South into Town, the content is specific to a route from the
northern Melbourne suburb of Coburg to central Melbourne and back; it
includes a number of iterations of the journey, as well as several means of
movement—walking, driving and public transport (tram). While the title
suggests a single instance of a one-way journey, the content of the artwork is based on these multiple journeys back and forth. This route is an
everyday part of my life, from suburbia to the city and back, the periphery
to the center; the journey is an almost daily occurrence and is very familiar, back and forth, back and forth. The daily nature of this route offers a
chance with which to consider what zoopoetics is or might be.

My concerns with the "zoo" part of the term are common noisy wild
urban birds. These birds are seen and heard during every journey along
this route. I understand "poetics" through my colleague Josie Arnold's
(2009, 8) definition of a feminist poetics as having a

> free and roving view of what a text is like, how it can be read, and the
> kind of information it conveys as important. There is no model way of

performing poetics: each experience consists of a reader coming to terms with her or his own self through a navigation of the writers' thoughts, ideas, feelings, wordskills and knowledge. There is no final authoritative conclusion in such works: they are offered for co-navigation for readerly-writing.

Arnold's definition is open and generative and suits the creative approach that propels *Heading South into Town*. Her idea of a co-navigation between reader and writer resonates with my creative approach, both in terms of the content and with how that content may be received by audiences. Audience reception is typified by Arnold's use of the term performing, which is particularly useful for my creative interests because while the artworks are transcriptions of what occurred in the field, they also function as experimental scores or compositions: They are prompts for what might occur during private readings and public performances. *Heading South into Town* combines the sonic characteristics of voice with the discursive properties of language, and through exchange and reciprocity proposes a kind of cross-species pollination of hearing/listening and speaking/writing. A non-authoritative inclusive approach establishes a level playing field between the birds and myself, where our lives overlap and mix during the repeated journey.

Listening

Heading South into Town is a response to listening to the birds. It represents an attempt at identifying a means of communication between the birds and ourselves. Based on listening, language, and voice, the artwork is sonic but silent. Using written language as a means of carrying sound is necessarily limited, but it is a constraint that is creatively productive. Sound is three-dimensional, expansive, fluid, and ephemeral. Using language as a conduit to convey sound is a limitation that forces a deep engagement with the sonic raw material. The textual realization of sound is a means of exploring "what literature might be, rather than what it is" (Gallix 2013, n.p.). Language can be inflexible and writing "is always constrained by something" (ibid.) and these characteristics fold in with the possibilities of sound in a cooperative and productive way. Restriction forces a response that may be precarious and uncertain but pushes at the boundaries of possibility, both in terms of the sonic and the writerly. In this way the artwork engages with Julia Kristeva's concept of subjunctive space which "acknowledges that language is an open structure that one can transgress and which continually produces change and renewal through discursive practices" (Luce-Kapler 2006, 8). Understanding language as a flexible iterative structure open to constant renewal enables me to speculate creatively on what language might be for the birds and how I might translate their exchanges into a kind of mixed language or pidgin between the birds and ourselves. Additionally, through restricting the sonic by using a textual rendering, a space emerges that facilitates the possibility of an exchange with the birds using listening as the trigger, where listening is "an activity, an interactivity, that produces, invents and demands of the listener a complicity and commitment" (Voegelin 2010, xv). Listening is "the beginning of communication" (ibid.).

Lorikeets fly over

nair   *reke oh really*   *haha because nees ree you're being a good boy bran nue*
seven ner szun lee haha

yeh   *szrah renum yeh*   *haha*   *ahh szoh ta kee yeh yeh*
haha no rates skee tsa ya ha ha

twee-twee-twee-twee   *crup-crup-crup-crup*   Myna   lawn
mower   siren   Syer and Bubles
Antonine   College   *eeeeeoooooooo* Starlings
eeee ee-ee ee-or ee-or ee-ah ee-ah ee-ah ee-ah   Starling complexity
wheeeeeoooooooo   Harding Street
wheeeeeeoooooooo
Akins Auto Service

trrrup   *trrrrup* Myna
anyway   *ee hee I wouldn't be able to walk*   *eepu eepu warp warp warp eek-ah*
eek-ah   Myna   *war-ku war-ku war-ku war-ku tre-tre yup-yup*
eep eep yup   *chup*   *chrrup trrup trrrup*   tram   boom of bass in
passing car   car horn   tram bell
ooo-ee   *ooo-ee ooo-ee-ooo*   Currawong around 2.30pm
Moreland Road   Yarra trams   Montano and Co   40 area

WRITING

As a method of writing the birds' voices, I use the phonetic words identified by naturalists in bird identification field guides. This is a scientific method but one that is speculative. Only two or three phonetic words are used to describe voice for a bird species and these words are rarely applied to strings of song or longer calls. In the *RSPB Handbook of British Birds*, the black-headed gull's voice is described as "a rather harsh 'kree-aaa'" (Holden and Cleeves 2014, 157). As anyone who has listened to a large group of black-headed gulls knows, they use a wide range of variations on the theme of "kree-aaa": their calls can be short and abrupt, quiet and intimate, or long and complex depending on the social interactions taking place. The herring gull's call is described as "a short kyow, kyow, kyow" (158), and while this is a good estimate of one kind of herring gull's sound, the range of sounds these birds make is far greater than a repeat of "kyow." As shorthand, these vocal prompts are helpful for bird watchers, but as sonic prompts they are limited. Despite (or perhaps because of these limitations), when I apply these words and build my textual versions of the birds' voices, the process reveals the birds as intelligent language users. The first three means of describing sound—pitch (frequency measured in hertz), amplitude (loudness measured in decibels), and timbre (the quality of a sound, less easily measured)—are not readily evoked in this textual process, but the fourth means of describing sound, duration—the acoustic envelope or how the sound develops over time—is. The number of words used and variations in their spelling conveys the length of the bird's song or call and this, in combination with the poetic considerations of rhythm, meter, pattern (such as repetition), verses/stanzas, and pauses/silences give a surprisingly good rendition of a bird's song.

What I hear of the birds' voices depends on my physical hearing ability as well as my level of concentration. During the transcription process, I avoid using recording equipment, because the struggle to write the birds' voices requires concentration and attention, which allows me to convey a layer of connection that is missing from a transcription taken from a recording. Transcribing the speed and intricacy of a bird's call is difficult, not least because of the choice of phonetic words that could be used and which of the many possibilities might fit the complexity of the sounds. Was the bird's sound a "pah" or a "bah" or a "bahh"? A "wa" or a "wah" or a "wahh"? There is no international agreement among naturalists about which words to use for certain calls and songs. Rather, it is individual choice,[1] giving the process a freedom and fluidity. Writing the birds' voices is imprecise: It is a guess, a supposition full of numerous possibilities, a sketch of estimates and impressions. But like drawing from life, this conjecture conveys the raw sense of being there: The mix of words illustrate the connection and immersion of lives lived bound up together, both human and bird. Full of layerings and foldings, this multi-plicity underlines the speculative nature of the possibility of communica-tion. By using textual methods to consider the sonic, the work engages with Donna Haraway's use of the word "muddle," which derives from Old Dutch for "muddying the waters." Haraway employs "muddle" as "a theoretical trope and soothing wallow to trouble the trope of visual clarity as the only sense and affect for mortal thinking. Muddles team with company. Empty spaces and clear vision are bad fictions for think-ing" (Haraway 2016, 174n7) and creating. Haraway uses the term to illustrate the interconnectedness and inarticulateness of all things mixed up together and, through this mix, their potential. Creatively, clarity and clear-sightedness are exclusive and restrict the first steps of the crea-tive process, into which everything has to be thrown, higgledy piggledy, without order or hierarchy or selection. Aurally, this co-mingling listens to everything and selects nothing.

> *Aye   ee wah ztrub tai   ah*
> *   ta dee ay tru rai   sorry? Uh?*
> * yeah   for   sure   Rachel's home   yeah   I saw you*
> *alright   yeah alright   um so maybe we can have some food as well   have*
> *some food? Alright bye*   Liberty Petrol *cha cha cha rrup rrup rrup rrup cha cha*
> *   rrup cha cha rrup   rrup   myna   yep I'm going up to*
> *   ch ch chee-owp* dingdingding dingding tram bell tram bell
> *   sitting there   get out stay out I know haaa   so does your sister need*
> *   I hope so I dunno   mm*   McDonalds   Albion St   *tra-*
> *eep tra-eep eep eep eep tra-eep eep chee chee chee chee chee che che che che cheeee* Myna
>   Hand car wash $8   Moreland Road Genovese IGA

Translating

Heading South into Town is a chorus, enunciating multiple iterations of an everyday journey into the city center through the voices of birds and people heard along the route. The text is a homophonic translation where sound is the focus rather than meaning. Jean-Luc Nancy (2007, 6) notes that the French "entendre" ("to hear") also means "to under-stand," "as if 'hearing' were above all 'hearing say' rather than 'hearing sound.'" I have no real understanding of the birds' sounds and vocaliza-tions but, as Nancy clarifies, "to listen is to be straining toward a pos-sible meaning, and consequently one that is not immediately accessible" (ibid.). I use speculation and imagination in combination with the phonetic words to translate the sounds into text. In this way, the artwork is aspirational in the double sense that Allora & Calzadilla use the word in their three-channel video, *The Great Silence* (2014), viewed as a part of *Making Nature: How We See Animals* at the Wellcome Collection in London (2016–2017). The narrative of this video, written by Ted Chiang and voiced by an endangered Puerto Rican parrot, identifies the two meanings behind the word "aspiration":

> It's no coincidence that "aspiration" means both hope and the act of breathing. When we speak we use the breath in our lungs to give our thoughts a physical form. The sounds we make are simultaneously our intentions and our life force. I speak, therefore I am. Vocal learners, like parrots and humans, are perhaps the only ones who fully comprehend the truth of this.
>
> (Allora & Calzadilla and Chiang 2016, 222)

The layered meanings of aspiration and entendre extend the reach of *Heading South into Town*: Through listening and trying to understand, I hope that communication will take place between birds and humans through the act of breathing, both the breathing that constructs the transcribed voices as well as the breathing by readers and performers of the final artwork. There is a sense of something previously hidden being revealed through this process: a tangibility bound up with the uncertainty that suggests a conduit between ourselves and the birds—a tentative link, a connection. Hearing, comprehending, hope and the breath support the text to be understood as an experimental score, a score written to be enacted, to be acted upon, to be performed and shared. As the Puerto Rican parrot observes:

> The humans use Arecibo to look for extraterrestrial intelligence. Their desire to make a connection is so strong that they've created an ear capable of hearing across the universe. But I and my fellow parrots are right here. Why aren't they interested in listening to our voices? We're a nonhuman species capable of communicating with them. Aren't we exactly what humans are looking for? (220)

Haraway answers the parrot's question using the term "kin" to establish a connection between all things and how we, as humans, can potentially respond to those around us:

Kin making is making persons, not necessarily as individuals or as humans. I was moved in college by Shakespeare's punning between *kin* and *kind*— the kindest were not necessarily kin as family; making kin and making kind (as category, care, relatives without ties by birth, lateral relatives, lots of other echoes) stretch the imagination and can change the story. (Haraway 2016, 103)

siren   siren

uh-uh uhhhh   uh-uh uhhhh   uh-uh uhhhh uh-uh uhhhh   uh-uh uhhhh uh-uh uhhhh   uh-uh uhhhh Dove

ohhhhhhhhhh   ohhhhhhhhhhh ohhhhhhhhhhh Magpie low dropping whistle

ak ock ka-chok ok   Wattlebird middle distance

ee-up eeup   Lorikeet   *uh mm ooh umm m m umm mm mahmah oo*

uh-uh   indistinct voice on radio in passing car

VOICING

Excerpts from *Heading South into Town* were read by Martin Ullrich at the conference "Animal Encounters" in Erlangen, Germany, November 25–27, 2016. This performance was a site overlay, where the text from one site (Melbourne) is sounded (or performed or read) at another, in this case the University of Erlangen-Nuremberg. Through the reading, the text operates as a score, and I encouraged Martin to improvise and interpret, to move around the text in a nonlinear way and to focus on particular words that appealed to him. There is neither an expectation of accuracy in mimicry nor are the readings/soundings intended to deceive the birds. There is no right or wrong way to read these texts, although some sonic renderings may be more successful for listeners/audiences than others, whether human or bird. Jessica Ullrich, coordinator of the symposium, emailed me her impressions of the reading:

> I didn't notice any noises in the room except for Martin's voice. It was very silent in the room and everyone listened very carefully. In the beginning people almost seemed to hold their breath. Then after twenty seconds or so some people started to laugh a little bit (not very loud) every time Martin voiced the bird sounds.[2]

The humor that Jessica identifies emerges from the absurdity of transcribing a language that is unknown. Martin's articulation of the phonetic words—sound words, words without meaning—would have been reminiscent of poems and rhythmic prose we read as children when we are learning our first language. There is an inherent humor at any attempt to articulate the birds in this way. Jessica also identified that "For me the whole piece had some kind of melody like a song in a foreign language." This suggests the reading was understood as an attempt to learn a new language, where the voicing of new vocabularies is humorous because of mispronunciations. The reading/performing of the artwork highlights this inherent humor; this characteristic is engaging and inclusive and invites audiences to participate in sounding out the works, both privately and publicly.

Jessica concludes that, "Right after Martin spoke the last words, there was a squirrel in a tree outside the window and people pointed to him or her and smiled. It seemed as if he or she has listened to the score from the outside." While focused on bird voices, initiating a connection by encouraging listeners to be aware of all species inhabiting and moving through their immediate surroundings is the intention of these texts, where "kin are unfamiliar (outside what we thought was family or gens), uncanny, haunting, active" (Haraway 2016, 103).

When I improvised with the delegates at the "Women in Sound/Women on Sound" conference at Goldsmiths, University of London, on June 16, 2016, birds' voices (wood pigeons and common pigeons) were heard outside the window during the reading of the second text. Interpreted as a response from the birds, their voices invigorated and inspired the participants in the room. The reason the birds called at that moment is unknown, but it was the chance experience of a vocal combination of bird and human voice that was memorable and suggested a very real possibility of communication. The sounding of the texts by readers is about what language can or might be as a means of communication. The texts consider the birds as complex language users that we cannot understand, and the readings and performances enact this consideration. The readers or performers are encouraged to improvise with the texts and use them as prompts rather than read word for word in a linear fashion. If a word or sound is appealing, participants are encouraged to repeat it; if the sounds from their neighbors are immersive they are encouraged to respond. A sonic response from the birds during any performance is highly rewarding, but these texts are not about performing with the birds: they are improvisational and are open to any and all possibilities that might unfold.

tra-eep tra-eep eep eep eep tra-eep eep chee chee chee chee chee che che che che cheeee   sun
            descending   get ter Ash's   yeah   ha   ha   meet up at like
        ha   ha   catch   ya yeah oh well that's it nah, for sure   did
        you call him back   shit   well   so   no seriously   well I mean
    no I knew that   I did bits and pieces   it's coming together a bit more   it could go one of
    two ways   Al-Taif   heyyy   and so   Jaz and I decided we're not gonna go out
                        ha   ha ha   eep eep eep eep eep eep eep eep eep
    yeah I will   traffic   yep um Tuesday night   ahhh   bye   yeh
                        traffic heavy, cars taxis trams trams trams headlights
            soft blue sky pinkening cloudlets Melbourne Cemetery   *no no I just   we*
        had to umm alarm call Blackbird *ink ink ink ink inkinkinkink the other ones came*
out   just wave to wait and see   um yeah   that was pretty good   my
voice was cracking   engine revs no burnout   *whaddya want whaddya wanna do*
            nothing trams traffic traffic trams trambells   *okay   I'll see*
        slow tram   *um yeah I think it went well   um sooo   yehyeh I mean*
        Lorikeets *Melbourne uni eep eep eep eep eep eep eep eep eep eep* and more
                            no Ravens

With some performative events I include a sound walk as a means of attuning participants to birds' voices prior to a collaborative reading or sounding. This approach immerses participants in the birds' worlds and establishes a direct connection prior to voicing the texts. I was invited to present as part of the sonic series "Points of Listening" coordinated by Salomé Voegelin and Mark Peter Wright in London on January 13, 2016. Voegelin and Wright describe "Points of Listening" as an event that

> seeks to promote and investigate listening together: to perform a "musica practica" of listening across disciplines. It is an expanded and nomadic arena for practice and research that facilitates experimental scenarios with a participatory and performative emphasis. (Voegelin and Wright 2014–2016)

My presentation consisted of an expanded lecture format that included reading and voicing together. It was preceded by a sound walk from Baker Street tube station to the southern part of the boating lake in Regents Park, where many waterbirds live. Meeting outside the station, loud with rush hour traffic, I asked the participants to listen to the birds as language users and to keep this idea in mind throughout the sound

walk. This impacts how participants listen, particularly in terms of paying careful attention to the birds. We walked as a silent group into the
quiet of Regent's Park, listening. Walking to the lake, we were outnum-
bered by the waterbirds who were vocal and curious. They included
swans, pigeons, black-headed gulls, Canada geese, a heron, mallards,
coots, and moorhens. The birds are regularly fed by visitors, so our
arrival was of interest and caused a cacophony of bird voices all around
us. Our ears became attuned to their calls and songs as we immersed
ourselves in what seemed like their world rather than ours. Sound artist
Ilia Rogatchevski was one of the participants. He describes the impact
of considering the birds as language users and how this idea encouraged
him to experience an increased sensitivity to the variety of bird sounds
heard. He recalls that the lake was

> where all the different breeds of birds were going about their day, squaking
> [sic] and singing. Knowing then that this would be (the) focus of our lis-
> tening experience, it felt as if each single bird and its voice could be picked
> out from the overall chorus. And so many different voices, each with its
> own story and timbral characteristic, bouncing off the winter sky like
> ghostly radio signals. Their interactions hung as they resonated through
> the air.[3]

Leaving the park and heading to our destination nearby, our subsequent collaborative readings were informed by the sounds of the birds'
voices ringing in our ears. This sonic experience enabled and extended
the collaborative voicing of the phonetic words. Rogatchevski added
that hearing the birds in their context "meant that attempting to recre-
ate bird song later in the day was a humbling experience rather than a
silly one—singing odes to linguistic markers beyond our understanding."
Paying attention to the birds by attentively listening to them influenced
Rogatchevski's attitude toward them.

As a part of the event I used an overhead projector and placed about
thirty sheets of acetate on the projector bed, each with a group of words
that included visual and vocal descriptions of birds, such as "crescent
white-plumed," "graceful," and a "sharp repetitive chattering cry." As
the acetate sheets were placed one by one on the projector bed, I voiced
the words. The written words became increasingly illegible as the lay-
ers of acetate piled up; the descriptions became indistinguishable as they
merged with each other. The letters became marks, less a decipherable

language and more a dense drawing: Haraway's muddle, full of potential and close connection. Salomé Voegelin found that this visual process signaled an absence of voice where "the overlapping words, and the increasing illegibility to letters, made a mute sound against the cacophony outside."[4] She does not use the word silence, and "mute sound" suggests a temporary absence of voice, like a pause or a quiet moment in a conversation. Mute sound also implies the continued presence of the birds—and the words—muddled into a dense pile of visual marks on the projector bed, full of potential, a chorus of bird voices waiting to be deciphered by the participants in the room.

Confab is artwork that is on display as part of a group exhibition *Human-Animal-Artist* curated by Janine Burke in McClelland Sculpture Park + Gallery (2016–2017), a regional gallery just outside Melbourne. The artwork is a site-specific text placed on the gallery window using vinyl lettering, and it is within easy reach of the birds and their lives in the grounds. There is no formal performance component to this text, and even though I have regularly visited the site throughout the exhibition, I am not monitoring the birds' reactions in a scientific, empirical, or data-driven way. The text may or may not be of interest to the birds. My presence at the site has some impact (the birds notice me) and may draw their attention to the text. When I visit I note occurrences, which may be triggered by the text or may be serendipitous; these occurrences might be birds singing near the window where the text is placed or interactions that may be initiated by my movements through the grounds. Every time I visit and listen, the sounds I hear are different from the last visit but also the same: the birds are the same, but their calls and songs vary; the place is the same, but the weather varies. Sound artist Peter Cusack observes, "the soundscape never ever repeats itself but […] some aspects of it are very consistent."[5] Reading the text in the gallery, at the same site as the sounds in the text, is like hearing an echo, where the site is sonically (textually) reflected back to the reader and is "a re-sounding or re-iteration that folds and re-folds over the site, providing a starting point for interaction" (Clover 2015, 186). Like déjà vu, a grey butcherbird may be seen on the grounds just as the words are read in the text or the "eep eep eep" of lorikeets flying overhead might echo in the reading, providing a disorienting sense of wonder through serendipity: Again, Haraway's (2016, 103) "uncanny, haunting, active" aspects of kin.

big crowd   Melbourne uni   *ahh dez zo ah dem ro   dut chu rin sher sher can re*
tzer   ran   ker   lo bo qua   yes um err a year ago yeh   you know
szer   raif chu   oh mwa   shu mu rah   szo   szor
waijo mm bu zu ka chn ko   zo ee ya   szan chow   ak ak ak

BECOMING-WITH

I work on the premise that the birds are intelligent equals, observing what I am doing in the way they constantly observe their environment, aware of all changes. My presence is one of those changes, and I am observed like everything else. What I am doing lies within the space that is articulated by Haraway when she describes Vinciane Despret's collaboration with Amotz Zahavi concerning the Arabian babblers:

> birds and scientists were in dynamic, moving relations of attunement. The behavior of birds and their observers were made, but not made up. Stories are essential, but are never "mere" stories. Zahavi seemed intent on making experiments *with* rather than *on* babblers. He was trying to look at the world *with* the babblers rather than *at* them […]. Birds and scientists do something and they do it together. (128)

My encounters with the birds are about sharing space using Voegelin's complicity and commitment. Haraway emphasizes a connection between all things and prefers the term sympoiesis or "making-with" over autopoiesis or "self-making" (2016, 58). Sympoiesis is a collaborative approach, an inclusive approach, one where we as humans are working together equally with other species. Making-with is how I initiate these artworks when I am "thinking of ecology as an expanded democracy, in which organisms of all forms might be acknowledged, valued, represented, and protected" (Boetzkes 2015, 200).

cold damp still low cloud   several Ravens calling to each other *Wah. Wah.*
Wah. Wah. Wah.   *Wah. Wah. Wah. Wah. Wah.*   *Wah. Wah. Wah.*
Wah. Wah. Wah.   Low pitch train horn chord   single   sound
Wah. Wah. Wah. Wah. Wah. Wah.   *Waaaah. Wah. Wah. Wah.*
intermittent traffic   cars   van   Doves varying rhythms   *cru-cruuu cruuu-*
cru   cru-cruuu cruuu-cru   cru-cruuu cruuu-cru
cru-cruuu cru-cru   cru-cruuu cru-cru   cru-cruuu cru-cru
cru-cruuu cru   cru-cruuu cru   cru-cruuu cru   cru-cru cruuu   cru-cru cruuu   cru-cru
cruuu   cru-cru cruuu

Haraway's understanding of "thinking" emerges from Hannah Arendt's condemnation of thoughtlessness as "an astonishing abandonment of thinking" (Haraway 2016, 36) where "the world does not matter in ordinary thoughtlessness" (Valerie Hartouni, qtd. in Haraway 2016, 36). In *The Great Silence*, Allora & Calzadilla's narrating Puerto Rican parrot also mentions the thoughtlessness of humans but refers to it as a lack of attention paid to the world: "Human activity has brought my kind to the brink of extinction, but I don't blame them for it. They didn't do it maliciously. They just weren't paying attention" (Allora & Calzadilla and Chiang 2016, 223). This thoughtlessness or lack of attention may be unintentional, an oversight, but it has grave consequences. It is the act of paying attention, of being alert, of taking note, with which *Heading South into Town* is constructed. An important part of paying attention includes a sensitivity to the unexpected and the marginal as artists Bryndís Snæbjörnsdóttir and Mark Wilson articulate:

> we are interested in allowing public conception and 'misconception' to resonate with the findings of science alongside more seemingly random or tangential factors along the way—a turn in the weather, a half-remembered hymn, a dream triggered by the experience of unfamiliar terrain, a familial bias, a flat battery ... (Snæbjörnsdóttir/Wilson 2015, 228)

This inclusivity is expressed when Haraway applies sympoiesis to Deleuze and Guattari's complex concept of "becoming." Becoming identifies beings as fluid and evolving where "life lived to its fullest is a life that actualises as many capacities and powers as possible, a life that makes the greatest number of connections to other things and alters itself in the process" (Cox 2016, 121). Haraway adapts the concept of becoming by adding the preposition "with": "Becoming-with, not becoming, is the name of the game; becoming-with is how partners are [...] rendered capable [...] Natures, cultures, subjects, and objects do not pre-exist their intertwined worldings." (Haraway 2016, 12–13)

During the attentive listening process of creating *Heading South into Town*, I stumbled upon many of Snæbjörnsdóttir/Wilson's tangential factors which are also opportunities to become-with, many of which are articulated in the text itself. Opportunities to connect arise frequently. Triggers are common, ordinary, and everyday as Snæbjörnsdóttir/Wilson indicate and could be a mouse running along the platform, a pigeon pecking on the ground, a sparrow landing at a café table, seagulls flying silently overhead at dusk, or a crow catching your eye.

ah shee juor   ah you mai ah tsai ah szow ee ree ng la ha ha ng dai rer ler je de ee or ai
lye ha ha   err dai zom dzom ee szi ee chum oo   yee or szer ai ee zee ya da
do   dzo jai yeow rum djul ha n adze ja lour   ah ha djo
dur lo   you no lo   szur   na la szer   na hoke na hoke hay la ay
nee jor ah   go ka   ee or ma   eh   now   szoo ee uh   ahhh   vey ah ne
sha vrer sho   dru sho djun mee-oh lay ah dun yoo   ah dow ya   doe shu ze
may-or ha   ha ha   zai   tchai ho   yeah it's fine
akak

The voices in *Heading South into Town* are conversational exchanges. Like the birds' voices, human languages with which I am unfamiliar are included using phonetic words. In the text, the vernacular is revealed through accent, dialect, and idiom. Songbirds also have accent and dialect and reflect geographic place in the same way as human voices (Clover 2015, 112). Blackbirds in Berlin sound very different from blackbirds in Melbourne: In Berlin the blackbirds' songs are melodic and complex, but in Melbourne the birds have to compete with loud native parrots, and their songs are simpler, shorter, and louder. language and landscape are deeply connected and the artworks reflect location through voice. Language emerges from landscape and is molded by the shape of the hills, valleys, riverbeds, and plains and by motorways, bridges, suburban streets, and drains. Cartographer Tim Robinson uses the term "geophany," which he defines as language that "shows forth the earth" (qtd. in Boetzkes 2015, 208). The conversational orientation of the voices in the text suggests informal exchange, idle chat, even gossip, which was not originally a word with a negative meaning. Easygoing conversation and exchange are considered important for social bonding in complex societies (Clover 2015, 201), so as a means of understanding social strategies, gossip is important: knowing who is where and doing what is vital; observing, watching, paying attention to each other and the relationships evolving between individuals is socially significant. I use this casual, familiar, and inclusive approach as a means of becoming-with the birds.

While based on transcription, *Heading South into Town* is preemptive and full of potential—it is what happens before something happens. The intention is to set up the possibility of a conversation with the birds. The work sets up a speculative condition for the possibility of exchange. It is a call waiting for an answer. I am not waiting for the birds to reveal themselves, but waiting for my own abilities to develop sufficiently to recognize an exchange when I hear it, one that I might comprehend.

I am also potentially offering a means of translation for when this occurs. There are likely to have been multiple responses from the birds that I do not recognize, just as Allora & Calzadilla's Puerto Rican parrot affirms; even at a physiological level I am unlikely to hear the range of responses because birds have a more extensive hearing range than humans (Clover 2015, 84) and, therefore, a more extensive vocal range to reflect it:

> Instead of picturing nature, then, contemporary artists are constantly watching and waiting for a way to reveal the earth without thematizing it through preconceived notions of what nature is (or should be) [...]. This tense encounter is the onset of a dialogue about how we perceive the earth and how it thwarts our perceptual expectations. (Boetzkes 2010, 18)

Bryndís Snæbjörnsdóttir describes this encounter as a way to "read what is there in front of you and read what else is there without necessarily seeing it" (qtd. in Boetzkes 2015, 206). Being attentive without understanding (but comprehending the potential) is not unlike how we know exchange is taking place when we hear a foreign language. Snæbjörnsdóttir describes this as the "conjuring of something outside of yourself and simultaneously the notion of sharing and being with it" (ibid.), and is perhaps a means of forming kin where we allow for not understanding those around us but make connections anyway.

Amanda Boetzkes describes the names of species that comprise Snæbjörnsdóttir/Wilson's artwork *Species Wall* (2015) as "more than words. They are propositions, in Latour's sense—an association of humans and nonhumans that seek better articulation" (Boetzkes 2015, 208). Haraway's becoming-with can also be understood as a proposition where we learn "how to conjugate worlds with partial connections" (Haraway 2016, 13). *Heading South into Town* is both a response and a proposition; it is generative and inclusive. It is aspirational—a call, a hail, of multiple bird and human voices, borne from attentive listening that encapsulates attentive thinking. Allora & Calzadilla underline an urgency for a change of thinking, for working with what we already have but do not realize it, and for paying attention to what is in front of us, through their narrating parrot's final comment: "I doubt the humans will have deciphered our language before we're gone" (Allora & Calzadilla and Chiang 2016, 223).

NOTES

1. Geoff Sample, email message to author. 22 September, 2008.
2. Jessica Ullrich, email message to author. 13 January, 2017.
3. Ilia Rogatchevski, email message to author. 26 January, 2017.
4. Salomé Voegelin, email message to author. 29 January, 2017.
5. Peter Cusack, email message to author. 25 January, 2013.

WORKS CITED

Allora & Calzadilla and Ted Chiang. 2016. The Great Silence. In Ramos, *Animals*, 220–223.

Arnold, Josie. 2009. Globalized e-Curriculum Making and/as Cyberfeminist Poetics. In *Contemporary Issues in Business and Organisations*. Proceedings for the Swinburne University of Technology, Faculty of Higher Education Research Symposium, ed. Steven Greenland, 5–8, June 3, 2009.

Boetzkes, Amanda. 2010. *The Ethics of Earth Art*. Minneapolis: University of Minnesota Press.

———. 2015. Visualising the Multitude: The Species Wall. In Snæbjörnsdóttir/Wilson, *You Must Carry Me Now*, 197–209.

Clover, Catherine. 2015. Tell Me Something: Unlearning Common Noisy Wild Urban Birds Through Listening, Voice and Language. PhD diss., RMIT University.

Cox, Christoph. 2016. Of Humans, Animals and Monsters. In Ramos, *Animal*, 114–123.

Gallix, Andrew. 2013. Oulipo: Freeing Literature by Tightening Its Rules. *The Guardian*. https://www.theguardian.com/books/booksblog/2013/jul/12/oulipo-freeing-literature-tightening-rules. Accessed January 31 2017.

Haraway, Donna J. 2016. *Staying with the Trouble: Making Kin in the Chthulucene*. Durham, NC: Duke University Press.

Holden, Peter, and Tim Cleeves. 2014. *RSPB Handbook of British Birds*. London, York: Bloomsbury.

Luce-Kapler, Rebecca. 2006. Creative Fragments: The Subjunctive Spaces of E-Literature. *English Teaching: Practice and Critique* 5 (2): 6–16.

Nancy, Jean-Luc. 2007. *Listening*, trans. Charlotte Mandell. New York: Fordham University Press.

Ramos, Filipa (ed.). 2016. *Animals*. London and Cambridge, MA: Whitechapel Gallery/MIT Press.

Snæbjörnsdóttir/Wilson. 2015. *You Must Carry Me Now: The Cultural Lives of Endangered Species*, ed. Ron Broglio. Gothenburg: Förlaget 284.

Voegelin, Salomé. 2010. *Listening to Noise and Silence: Towards a Philosophy of Sound Art*. New York and London: Continuum.

Voegelin, Salomé, and Mark Peter Wright. 2014–2016. *Points of Listening*. https://pointsoflistening.wordpress.com/. Accessed 31 January 2017.

Coda: Speaking, Reading, Writing

Marcel Beyer

If it alights on the doorstep I hear a gentle *clack!* when its claws touch the metal. An accidental sound, which nevertheless serves to establish contact, and which over the years has become a sort of signal: I look up from my computer screen and see the tit looking at me. That is all it needs to do in order to address me. Except when, immersed in my work or in a book, I prove to be temporarily unreceptive to sounds and signals. In that case, after waiting there quietly for a while, the tit will fly up and hover above my screen, thus drawing attention to itself not only acoustically with the beating of its wings but also optically, borne by the basic assumption that no social animal can remain aloof for long.

Unless, of course, I am asleep. In that case, on an early summer morning, the shade of my bedside lamp will be transformed into a combination of language organ and observation point. Not only can the bird use the weight of its own body on the taut canvas to produce a sound, from these close quarters it can also check to see whether the sleeper—given away by the head plumage (what else?), sticking out from beneath the covers—opens his eyes at this gentle yet unexpected *boing boing*.

In winter, when the balcony door remains shut and I can no longer observe the situation on the table outside, playthings become tools.

M. Beyer
Dresden, Germany

© The Author(s) 2018   271
K. Driscoll and E. Hoffmann (Eds.), *What Is Zoopoetics?*,
Palgrave Studies in Animals and Literature,
https://doi.org/10.1007/978-3-319-64416-5_15

From the late summer onwards, I will regularly use walnut shells to "hide" feed on the table. If these shells have been empty for too long, the bird will gradually nudge them over the edge. When they hit the ground, even though I cannot see what is happening on the other side of the door, I nevertheless know that the shells are empty. Should I fail to react within a certain amount of time, another empty shell will be pushed over the edge, then a third, and a fourth. In so doing, the unseen sparrow is not merely announcing its presence; it is sending a message, it is addressing me, a member of another species. The walnut shell is its telephone to another world.

The most fascinating thing to observe, and it is newly fascinating each time because of the enormous space it opens up, is how a bird will grow increasingly impatient, exasperated, and helpless, when, despite repeated attempts to express a desire or a demand, it fails to elicit the appropriate response from its human interlocutor. What does the bird think of me at such moments? That I am just lazy? Or a bit slow on the uptake? That I've lost my mind? To me, the bird appears to demonstrate something like an awareness of foreign languages: when the young tit sees that I don't understand, it tries harder, with increased vehemence, like a human who thinks he can compensate for his inability to speak the language by raising his voice, until, having shouted himself hoarse, he begins to cough.

Movement, curiosity, play, address, and response—communication is taking place. Faced with such experiences on a daily basis I can easily begin to imagine what it might mean to lead a life without the ability to talk like a human. There is nothing frightening about this idea; on the contrary, there is something seductive, a glow.

Presumably, I would be endowed with sharper eyesight and more acute hearing. Considering the largely ritualized speech acts on which I rely in my daily life, it would hardly be an impoverishment of my expressive repertoire, especially if I had command of the vast array of sounds available to a crow. As for my nonvocal behavior, my beak and feet would take over what my hands and facial musculature do now. Flapping my wings silently or gently, or else raucously, would communicate my mood and betray my intent—including that of deceiving my surroundings. My every movement, every sound I made, deliberately or otherwise, could be interpreted as a speech act, plus I would be able to make use of instruments such as walnut shells or lampshades in order to communicate across species lines. What a perspective. What a world.

Comparative linguistics teaches us that you can say anything in any language, regardless of how many tenses it has, or whether it has five distinct tones or just one, or the subjunctive mood, or an expansive vocabulary, or any other distinguishing feature. This language is no different. So what would I have to lose? Anything I wanted to say I could just as easily say as a bird, albeit in a different way.

Of course I know that this animal I am imagining has no exact counterpart in reality. It is an amalgamation of radically disparate observations and experiences: the inventiveness of the tit when it is seeking to establish contact and the unmistakable interpellation ("yes-I-mean-you") of its address; the unruffled pragmatism of the house sparrow's interactions with other birds, whether they are members of its own species or not—completely unfazed by what from its perspective must seem like outlandish behavior. Over time, this sparrow's resolute tolerance of foreign idioms can even prompt non-sparrows such as blackbirds and great tits to abandon their aberrant behavior in its presence, in other words to put up with, if not to learn, the language of sparrows. The crow's ability to imagine the perspective of a human, who does not know its or perhaps any language, to a sufficient extent that it will attempt to teach him to speak crow. In this procedure, part communication game, part socialization experiment, the crow exhibits a certain openness to developing common exercises and to integrating the pupil's behaviors into its own vocabulary. Taken together, mine is a bird that does not exist because each species lives in its own sphere and is tethered to its own behavioral patterns, just as I, the human, do and am.

One thing I do not know and am also not in a position to find out is whether this fantasy of mine is not in and of itself a thoroughly linguistic event, whether it is possible only on the condition that it be thought up by a linguistic being, more precisely by a representative of a species which is aware of a sphere that lies beyond vocal and gestural communication, namely writing.

I would have no objection to being some other creature or to speaking like some other creature. But I find the idea of having to live without the ability to read and write profoundly disquieting. Deep, irrational fear: to be a creature that does not write.

Perhaps it is only human language that can dream of its own absence.

I see two states of affairs, one imaginary, the other real: either to be an animal and to know nothing of semiotics, the philosophy of language, phenomenology, or epistemology because these do not exist in

my sphere, or, the more appealing option, to be an animal and to be
aware of the existence of semiotics, the philosophy of language, phenomenology, and epistemology, but not to know anything else about them
because they belong to some other sphere. But precisely this, I realize
even as I am formulating this sentence, is writing.

Translated by Kári Driscoll

INDEX

A

Adams, Carol J., 42, 155
Adorno, Theodor W., 169
Aesop, 61, 89
affect, 150, 152, 157, 160–162, 180, 217, 219, 221, 226, 228, 231, 239, 243, 258
Agamben, Giorgio, 85, 124
agency, 7–9, 59, 60, 83, 131, 137, 168, 182, 196, 216
aggression, 71, 72, 75, 76
Ahmed, Sara, 241
allegory, 4, 5, 18, 29, 56, 86, 195, 200, 204, 206
Allora & Calzadilla, 259, 266, 268
Allora, Jennifer. *See* Allora & Calzadilla
American poetry, 237
anagram, 200, 201
analogy, 10, 82, 85, 90, 92, 95, 140, 157, 163, 176, 209
Anderson, Susan, 156
animal, 1–12, 17, 18, 21, 27–31, 33–36, 38–42, 45–54, 56–61, 64–66, 69, 70, 73–75, 81–85, 88–90, 92, 93, 95, 96, 104, 106, 107, 109,
110, 112, 115, 116, 119, 121, 122, 124–126, 130–145, 149–155, 157–164, 167, 169–178, 182–184, 194–196, 199, 200, 202, 205–207, 209, 210, 215, 216, 224–228, 236–241, 246, 249, 260, 264, 271, 273, 274
animal studies, 3–6, 10, 18, 81, 83, 96, 130, 151, 155, 157, 174, 193–195, 207, 249
  charismatic megafauna, 195
  diegetic vs. semiotic, 51–54, 56, 133, 135, 137, 142
  disappearance, 4, 11, 48, 82, 167, 169–174, 177, 182, 207
  human, 223
  as medium, 4, 11, 31, 131, 193, 206, 208, 209
  trace, 33, 184, 186
animal grimoire, 34, 35
animality, 3, 4, 6, 9, 11, 30, 45, 74, 103, 104, 110, 130, 151, 152, 154, 155, 157, 163
animal rights, 177
animal trainer, 150

© The Editor(s) (if applicable) and The Author(s) 2018
K. Driscoll and E. Hoffmann (eds.), *What Is Zoopoetics?*,
Palgrave Studies in Animals and Literature,
https://doi.org/10.1007/978-3-319-64416-5

animetaphor (Lippit), 45, 46, 51
animot, 6
Anthropocene, 171, 238
anthropocentrism, 10, 28, 49, 50, 57,
  60, 61, 70, 71, 81, 82, 138, 154,
  155, 168, 171, 195, 196, 199,
  207, 209, 228
anthropological difference, 28, 30, 38
anthropological machine, 124, 125
anthropology, 28, 236
anthropomorphism, 64, 65, 73, 74,
  90, 93, 141
ape, 16, 18–22, 124, 125, 141, 155,
  156
  chimpanzee, 18, 19, 21, 23
  gorilla, 20, 21, 178
  orangutan, 21–23
aping, 124. *See also* imitation; mimicry
Arachne, 197–201, 203–205, 207
arachnids, 193–195, 206
arachnophobia, 194
arche-animality, 7, 11, 104, 105, 107,
  108, 112, 113, 119, 123–125
arche-writing, 7, 104, 106, 107
Aristotle, 38, 85, 171, 194, 198, 199,
  202, 206
Arnold, Josie, 254
Arsić, Branka, 219
auto-affection, 120, 121
autobiography, 150
autopoiesis, 265

B
Barad, Karen, 216
Barnes, Djuna, 9, 11, 213
Barthes, Roland, 193, 208
bear, 150, 151, 156, 158, 160–164
  polar bear, 149–161, 163
beast, 32, 35, 38, 85, 116, 137, 184,
  199, 215, 223, 224
beauty, 21, 48, 60, 89, 219

behavior, 27, 28, 31, 32, 34, 35, 39,
  40, 63, 65, 68, 71, 72, 74, 75,
  77, 265, 272, 273
Benjamin, Walter, 2, 41, 195
Bennington, Geoffrey, 107
Berger, John, 1, 172
Bergson, Henri, 218
biopolitics, 8, 46, 55, 221
biopower, 48, 58
bipedalism, 71, 77, 156, 161, 222
bird, 12, 29, 47, 93, 167–169, 172,
  176, 254, 256–258, 260, 261,
  263, 264, 268, 271–273
  albatross, 167, 172
  Arabian babbler, 265
  blackbird, 262, 267, 273
  black-headed gull, 263
  Canada goose, 263
  common myna, 253, 258
  coot, 263
  corpse bird (aderyn corff), 184
  crow, 184, 187, 266, 272, 273
  curlew, 184–186
  dodo, 172, 187
  dove, 260, 265
  great auk, 178
  grey butcherbird, 253
  heron, 263
  lorikeet, 253, 256, 260
  magpie, 253, 260
  mallard, 263
  moorhen, 263
  parrot, 259, 268
  pigeon, 47, 48, 54, 97, 176, 263,
    266
  raven, 265
  seagull, 187, 266
  songbird, 267
  sparrow, 266, 272, 273
  swan, 263
  swift, 184
  tit, 271–273; great tit, 273

waterbird, 262, 263
wattlebird, 253, 260
Blumenberg, Hans, 34, 40, 229
boar, 31, 32
body. *See* corporeality
Boetzkes, Amanda, 268
Borgards, Roland, 6
Braidotti, Rosi, 214, 216, 223
Breitinger, Johann Jakob, 83
Buffon, Georges-Louis Leclerc, Comte
    de, 90
Burke, Janine, 264
Burke, Kenneth, 224
Butler, Judith, 151, 152, 158

C
calf, 114, 117, 205, 206, 240–245
Calzadilla, Guillermo. *See* Allora &
    Calzadilla
care, 58, 60, 161, 231, 232, 242, 245
carno-phallogocentrism, 3, 38
Carroll, Lewis, 172
catachresis, 207
cat, 18, 23, 41, 69, 74, 82, 161, 228.
    See also lion
    wild cat, 35
Cervantes Saavedra, Miguel de, 65
Chen, Mel Y., 154, 157, 159
Chérau, Gaston, 29, 30, 36, 37
civilization, 93, 170, 231
civilizing process, 155
clarity, 51, 87, 88, 106, 108, 112,
    113, 115, 247, 258
Clever Hans fallacy, 63
Coetzee, J.M., 249
Colebrook, Claire, 171
Coleridge, Samuel Taylor, 167
communication, 12, 36, 64, 239, 272
    inter-species, 254, 271, 272
consumption, 38, 137
corporeality, 3, 9, 119, 194, 206

cow, 114–118
cricket, 108, 109
Cusack, Peter, 264, 269
Cuvier, Georges, 170

D
Darwin, Charles, 77, 170, 217, 220,
    221
    Social Darwinism, 221
Dathe, Heinrich, 15–17, 19
death, 2, 32, 86, 110, 111, 116,
    118–120, 160, 168, 173, 176–
    179, 182, 200, 207, 208, 210,
    213–216, 218, 221, 225–227,
    230, 231
deception, 33, 59, 87, 120, 121
    self-deception, 114
deciphering, 33, 35. *See also*
    interpretation
deer, 30, 34, 121, 122
degeneration, 221, 222, 231
    degenerate art, 21
Deleuze, Gilles, 54, 158, 159,
    223, 226, 227, 266. *See also*
    deterritorialization
Derrida, Jacques, 1, 60, 81–83, 85,
    88, 104, 105, 107, 120, 172,
    180, 186, 199, 216, 227. *See
    also* carno-phallogocentrism;
    hauntology
Descartes, René, 151
desire, 17, 36, 38, 39, 108–111, 120,
    134, 141, 143, 150–152, 157,
    160–163, 207, 214, 215, 217,
    223, 224, 226, 229, 230, 238,
    259, 272
Despret, Vinciane, 265
deterritorialization, 57, 158
diegesis, 134, 142
Diogenes of Sinope (Diogenes the
    Cynic), 65

CPSIA information can be obtained
at www.ICGtesting.com
Printed in the USA
LVHW031751060619
620410LV00009B/258/P

9 783319 644158